Educating the Young Thinker

Classroom Strategies For Cognitive Growth

Carol Copple

Irving E. Sigel

Ruth Saunders

Educational Testing Service

 LAWRENCE ERLBAUM ASSOCIATES, PUBLISHERS

1984   Hillsdale, New Jersey   London

Text photographs by Bob Harris, Gary Saretzky, and Larry Stricker.

Lawrence Erlbaum Associates, Inc., Publishers
365 Broadway
Hillsdale, New Jersey 07642

Library of Congress Catalog Card Number 79-89436
ISBN 0-89859-523-1

Printed in the United States of America
10 9 8 7 6 5 4 3

Without the collaboration of our teaching staff this book could not have been written. In particular, we gratefully acknowledge the extensive contributions of

Catherine Moore

Colleen Natalie

Eloise Warman Riley

Preface

Most people recognize that teaching is a tough job. They usually think it's tough because of the stamina it takes to be with a group of young children for many hours a day. What is often unrecognized, however, is how intellectually demanding the job is, what complex and difficult decisions teachers continually face. We find that too much of what is written about curriculum conveys the impression that good teaching is a straightforward matter. Dealing with children's emotional and social problems is often viewed as requiring great sensitivity and thoughtfulness (which it does!), while fostering children's intellectual development is seen as a matter of having a good set of activities or the right prescribed model.

Perhaps this misconception is rooted partially in the view of the teacher as the *transmitter* of knowledge, a view which we are rejecting in this volume. Rather, we see the teacher as involved in the child's *construction of knowledge* in a variety of crucial ways. Teachers are not fillers of empty vessels. But they can and do play an active role in enhancing children's intellectual development. In this book, we describe how the teacher can play an active role in educating the young thinker.

We are convinced that unless teachers are armed with an understanding of *why* a certain activity or strategy is successful with children, their effectiveness will be limited.

Teaching is an art, it is true, but it is a very conceptual one. The teacher's artistry can be improved only by understanding why certain things work—why some events or materials intrigue children and others do not, why children have this misunderstanding and not that one. With such understanding the teacher can go further in pursuing a line of inquiry with a child, can choose successful activities and materials more often, and can explain the method to parents and others.

For these reasons, this volume focuses on the teacher's thinking with each situation. The how should follow the why. A teacher who has a philosophy of what should be done in the classroom is ahead of the teacher who merely "goes by the book," trying to adhere to a set of procedures or activities not grounded in a firm notion of purpose.

With this end in mind we have organized the book in the following way. Chapter 1 describes a group of teachers dealing with a classroom problem. It gives the student the opportunity to see the importance of making decisions based on a clear identification of the problem at hand and provides a model of the problem-solving process in action. Since we emphasize the importance of teachers working from a strong "sense of why," we ourselves clearly need to present our own whys. We have done so in Chapter 2.

In Chapter 3 we enter the classroom of two teachers and focus on the decisions they face, along with why they decide to act as they do. The next five chapters look at particular curriculum domains: Art and Construction (Chapter 4), Music and Movement (Chapter 5,) Science (Chapter 6), the Social-Affective Domain (Chapter 7), and Imaginative Play (Chapter 8). In each of these chapters, we begin by examing ideas useful for the teachers in planning activities and learning encounters. We then move to illustrations of how the two teachers translate these ideas into action. As we go through the teachers' planning and implementation of activities and their spontaneous encounters, the *reasoning of the teachers* is the focus.

In the final chapter, we draw together some of the principles for teaching strategies that are implicit in earlier chapters. Teachers often listen to theoretical proposals and then say, with good reason, "But what do I do Monday morning?" We have tried to deal with this question in Chapter 9. For teachers (or aspiring teachers) who would like to begin putting the previous chapters into practice, we have included suggestions for how to work on their own development. (Some instructors may wish to consider using Chapter 9 or parts of it earlier in the course, for example, after Chapter 3, and then returning to it again at the end of the course.)

The book is appropriate for undergraduate courses in early childhood education, child development, developmental psychology, or philosophy of education. For courses that include some involvement in a classroom, the book provides a challenge to search beyond the behavior of children for what they are thinking and take actions to clarify and extend their thoughts. Using this book in conjunction with classroom observation and/or experience should thus be particularly fruitful. We also suggest the book as a supplement in courses concerned with educational philosophy or psychological theories of development. We have found that being engaged in day-to-day educational decisions and dilemmas has continually provoked our own theoretical growth. As a result, we believe that an account that follows the teacher into the classroom, raising the question of "why" at all junctures, is an excellent way to sharpen theoretical focus and give some body to the dry bones of theory. Another interesting possibility is using this book along with other attempts to describe Piaget-based programs or contrasting perspectives.

We do not expect that everyone will agree with everything we have written. Educators should not be that agreeable. We do hope that we have found a means for activating the thought of our readers about the intriguing business of educating the young thinker.

Contents

Chapter 5

Chapter 6

Chapter 7

Chapter 8

Chapter 9

Foreword

By David Elkind

Erik Erikson once wrote to the effect that in order to be heard in America, it is necessary to take an extreme position. A moderate stand is simply not news. Intuitively, I suppose, many of the early supporters of Piaget in this country were aware of the dictum which Erikson articulated. In order to get Piaget a hearing, therefore, the case for cognitive structures in learning was overstated. In addition, to make the case even stronger, a scapegoat was found, namely, representational processes in general and language in particular. Language facility it was argued, often masks cognitive ineptitude and could not be trusted either as a means or product of learning.

The curriculum work of the 1960's was a rough and ready attempt to apply cognitive theory to school subjects. The emphasis was upon discovery, upon general principles and concepts and little attention was paid to language per se. Jerome Bruner, in part responsible for the strong cognitive emphasis in this curriculum effort, may have sensed the extremeness of the position. Perhaps in order to counterbalance it, he offered an alternative scheme, one that overstated the role of representation. But cognition was already too entrenched and Bruner's representational theory never acquired much of a following.

The failure of the cognitive curricula of the 1960's and the "Back to Basics" movement of the seventies have made it possible to reconsider the role of representational processes in learning. In this regard it should be said that Piaget himself always acknowledged the role of representational processes and was not responsible for the exaggeration of his position promoted by his supporters. Indeed Piaget's recent work on the figurative processes (imagery, memory and consciousness) shows the significance he attributes to representation.

This brief historical note, it seems to me, is required to place the present volume in perspective. What the authors have done is to make a case for the role of representational processes in learning and to show that such an approach can be consistent with one based on cognitive development. The book thus reflects the contemporary "rediscovery" of representational processes in learning. In developmental psychology it is reflected in the new interest in imagery, memory and "metacognition." In education it is shown in the new interest in "schema" theory and in language comprehension.

So the theme of the present volume is quite contemporary and its major concept "representational competence" is an important and useful construct. The idea that representational competence is an essential ingredient in learning is not new, of course. Dewey, who already said much of what most contemporary educators are saying, long ago argued that learning is the "re-presentation of experience." And I have echoed this point with my own concept of "connotative learning," learning through expression.

But "representational competence" is a more articulated concept and is conceived as a multifaceted skill which can be improved with practice and which can mediate the acquisition of other knowledge. Indeed, it seems to me that "representational competence" is best viewed as a "mediating structure" that intervenes between the cognitive structures described by Piaget and the material to be acquired. Although it is broader in conceptualization, as I understand it representational competence functions like a learning style or a cognitive style in facilitating the acquisition of knowledge.

The concept of "representational competence" is thus important because it recognizes what the early cognitive curricula did not recognize, namely, the role of the teacher in instruction. A teacher cannot teach or instruct children in the attainment of cognitive structures. He or she can, however, help children attain representational competence. Hence the new conceptualization which is emerging is that what teachers can help children to acquire, in addition to specific content, are strategies for learning. In other words what children need, in addition to operations, are skills for the utilization of these operations.

I would be dishonest if I said that I agreed with everything that is said in this book, or how it is said. Yet I think it is important because it presents a healthy counterpoise to the overly manipulative curricula that are often promulgated in Piaget's name. Language and representational processes are important in learning. And this book makes that point most clearly. But there is always the danger of overstatement in the other direction. My guess is that this book will be useful to teachers who wish to broaden their approach and to acquire a knowledge of how to improve children's representational competence, a competence which is basic to much of school learning.

A Historical Perspective

By Irving E. Sigel

In writing the introduction to this volume, I am aware that it is unusual for one of the authors to undertake such a foreword. The circumstance in this case is unusual because this book reflects a unique and exciting collaborative venture which will unfold as I tell the story of the how, what, and why of this effort.

This is a book dealing with a *way* of education. It represents a way of thinking, observing, and participating in the educational effort. The fundamental purpose of this volume is to free you and the children you work with from fixed, prefabricated experience and to help you become oriented to the significance of inquiry and discovery.

How this Book Came to Be

This book reflects the refinement, elaboration, interpretation, and application of a set of theoretical concepts derived from Piagetian concepts and my own research (Inhelder & Piaget, 1966; Piaget, 1966; Sigel, 1970). It has been a long and slow process influenced by many thoughtful colleagues and finally brought to fruition under the creative leadership of Dr. Carol Copple, the first author of this volume. Her careful and thoughtful in-depth approach, along with that of Dr. Saunders, resulted in an integrated book describing the ingredients necessary for developing an exciting and meaningful educational experience for young children.

To further help put this volume in some historical perspective and identify its place in the child development arena, let me proceed to a discussion of its background.

Each of us is an intellectual debtor, indebted to many known and unknown scholarly forebears. The ideas expressed in this volume have as their major source the work of Jean Piaget, without doubt the foremost contributor in the twentieth century to the understanding of the intellectual and social growth of young children. As with all great thinkers, Piaget could not cover the entire spectrum of what had to be understood and developed in order to apply his ideas to the practical world of education. What he provides is a systematic perspective for understanding and interpreting how children develop intellectually and socially. He indicates, if sketchily, what environmental conditions contribute to fostering optimal cognitive development.

In 1965, with the advent of Head Start and the renewed interest in cognitive development and preschool education, Piagetian theory came into its own in educational circles. Ironically, since little was known at the time about the cognitive development of young children the orientation toward Piaget was a logical choice. He was the only major writer at that time who addressed the subject of the intellectual development of young children in a comprehensive manner (Sigel and Cocking, 1977). An increasing number of American educators and psychologists became interested in studying Piaget's theory in terms of its applicability to the development of curriculum materials, to teaching strategies, and to a philosophy of education for children of all ages.

It was during this period, one heavily influenced by Piaget's approach, that I engaged in a series of studies investigating the development of classification skills among young underprivileged children. My particular interest was in studying their ability to work with different types of symbolic material. For example, did the children classify pictures (representations) as readily as three-dimensional items, and what differences were obtained when they worked with meaningful as opposed to nonmeaningful material (Olmsted and Sigel, 1970)? The point of this research was to identify the developmental changes and competencies of these young children in engaging in a critical intellectual activity.

The research studies revealed that preschool children from low-income homes had considerable difficulty in creating logical and/or rational classifications when the materials were photographs or drawings. This finding posed two questions: (1) Why do children from low-income groups have difficulty in working with representational material? (2) Is there something in their environment that inhibits the development of this competence? Studies were undertaken to investigate how the parents of these children interacted with them. It was discovered that these parents tended not to encourage their children to engage in using internal representations—such as imagining, creating mental pictures of experience, and reflecting on the material they might be working with. In general, the parents were didactic and authoritarian in their approach, providing little opportunity for the children to participate in give-and-take discussion and problem solving.

On the other hand, children coming from privileged homes where the parents did engage them in give-and-take discussion, explanation, planning, and so forth had less difficulty in working with representational materials. Coupling these observations with the readings from Piaget and with discussions with teachers, it seemed reasonable to propose that what might be needed to foster the development of representational competence was an environment that encouraged children to think for themselves, to appreciate options in solving problems, to understand that ideas can be represented in many forms, and to represent mentally non-present situations, objects, and events.

The next step was to identify and to hypothesize ways to achieve such developmental objectives. It seemed reasonable to postulate that if children are expected to achieve such competencies, an educational environment should be created which would encourage imagining, creating mental pictures, identifying options to solve problems, etc. Using Piaget as a backdrop, and again discussing these issues with numerous "master teachers," I concluded that a systematic inquiry process would be the appropriate type of teaching strategy. Inquiry techniques require that the child come up with answers or suggestions and be actively engaged in discovering alternatives (Sigel and Saunders, 1979). Inquiry strategies require the child to generate answers, especially when the question is one which calls for reflection and interpretation, not just association. The idea began to emerge that using an inquiry teaching strategy, *systematically applied*, could make a significant contribution to the child's representational competence. Prior to establishing such a program, however, other types of research were needed to justify the inquiry approach.

Some teachers to whom I spoke indicated that they always asked questions. They asserted that they did encourage children to think for themselves and that they always encouraged thinking of alternatives. Their contention led to a series of studies, both observational and experimental, to check out these assertions before a final commitment to the preschool route was made. We investigated whether teachers did in fact employ an inquiring strategy as they described. Further, I was interested in determining whether children could participate in this process.

It was found that teachers did *not* use inquiry in an open way with young children even when they believed they did. Rather, questions were highly structured, clearly requiring a right answer, and were more like "checking" what the child knew, not generating thinking and reflection (Sigel & Olmsted, 1969). Some short-term training studies also supported my confidence in open-ended inquiry (Sigel, Roeper, and Hooper, 1966).

These studies supported my theoretical conceptualizations. Some other issues were still open: can these ideas be put into the form of an educational experience, engaging relatively large numbers of children, and is this type of educational experience possible with children from underprivileged backgrounds? The first step was to create an educational environment that would put these ideas into practice and make adaptations as needed. A related issue was the age which children should be when they entered the program.

Piaget helped answer the latter question. Since children of about two years of age are just beginning to engage in representational activities in their play and in their developing language, it would make sense to begin with this age group. Armed with the theory and the decision to work with two-year-olds, I sought and received financial support from the then Office of Economic Opportunity, Research Division. Dr. Edith Grotberg helped launch the program with the appropriate amount of financial support. The State University of New York, Department of Psychology, sponsored the program, and we were off and running. Twenty-two two-year-old children from inner-city Buffalo, New York were recruited, as well as experienced teachers who were willing to try to develop my ideas in workable educational practices. It was an exciting time, full of experimentation and challenge. Four years of such activity, with the program growing as the children grew, provided a solid basis from which to advocate such a programmatic effort (Sigel, Secrist, and Forman, 1973).

That effort, simply put, has been to create an environment in which the teachers engage the children in a variety of representational experiences, using inquiry systematically and carefully to encourage the children to "distance" themselves from the here-and-now in time and space. It came to be known as a *distancing* program. The program proved to be successful (Cataldo, 1978).

Is what works with preschool children from improverished backgrounds appropriate for children from more privileged backgrounds who often already have the advantage of parents who are open, free to inquiry, and willing and able to afford the luxury of interactions with books, projects, and the like? The chance to test this question was made possible by an invitation from D. Samuel Messick, Vice President of Research at Educational Testing Service, for me to set up an experimental preschool program—the Child Care Research Center. The Educational Testing Service provided the wherewithal for the Center to get underway. Dr. Rodney R. Cocking joined me as the Director of the Research and Evaluation. We quickly discovered that the application of the ECEP program from Buffalo had to be modified to meet the needs and interests of a more privileged group.

The process of development was a careful and slow one, involving the thinking of many individuals, initially with Betty Bryant, the first Educational Director, who began setting program strategies for the middle income group. Ruth Saunders, succeeding Betty Bryant as Educational Director, made a significant conceptual and organizational leap forward by articulating some of the developmental principles for representational thought (see Chapter 2). During the past year, the time seemed ripe to abstract the basics from the program and place them into the context that is reflected in this volume. Carol Copple, who worked with Ruth Saunders and then followed her as Director of the Educational Program, has collaborated with the 1977–1979 teaching staff (Catherine Moore, Colleen Natalie, Eloise Warman Riley, Rosemarie LaValva, Jean Sander, and Kalina Gonska) in making further modifications and integrations of the theoretical notions. The classroom continued to be an exciting and indispensable laboratory for this evolution as issues needing further elaboration and development continued to present themselves. The final product, this volume, represents a formidable effort, written to a large extent by Carol Copple with the close collaboration of Ruth Saunders and me, with close readings by the teachers.

What is this Book?

This volume reflects the application of the program conceived at the State University of New York at Buffalo and developed and matured at Educational Testing Service. During the four years of work at Educational Testing Service, the program evolved in the following ways: the understanding of how to pose questions to the children became increasingly specific and relevant (discussed in Chapters 2 and 9); the approaches to the various subject or content areas such as science, social-affective understanding, art and construction, and dramatic play were developed with specific and general approaches (see Chapters 4, 5, 6, 7, and 8). These chapters could only be developed because a conceptual framework was created within which to derive the details. This is an important point to keep in mind. Practice in education, I believe, can move forward only when teachers become able to develop their own approaches. To achieve this freedom as a teacher requires an underlying set of principles as the foundation for the practice. This is evident in the early chapters, particularly in Chapter 2. Finally, teachers make decisions, and these decisions are part and parcel of the everyday life of the teacher. How these decisions are made is presented in Chapter 1, and in the other chapters as well, showing how they are related to the basic viewpoint. We conclude this volume by pulling together the major points and by considering how a teacher can get started in incorporating the new perspective in the classroom.

What you will see in this volume is a collaborative effort between research and practice, each contributing to the growth of the other. It should also be kept in mind that the research which directly undergirds this program is integrated with research in a number of other areas related to the central theme of this volume, educating the young thinker.

You may be surprised that some material is not included as a separate section. For example, we do not have a separate section on language development or the acquisition of number. The reason is that these skills and capacities are integrated in each of the major sections of the book. What we have done is taken a number of what we hold are relevant areas of experience and knowledge, areas of genuine interest to children and important for their intellectual and social growth, as the substantive framework for this book.

This book is a statement of a point of view, a conceptual orientation to the education of young children based on a set of principles and guidelines built on conceptual and empirical bases.

Thus you may ask how this program differs from other programs and what makes it unique. I have indicated that it has a long history of specific research to undergird its particular approach. The program was consistently monitored by research psychologists. Dr. George Forman, now at the University of Massachusetts, worked with me during its development at SUNY/Buffalo; during the program at Educational Testing Service, Dr. Rodney R. Cocking was the Director of the Research Program. The results of their work provided the assurance that the program was, in fact, accomplishing what it set out to do.

The approach emphasizes the teacher as basic to the educational process. Our orientation focusses more on the teacher than on materials. It is a teacher-child interactional perspective where materials are only a means to enhance that relationship. Materials become a vehicle for learning. It is how the teacher and the child interact with materials that constitutes the learning environment. Finally, our emphasis is on the decision-making approach, where the teachers have to be aware of themselves as individuals capable of employing their own problem-solving processes in working with the children. The teacher is in the center position.

It may appear that the perspective advocated insists on constant teacher involvement. As you will see, how and when teachers get involved are carefully described throughout the book.

How to Use this Book

Since this is a book based on principles from theory and research, how can it best be used? It is useful on at least three levels. First, this is a volume that will provide you with a particular orientation to the education of young children. It is not age specific; it is relevant to children of a wide age span, and principles are not tied to particular ages. The examples and the dialogue of the teachers, and some of the content, focus on the early childhood classroom, but the conceptual model for the development of thinking skills is applicable to the young and the old. Second, the book provides vignettes and models for thinking about curriculum planning, teaching strategies, decision making, and the other critical features of educational programming. But it is not done in a cookbook manner. Rather, it is a statement that intends to engage you, to make you think and wonder about educational processes and about young children as you proceed. Finally, the statement should provide you with a basis from which to develop your own creative teaching style. The principles provide the broad guidelines. Chapter 9 shows a way of expressing those principles in a practical way. The final decisions in the classroom emerge from the interaction between the teacher and the children. You and the children you are working with will become, in the long-run, a partnership in the process of mutual learning, mutual thinking, and mutual understanding.

So I come to the end of my introduction. I have taken the liberty of making this, in part, a personal saga because the whole effort has been a meaningful and powerful intellectual experience. To have witnessed the development and application of an approach to education that has attracted a number of able and dedicated professionals, that has inspired their confidence to contribute so much of their time and energy to producing this volume, has been a moving experience for me.

Acknowledgements

The volume could not have been completed without the tremendous input of talent, energy, and organizational ability of Carol Copple. The best ideas are of little value unless communicated clearly and potently to a public. Dr. Copple has done that. Working with her and Ruth Saunders, two exceptionally talented and wonderful people, brings to a close a chapter in the development of the educational effort. The evaluation of this endeavor, which will be reported in other writing, was the responsibility of Rodney R. Cocking.

His sensitive and talented approach to evaluation provided us with the necessary confidence that the program is effective. Now it is time to turn to building on what we have learned.

Of course, all our efforts would have been for naught had not the parents of our children in Buffalo and in the Central New Jersey area had the confidence that we would be of service to their children. Last, but most important, are the children themselves. Their enthusiastic responsiveness and their communication with us taught us much. And it is to them that we owe our greatest thanks for sharing their excitement, enthusiasm, and wisdom as we embarked on this educational adventure.

No book or program can be carried out successfully without a large group of support staff, individuals who in their quiet way make programs work. Particular appreciation goes to our secretarial staff of Linda Kozelski and Betty Clausen, whose steady hands and temperament carried us along for many a year; to Jan Flaugher and S. Erik Holme for their help in maintaining our technical facilities; and to James Norris and Jonathan Rightmyer for their help in collecting useful and important information about our children. To all these, and everyone unnamed in the last ten years—Thank You!

To you, the reader, I hope that these few words have provided you with the what, why, and how of this volume. I hope that it will be as exciting and as profitable for you to read as it was for us to write.

The Teacher as a
Decision Maker

Susan Cook, one of the teachers of the four-year-olds at the Edgehill Day
Care Center, says to her teaching partner, Michael, "There it is again today.
The block corner is in the hands of The Gang and the air is ringing with the
noise of gunfire." Michael agrees, "I think it's time we asked for some time in
the next staff meeting to discuss this problem. Gail said that she and Kate had
a situation somewhat like ours on their hands. I'll speak to Anne [the director]
about it right after class." So, it is agreed that the four teachers who have been
having trouble with the block corner will meet, along with the director of the
day care center, on Monday while the children are napping. Susan begins with
a description of the situation with which she and Michael are having trouble.

Susan: We've been in school two months now and for the last three weeks
we've been more and more aware of the way the room has been
during free play. There's a group of boys who spend every free
play in the block corner.

Michael: They always build pretty much the same old fort and play the same
loud gun games. The rest of the class seems to get more hyperactive
and "zooey" as a result. There doesn't seem to be that much terrific
building or even dramatic play going on, but there are a couple of
things that bother us even more. One is that this gang has the other
kids thinking that they own the block corner.

Anne: Are they shutting out other kids or are the others just staying away?

Susan: Some of both. Rarely does a girl even venture into the area. When
she does, she's told in no uncertain terms "boys only." And we
thought this classroom was the bastion of non-sexism in a sexist
world!

Michael: But not all the boys go there either. It's a small group and always the
same ones. There are some attempts of others to join and some
interesting negotiating about that. Like one boy will say when told
by the others that there's no room in the fort, "Well, I'll be the guard
and later we can switch and somebody else will be the guard" and
so on. But this is only one or two boys and after a while they'll either
be permanently accepted or permanently shut out. All the others
stay away.

Susan: As Michael mentioned, the *building* of the fort isn't really very
important. They build it quickly with no reflection or elaboration
of it from day to day. They use all the big blocks if allowed and all
the space too. The small blocks are often not being used but the
other kids don't have good access to them across this "war zone"
and no room to build with them if they could get to them.

The decisions teachers make are complicated ones. As we will see, the
problem at hand for these teachers is just beginning to unfold and they will be
discussing through the entire nap time. Is it worth it? Let's consider another pair
of teachers confronted with a similar classroom situation. Jane, the head
teacher, realizes that day after day the same gang of four boys is in the block
corner building their standard fort and excluding other children, especially

girls. She decides she'll provide a diversion in another area of the classroom—a throwing game that she knows will be of great appeal to these boys. She tells her teaching partner her idea and they begin making the game. This idea may have much to recommend it. It may work as well as anything our other teachers arrive at after an hour of discussion. So why are they taking up valuable time with such an exercise? What will they gain by taking their recuperate-and-prepare time to talk this problem through? Anything other than an outlet for their frustration? Let's return to the discussion.

Anne: (To Kate and Gail): Is the situation with your group a lot like this?

Kate: Some of it is but I've been thinking of differences too as Susan and Michael described their situation. It sounds like a part of their problem is the kids being wild and loud in that area and the whole classroom atmosphere being affected. Our set of block corner cronies, which by the way includes Laurie, is quiet but exclusive.

Gail: We were thinking about the fact that these three or four children don't explore anything else much in the classroom. We can tell you about a few things we've tried when we're ready for that. But we'd thought of it in terms of the limited range of things that those children are experiencing, and the fact that the other kids can't play with the blocks. The other kids get little or no block play and these kids get nothing else.

Kate: Their social interactions seem so repetitive too. All day long it's barking orders and "pecking order" interchanges of one kind or another.

Gail: We've talked about that part of it, though, and we're not sure what to think. I sometimes wonder how we know this doesn't serve a valuable function for them. If we believe that children seek out and engage in those experiences that they need developmentally . . .

Michael: Would you say that about loud gun play? Or jeering at one child in the group?

Anne: I think we're up against a really difficult issue here and, if you think of it, it tends to come up almost everytime we meet, in one form or another. How do you decide what a child or a group of children need? As Michael points out with his examples, these are decisions that rest with us to some degree. We can't just say that the child always seeks out what he needs. Sometimes what one or more children need is clearly detrimental to the other children. That may be involved to some extent in this block corner thing. But suppose you can come up with a solution in which the daily fort building of these boys doesn't interfere with anyone else's block play. What's harder is to ask yourself the question Gail is raising. Do those children have "reasons" for spending so much time with that activity—developmental reasons? Or are they not familiar enough and comfortable enough with the other choices? Are they just in the habit of coming to the block corner, etc.? How would you tell?

Susan: It's inference at best, but we do sometimes get a clue from watching what they're doing as closely as we can. Like right now with our block corner group I'd say that they aren't that much involved in constructing. The slapdash way they build the fort makes me think it's a secondary thing. Where the attention seems to be is on who gets to play, who's boss, that us-against-them kind of stuff.

Anne: Would you say the fort gives them a territory; that the territorial motivation is a part of it? After all, they could be a gang in different areas of the room.

Michael: Yes, I do think territoriality, as you call it, is a big part of what's involved for our kids.

Gail: I think that's part of it for ours too. Their sense of belonging seems to be fortified by having a regular place. I think it adds a lot for it to be a closed-in place.

Kate: And one that they built and thus have rights to. You don't see them banding together under the loft, for example.

Anne: OK, let's see what we've said so far in terms of describing what the various problems are. As I've been hearing you it sounds like the problems are not identical in the two classes; similar in some ways, different in others. Both groups have some concern with the monopolization of the block corner by a small number of children, the lack of access to the blocks for the other children. Both groups are having the excluding of children to deal with but you all have some mixed thoughts on it and on how to deal with that. Michael and Susan have the additional concern with loud and rough play. Gail and Kate were concerned with the limited range of experiences those in the block corner were getting and Michael and Susan seemed to feel that might be happening with their group too. In one class—is it yours, Susan and Michael?—there's a sex barrier involved in this excluding of children also. And I suspect that may be there for the other class too but with an exception made for Laurie who the boys sort of acknowledge as one of their own. So there are a number of concerns as well as some "concerns about the concerns"—for example, *should* we worry about children spending most of their time in one activity?

Up to this point the teachers have primarily been attempting to identify the problem. What may have initially bothered them, loud gun play, let's say, was first of all observed for a period of time by the teachers to determine more about what was going on. Susan and Michael talked it over between themselves and now through describing it to the others and hearing of their similar problem, they have clarified the various interrelated problems more explicitly. They are ready now to begin generating alternatives for solving the problem at hand. The four teachers will also be reviewing what they've tried and what has happened with these attempts.

Anne: Well, what have you tried so far?

Susan: One thing we did was try to put activities in other places in the room which would interest these children—like a "dart" game with rubber darts. That worked for exactly a day.

Michael: The Christmas morning effect. And even then that same group, of the "Good Old Boys," stayed together.

Kate: We've tried to interest our block gang in other things also and we've sometimes had some luck with it. There are two kids out of those four or five that really like to do a number of different things like drawing, looking at books, etc., when they aren't pulled into the block corner from the beginning of each free play. When Wesley is absent, I've noticed that Scott is much more likely to do other things in the class.

Gail: That's tied in with why I think we had some luck last week with getting some of these guys to do other things. What we did was say at the end of the first circle that we were going to take Phillip, Diane, and Sharon into the block corner—three kids who never play with blocks. We sort of matter-of-factly told them that anyone who'd had it in mind to play there would have to find another place to play for that one free play.

Kate: When they had to find other things to do, they did. If they looked over in the block corner, they would see it was occupied and they couldn't go running right over there and fall back into the same old patterns. We're just starting with this but our feeling was that we'd try it for long enough to give some new interests a chance to develop.

Gail: Not everyday—I think maybe we'd feel too directive placing these kinds of constraints everyday—but once or twice a week.

Michael: We haven't tried that but I can anticipate a couple of kids that it would really be a bust with. Have those ousted kids really started doing new things? (Gail and Kate nod and Gail murmurs, "much to our surprise"). We have one child who I'm sure would wait it out. He'd sit in the big chair or lie on the floor until he was allowed to return to the blocks.

Susan: You mean Adam. Well, he's a story unto himself. But even with other kids, I think there'd be something of a hostile reaction to a restriction of that kind and I'm not even sure I'd be comfortable with it myself. The same with teacher rules like you can only tie up the blocks for one free play, you can only choose that area two days a week, etc.

Anne: Susan, you're giving us some other things to think about with those ideas. Even though you don't like the idea of imposing them from a me-teacher-you-children stance. We've identified our problems. Before we get to more evaluation of the pros and cons and hows of each idea, let's think some more about the range of possibilities. Susan is mentioning one set of things you could manipulate to bring about change—limiting or distributing the *time* that kids have access to the area. Whether there'd be other ways to bring that about besides teachers laying down the law is also something to explore. But what other aspects besides *time-of-access* could be changed to potentially have an effect on the problem?

Michael: Well, we mentioned diversions elsewhere. I guess that would fall under the category of *materials changes.*

Anne:	OK, what other materials changes might there be?
Kate:	Are we brainstorming—any idea that comes to mind, right? Well, you could remove the blocks entirely for several weeks.
Gail:	I can see all sorts of problems with that, such as mutiny, but it's interesting to speculate on what might happen. Let's keep on tossing out ideas. What about having more space devoted to blocks, but limiting the amount of space and the quantity of blocks that a child or group could see?
Michael:	So the idea would essentially be to allow the current block kids to continue but try to provide a way for the others to get their chance? It seems to address only some of the original concerns plus there are obvious space problems. Just for the space problem something just occurred to me that might help some. Those smaller unit blocks that never get used because they're stored on the other side of where the fort gets built—why don't we arrange things so that those small blocks are accessible at the same time the large blocks are being used? They don't take up nearly as much room as large blocks, so there'd be enough space, I think, for a sort of modification of Gail's idea.
Susan:	Also, I think they build very different *kinds* of things with those smaller blocks and they may well appeal to quite a different set of kids.
Gail:	There are definitely a bunch of kids who like to use materials like plastic building blocks. They might really like to do things with the blocks and right now they can't get to them, never think of them because they're too remote. In fact, that might be a good bridge for getting those children more interested in the large wooden blocks. I have a feeling that more dramatic play would be an additional benefit of that change.
Michael:	It's true that some of the kids who do a lot with those small manipulative toys do less with dramatic play. I hadn't thought about that.
Anne:	One more aspect of the problem that we hadn't identified before. But now, so far what have we looked at that can potentially be changed? I keep pushing this because I want to be sure we have all our options before us. I have a feeling we may need a handful of strategies and alternatives which we'll have to combine, try and learn from, etc.

We haven't talked much about changing children's behavior directly. If we were behavior mod people, we would have started right out thinking about just what specific behaviors we wanted to eliminate, which ones we wanted to increase, and with what rewards should we set about shaping the desirable behaviors while we extinguished the undesirable ones. But this is only one approach to *behavioral change*. That's an area for us to think about. And it may be most useful to think not only of the individual child's behavior as the target but also of the way the whole class functions. So there might be the ways you'd influence behavioral change in

	individual children—like sharing in someone's excitement when he does a painting for the first time, etc.—and the ways you approach the thing as a group problem.
Susan:	That makes me think of something we thought about. We like the idea of having the children themselves in on these problem-solving situations and we've been considering the idea of getting them involved in working through this with us. It's really a class problem and it seems they should have input.
Michael:	Susan and I have talked this over. I like the idea but I want to be sure it's a genuine group problem-solving session, not a phony one.
Kate:	What do you mean a phony one?
Michael:	I mean that if we really know what we want them to do ahead of time we'd only be pretending to involve them in the decision-making process.
Susan:	I agree and I think this is a recurring problem for us. Not anything they decide on is okay. There are some things that we wouldn't be willing to have as class policy. For example, only boys can play with blocks.
Gail:	But they'd never decide on that as long as some girls were protesting.
Susan:	Maybe that isn't the best example then because we do have some red-hot little feminists, thank goodness. But they might decide, let's say, to move the blocks outside where there would be more room and have free plays out there. For a number of solid reasons that wouldn't be something we could go along with.
Anne:	I think there may be ways of having a real group problem-solving session and still have teacher limits. These are the things to think ahead about, though, so you'll have an idea how you'd react when suggestions you can't act on do come up. This idea of a group discussion will be something to come back to and think about more. You've been having group discussions of a sort already, haven't you?

The teachers were sometimes getting ahead of themselves to evaluate the ideas but they were primarily at the stage of problem-solving where *generating solutions* is the task. There are a variety of things which teachers can vary or work with to bring about a change in the classroom:

1. type and quantity of materials
2. arrangement of space and materials
3. rules/schedules for use of space and materials
4. teacher presence and role in facilitating change—through interactions with individuals and/or through group dynamics.

Notice that there is a relationship between the problem as it has been identified and the kinds of solutions generated. If the problem had been defined as loud and disruptive gun play, a very different set of potential solutions would have been suggested. This is why it is so important to carefully observe and to specify the problem or problems which are important to do something about. Even when you are a lone teacher (or in the parent role for that matter) you can still go through the process of observing and identifying the problem. Group meetings or meetings with a teaching partner have advantages but they are not the only way.

Now the group will proceed to more focused evaluation of the solutions which seem to them to have the most applicability to their classrooms. We will not follow this exchange from start to finish but let's look at a couple of parts. Both classes are thinking of changes of arrangement of materials, following up on the idea of moving the small wooden blocks to a more accessible spot. The question now is where, but that too involves returning again to why.

Susan: I like the idea of moving the small blocks to where they'll be more accessible and separate. Originally we generated that idea for an "access" reason but I'm thinking now of a number of potential benefits. But I may be getting carried away. See if this makes sense. I was thinking that I rarely see any small blocks used in the same constructions as the big ones. For the children playing with large blocks, the small ones become guns, etc.

Michael: That's true. And the choosing of blocks to serve as props could have good representational demands. [More on this in later chapters, but in simple terms Michael is saying that pretending one object is another and finding one that would adequately represent the other are mental tasks in their own right.] Only the way it has been happening it's the same thing everyday—the medium-sized skinny blocks for guns and the small ones for C-B radios.

Susan: Right, but what I'm thinking is that use of the small familiar blocks for building is actually sort of inhibited by the large blocks—not just space-wise but because of the scale in which building is taking place. There is this big fort and the kids never seem to think in terms of adding any elaboration from small blocks. It's partly what they're building and their purposes being less a matter of accurate construction than of getting a territory to call their own. But it's also the very presence of that grand-scale fort seeming to get in the way of them or other kids thinking of working with small-scale roads, bridges, etc., with the smaller blocks. I've seen kids this age do a lot with those small ones.

Anne: Do you think maybe it's less advanced or less demanding to work with things of roughly the same scale first? Maybe you can build a plane of large blocks or one of small blocks more easily than you can build one where large blocks are used for the body and wings, while smaller blocks are used for making the instrument panel, wheels, lights, etc. I don't know—that's a thought to keep in the back of our minds in observing the block play. But I think Susan's major point is something we should consider—that the small blocks seem to be conducive to different construction potentials that

	aren't now being used. For example, intricate roadways are not as practical with the large blocks.
Michael:	So we want to think about having the small blocks accessible and providing adequate space for the children to use them for separate constructions if they wish. Susan, your point about the large blocks possibly "inhibiting" this kind of play with the smaller blocks would seem to indicate putting them in a different area of the room might have some advantages. . .

As the teachers go on to evaluate alternative placements of the small blocks, a number of points come up that are considered before decisions are made.

—If the small blocks and the large blocks are separated to different areas of the room, the use of them together may not be as likely to take place. As Anne has mentioned, constructing with large and small blocks together seems to involve a different kind of mental demand and in many cases to allow for more elaborate representation. This potential for use of the large and small blocks together is one factor to weigh into the decision on placing the small blocks.

—It appears that in both classes to some extent the children who play with large blocks are on the whole older, are usually boys, and are currently more involved with dramatic play. The children who spend their time with the small manipulative materials—Legos, bristle blocks, etc.—are heterogeneous in age and sex, including a number of the younger children, both boys and girls. Many of them do not engage in dramatic play except at the simplest level. At the moment, then, the groups involved with large blocks and small blocks are rather different. Will they benefit from playing nearby—from seeing what their classmates are involved in and thereby learning new possibilities? Or perhaps the proximity will cause a great many management problems, with the noisier, space-consuming, large block play impinging in various ways on the small block play. Some children may even stay away from the area.

—Another "proximity" consideration is the facilitation of children's using the props and costumes together with the blocks in engaging in dramatic play. The potential for such integration of materials is another factor to be weighed. The teachers wonder whether children would be as likely to use these items together if they were not located close at hand.

—Another set of considerations to take into account are the other areas of the room, which are arranged as they are for good reason. For example, the "wet art" area (easel, finger paints, etc.) would be difficult to move away from the sink, especially if children are to be able to be independent in their clean-up, in working with paint consistency, etc.

Such constraints are involved in making a decision about a new room arrangement.

Anne: Our hour is almost gone. We've come up with some room changes that Michael and Susan are going to try. Kate and Gail, you've decided to observe the block play in your class more before moving areas around. Also, by then we'll have an idea of how things are working out with Michael and Susan's room switches. In the meantime, do you have anything else in mind for dealing with the block area situation?

Kate: We want to know more about how the children themselves perceive the current situation. We'd like to do some group problem-solving with them if some of them do feel there's a problem. But first we want to see what they think.

Gail: We have had some fights and hurt feelings when kids have been excluded from the area —enough so that I think there is some unhappiness with the situation that will be voiced by the kids themselves.

Anne: As your thoughts progress on this or as you try out your discussion ideas, we'll be anxious to hear how it goes. I think this involving of children in thinking about classroom problems is an exciting idea we've all been attracted to but one in which we're in uncharted territory. Unfortunately, there's no more time today. Let's keep each other up to date on how these situations are shaping up in a few weeks and we can go back to the drawing boards if none of these things are working out.

By the end of this meeting each pair of teachers has decided on a "plan of attack" which seems the best place to start in the classroom. As you can see, what the teachers decide stems from the perception they have of the problems, their values and beliefs about children's development and behavior, and their previous experience with this specific problem—what they have tried, what factors they've observed affecting the situation, what they know about the individuals involved. There are many considerations to take into account. Teachers often find that the more they teach, the more different factors of this kind they notice and consider in their planning and decision-making.

Let's return to the other teacher, Jane, who had a similar situation in her classroom. By this time, she has an attractive new throwing game completed and ready to hang in the classroom—while these five are still talking. And what do they have to show for their time? The four teachers and the director have gone through a problem-solving process which has several potential advantages.

1.   Through their discussion the teachers have been *alerted to sources of information* that they might have otherwise overlooked. Most important, they have become aware of some *things to watch for in the classroom*. In addition, they have seen that there are *observations reported by other teachers* which they can learn from. It is useful to see how a situation is similar to and different from one's own when a different group of children and teachers is involved. Another source of information of which the teachers may become more aware is parents. This source of information is less prominent in this particular situation but often in carefully working

through a problem teachers find themselves thinking of *information and impressions they need to obtain from parents.*

2. In this discussion the teachers have more *specifically identified the problem.* They force themselves to be explicit in not only describing each problematic aspect, but in specifying why it is a problem. Sometimes the problem is different from what was initially noted; almost invariably it is more complex. As can be seen in the above discussion, it is critical to know what problem or problems you are trying to solve before rushing in with a solution.

3. The *generating of a wide range of alternative strategies* is a very useful step. The first idea one thinks of is not always the best. Pushing oneself to brainstorm for a while before deciding yields two benefits: (1) the quality of the initial idea adopted is likely to be higher and (2) if the first plan doesn't work, one is armed with a repertoire of other options to reconsider.

4. The teachers have subjected potential plans to *more careful evaluation* than Teacher Jane who jumped into making the materials before she had subjected her idea to scrutiny. Many ideas which sounded good initially broke down when they were thought through by the individual or the group.

We will be seeing this problem-solving process again as we proceed. It is the same process that the teachers work to facilitate in the children—*careful observation, identification of the problem, generating a number of solutions, and evaluating the alternatives.* An individual cannot always go through the process in its full form, at least not aloud and with the benefit of group reactions. But it can become second nature to go through the steps of problem-solving, at least in capsule form, at many stages of the teaching process—whether trying to figure out what to do for an individual child who's having trouble making friends, which of several field trips to plan for the month of October, or what puzzles to buy for the classroom. Stopping periodically to work through a problem together helps teachers clarify the guidelines they will follow in the day-to-day arrangement of materials, planning of activities, and interaction with children. The experience of periodically making such attempts to clarify one's perspective makes it more likely that actions "in the heat of the moment" will be in tune with the best judgment of the teachers.

In the following chapter we will be describing a particular perspective on educating young children as thinkers. Not every early childhood educator has the same perspective. As teachers in the process of formulating your own perspectives, you may find some aspects with which you disagree. This is as it should be. What is crucial is that we communicate the importance of asking yourself the why question in tackling any of the decisions you as a teacher will confront.

2

On Educating
the Young Thinker:
A Perspective

Mrs. Jamison, Mr. Schroeder, and Mrs. Riley are sitting on a park bench discussing schools and children. Mrs. Jamison asserts, "Just turn them loose in a roomful of assorted 'stuff' and they do fine! The less you do beyond keeping kids safe, well-fed, and loved, the better they learn. Look at how they learn a complicated thing like talking—it's a good thing schools don't have the job of teaching them that. They'd get in the way so much the kids would never learn!"

Mr. Schroeder objects, "But it's not that way with most things. I guess things like walking and talking will get going pretty much from growing up around people who walk and talk. But what about learning to read and write and learning how to behave in society? A kid's not going to pick that up without someone sitting down and teaching him. The job of the school is to teach kids what it's taken centuries for human beings to learn." Mrs. Riley takes her turn. "I don't agree with either one of you. You don't just keep out of the way. But setting out to 'teach' them everything *you* think they ought to know doesn't work. The only learning kids do is, as far as I can see, on their own terms. They aren't just sponges you fill up with learning. The teacher makes a big difference, sure. But so does the way kids are and where that particular kid is when she's asking him something or when he's working on that problem. What the kid is like at the moment makes a big difference to what kind of difference the teacher makes!"

You've probably heard people make these kinds of statements before and perhaps made some of them yourself. You probably didn't think of the Mrs. Rileys and Mr. Schroeders on your block as theorists. But they are stating their theories, their beliefs, about the development of children. This particular threesome have, unbeknownst to themselves, given rough-and-ready versions of three general perspectives which Kohlberg (1968) sees as the "three broad streams of educational thought over the generations."

The first of these, which is reflected in the opinions of Mrs. Jamison, is a "maturationist" view of what education should be. Although Mrs. Jamison may be more extreme than many of this general view, this stream of thought sees the best educational environment as the one which allows the development of the child to take place as it is its nature to do. Although not denying the effects of environment entirely, this school of thought sees development as an unfolding of the abilities and qualities inherent in the human being. The best situation is a benign but unobtrusive environment in which the "good will out," the natural course of development will unfold. Shapiro and Biber (1972) list representatives of this viewpoint from its early proponent, Rousseau, to Gesell and Freud and their followers, to A. S. Neill (1960) of Summerhill fame, C. Gattegno (1970), and, to a degree, John Holt (e.g., 1964) and Herbert Kohl (e.g., 1969).

Mr. Schroeder speaks for another enormously prevalent and influential view of education, which Kohlberg calls "cultural training." In Kohlberg's words, for this viewpoint "what is important in the development of the child is his learning of the cognitive and moral knowledge and rules of the culture, and [therefore] education's business is the teaching of such information and rules to the child through direct instruction" (1968, p. 1015). Although one cannot generalize about something as vast and diverse as the U.S. educational system, this viewpoint is probably the closest to being the prevalent belief system underlying our schools, at least from the elementary grades on. As Kohlberg (1968) points out, the representatives of this view over generations include Locke, Thorndike, Watson, and Skinner, and on a more applied level, Bereiter and Englemann. The behavior modification and programmed learning programs and television programs such as "Sesame Street" also fall within this tradition.

The third major stream of thought, which Mrs. Riley stumps for here, is called by Kohlberg the "cognitive-developmental" or "interactionist" view. This view assumes that the educational environment has an important effect on development, but does not determine its basic pattern or sequence; it stresses that the child comes to each educational encounter *with* a mental structure which determines to a very large degree what will come of that encounter. As Kohlberg puts it, "the cognitive and affective structures which education should nourish are natural emergents from the interaction between the child and his environment under conditions where such interaction is allowed or fostered" (1968, p. 1015). This view of the child's development has a considerable following in education today, largely due to the impact of the Swiss psychologist Jean Piaget. The British Infant Schools exemplify this view of education, as do numerous U.S. programs such as those identified with C. Kamii, C. Lavatelli, D. Weikart, I. Sigel, and with Bank Street College.

It is with Piaget and Mrs. Riley that we agree. Our perspective is firmly "interactionist." Those who have an interactionist perspective on the development of the child share a number of fundamental assumptions. When we narrow the pack to those who approach education from a Piagetian perspective, there is even more commonality of basic beliefs. At the core of these shared conceptions is the view that the child's development is the result of his own active construction.

A Constructivist Perspective on the Education of the Young Child

Active Construction

Does the statement "the child actively constructs knowledge" make you do a double take, sit up in your chair and say to yourself, "Hey, this is a way of looking at learning that's different. That's not the way everybody looks at it"? Probably not. Unless the meaning of the statement is well understood it may sound like a bland statement with which everyone would agree. It most definitely is not. To see the distinctiveness of this view of children's development, it is useful to examine the contrary view.

George Forman and David Kuschner (1977) make the contrast clear in their description of the alternative conception as the *copy theory of knowledge*. In this view, knowing is something like a photographic process. In the words of Forman and Kuschner, "wisdom, useful knowledge, and adaptation result from getting clear focus on the object. . . . Improvement takes place when the lenses are adjusted—that is, when the viewer makes some change in the way he looks at the world" (1977, p. 47). Knowledge, in this view, is the result of more refined perceptual discriminations.

For those of the constructivist perspective, what takes place is of a more active nature. The mind actively constructs relationships among objects (or events, bits of information, etc.). *Knowledge is the result of this active process of construction* (Sigel and Cocking, 1977). This does not mean that the child does not need to learn to notice features of objects and events. According to Piaget, this noticing is important but not sufficient. To illustrate this point, let's look at an example.

Suppose the child is confronted with a situation like those involved in Piaget's conservation tasks. In these tasks the child sees that two identical glasses of water are filled to the same point. She acknowledges that the amount of water in them is the same. When one of the glasses is emptied into a tall thin container and the other into a shallow wide one, the child asserts that the first container has more water in it. Does the child need to learn to observe the containers more carefully, or perhaps watch more closely when the water is being poured? Does she need to have the water reversed and then repeated until she sees the equivalence? There have been those who have thought that drawing the facts more clearly to the child's attention in these ways would correct the child's misconception. Piaget's careful research has indicated otherwise. As he has claimed, no amount of attention to detail will suffice for giving the child an unshakable conviction that the two amounts must logically be equal. The child must construct this knowledge and he cannot do it overnight. Successive steps along the way provide the basis for further steps. Until something makes the child uncomfortable about his present construction of the situation he does not learn much from observation. In conservation, as in all of the child's continuing construction of reality, a key concept is *discrepancy resolution* (Sigel and Cocking, 1977).

Discrepancy Resolution

Development takes place through a process of discrepancy resolution. A discrepancy may be thought of as an inconsistency, a gap, or an expectation which is upset. Suppose a young child has a concept of what a dog is. From the dogs he's seen before, he thinks dogs are furry, four-legged animals larger than cats and rabbits though not as large as cows and horses. He and his mother see a chihuahua on the street and his mother says, "What a cute dog!" BOING—something doesn't fit. This is one kind of discrepancy, an inconsistency between the child's construction of a dog and this current minuscule contender for the label. When an individual is faced with such a discrepancy, his mind goes to work to resolve the discrepancy. One way or another, the discrepancy is dealt with, usually by the construction of an understanding which is more accurate, and often more elaborate, than the previous one. In our example, the child realizes that his earlier concept of dog was inadequate. Some dogs apparently are no bigger than cats, so that criterion is no good. The child is intrigued enough to inspect the odd creature more closely. Admittedly, it doesn't look much like a cat either. The pointed face, the wagging tail, and the bark fit with his own dog and his neighbor's dog. These features are shifted to a more central role in the child's new construction of dogness. The new generalization encompasses more cases; it is more in accordance with the way things are.

This is, by the way, the same process that takes place countless times every day for adults as well—in big ways and small. Your roommate tells you that her blind date was a tuna. Even as blind dates go you cannot accept that her date was a fish, so you realize that she's speaking metaphorically. Discrepancy resolved. Your bank balance is $200 more than you thought you had. The new figure is more appealing, but the inconsistency keeps coming to your mind until you remember a possibility. The $200 you sent your parents is sitting in their mailbox while they're on vacation. Discrepancy resolved.

A discrepancy is only perceived as such in relation to the individual's current expectations or knowledge. You can't have a violation of expectations where none exist; a bit of information is not incongruous unless the individual has some knowledge with which it doesn't fit. For example, it will not seem strange that a platypus both lays eggs and has fur if I know very little about mammals and birds.

Consider an example in the child's play. Lynne is rolling objects down a ramp. The first object she picks up to roll happens to be a cone so it rolls off the edge of the ramp. Picking up objects at random, she rolls balls, hoops, and cylinders. Picking up another cone, she again sees it roll off the side. None of the others have done that! She repeats it several times, taking care to hold it straight before releasing it. She tries the experiment with the cone's large end toward her and then the other way around. This seems to make a difference in which side of the ramp the cone curves toward. She continues until she has an idea each time of which way the cone will roll. Notice that the first time Lynne rolled the cone she did not find its pathway discrepant. The discrepancy was not perceived until the child had constructed the idea that objects roll straight down the incline. It is also important to note that Lynne's baby brother could watch this whole sequence from start to finish and find nothing discrepant at all. His representational abilities (among others) are not sufficiently advanced for him to form the same kinds of predictions that Lynne does, but he might find it discrepant if one of the objects suddenly took flight. A discrepancy is in the eyes of the beholder.

Let's look again at the major points we have been making about the constructivist perspective in relation to the child's development:

1. *The individual develops by actively constructing his reality.*
2. *Development takes place through a process of discrepancy resolution.*
3. *A discrepancy can only be perceived in relation to the individual's current expectations or knowledge.*

Our purpose in this chapter is to acquaint the reader with our general framework for viewing the education of the young child. To complete our description of this framework, we need to introduce another basic concept: representational competence.

Representational Competence and the Education of the Young Child

A Scenario

Sarah and Jamie are undergraduate students who have never met, sitting at nearby tables at the student union. Sarah has just finished a final and is feeling frisky, so the next time Jamie looks over at her, she winks. Jamie grins and immediately comes over and introduces himself. He thinks (or pretends to think) he has met her before and tries to think where. They consider classes they might have had together ("What a dazzling topic of conversation," Jamie thinks). They discover they are among the horde in Psych 101 and are both celebrating the completion of its final. They talk about some of the professor's eccentricities and Sarah tells Jamie about a hilarious thing Professor Hinkle was said to have done in a previous semester. They talk about what they plan to do when they graduate, though their respective thoughts are turning to what they plan to do Saturday night.

Finally, needing to leave, Sarah says, "Well, I winked at you but that's as far as I go in shameless aggression." Jamie finds himself with a date.

He asks for directions and Sarah draws him a map on a napkin. After some discussion of what movies are playing, etc., they set a time for the date. Sarah dashes away. Passing a mirror, she smiles at herself. And winks.

Are we employing this scenario as an example of Boy Meets Girl? Of Women's Lib On Our College Campuses? Guess again—it's an illustration of what we will be calling *representational competence* as the Cornerstone of Life and Love. Consider the following events in this scenario, astounding occurrences when you think of it, and in what way each is dependent on the ability of Sarah and Jamie to use *representational processes*.

—Sarah's wink propels a 6'2" sophomore across the room.
—By running through their class schedules, Sarah and Jamie determine that they are both in Psych 101.
—Mr. Hinkle, although he is not with them at the Union, causes Sarah and Jamie to laugh—about something neither of them ever saw.

—Future career experiences, three years and many final exams away, are discussed and evaluated as to how enjoyable they will be for Sarah and Jamie.

—Jamie learns where Sarah lives by gazing at lines she has drawn on her napkin.

There are a multitude of happenings here that would not have been possible without Sarah and Jamie's abilities to represent. Just thinking of Professor Hinkle and his oddities requires mental, or *internal,* representations. And what about the fact that Sarah knew a particularly rich example of the Professor's flair for the bizarre from the previous school year? For this to be possible, an upperclassman friend of Sarah's had used language, perhaps a bit of gestural embroidery, to recount what he had seen take place. Now Sarah has put together his words and her own experiences of Professor Hinkle in order to construct her own *internal* representation of the event which she is able, months later, to communicate to Jamie. Together with Jamie's own experiences with Professor Hinkle (the innocent object of all these representations), Sarah's words help Jamie construct vivid mental pictures of the original event. Jamie reacts almost as if he were there. Sarah, her upperclassman friend, and Jamie all have different but related *internal* representations of the same event.

The different *internal* representations have been communicated through *external* representation systems. The *external* representational systems of language and gesture contribute to the shared enjoyment of the anecdote. Another *external* representational system is employed when Sarah draws Jamie a map to her apartment. She could have given him verbal directions alone (another type of external representation), but she elected to use a drawing as the medium in which to represent spatial location. This kind of representation seems particularly efficient in giving him a sense of the layout of the complex where she lives—where it is in relation to other places with which he is familiar, how it is arranged, etc. With a map he'd also do better at figuring out an alternate route if he should find one of the roads closed for repairs.

Different external systems are most effective for different communication tasks. Imagine Sarah having to communicate the Hinkle anecdote through pictures. Certainly some well-drawn sketches or cartoons, if she had the time and talent, could be good for illustrating facial expressions, but the events—for example, what was said—are far more efficiently communicated by language (even the eccentric Professor Hinkle would have trouble discussing the theories of Freud and Skinner by pictures or pantomime alone).

We have invited you to consider how representational thought and communication underlie even the most commonplace everyday events in the lives of adults (if we can be so unromantic as to regard Sarah's and Jamie's meeting in this light), and we have hinted at the value of competence with different kinds of representation (language, gesture, maps, and pictures). Sarah and Jamie were able to communicate because they have learned how to interpret each other's actions and words. They share an understanding of the meanings of winks, words, and wisecracks.

Our Usage of Five Crucial Terms

Let's take a moment at this point to clarify some of the terms we have used and will be using. This is especially important because not everyone who writes in this area uses the same terms or uses them to mean the same thing. We are using the term "representational" where some other writers use "symbolic" (e.g., Bruner, 1973; Gross, 1974; Olson and Bruner, 1974). There are reasons for our choice, of course, but the differences in what is being referred to with the two terms is minimal. The ability to employ representations we refer to as *representational competence*. In thinking, we are engaged in *internal representation*. In conveying our ideas to others or recording them for our own pleasure, manipulation, or later use, we use some system of *external representation*. The various *representational systems* or *modes*, e.g., linguistic, pictorial, musical, etc., each have their own unique characteristics and within each there are a variety of possible media. The *medium* is the specific means of expression. For example, linguistic representation can be in the medium of a poem, a story, a play, and so forth; for the pictorial mode, the medium might be paintings of various kinds, collage, etc.

Development of Representational Competence: General Principles

Developing the skills which our undergraduate couple Sarah and Jamie showed is not as automatic as it might seem, and these abilities are not acquired equally by everyone through maturation alone. For the growth of fully developed skills of representational competence an environment is necessary which fosters such competence through the kinds of interactions and materials it provides. These assertions are based on a large body of research you may want to read (Arnheim, 1974; Bruner, 1973; Olson, 1970; Piaget, 1971; Sigel and Cocking, 1977).

We will now look at three points about representational competence which are important to developing an educational program.

1. Human beings understand their world through representations of it.

Both internal and external aspects of representational competence are necessary for us to cope effectively with the world. We use our internal representations to help us remember experiences we've had, to think about those experiences, and to apply what we learn in one situation to new situations. Our internal representational system helps us to use past experience in adopting behaviors and beliefs that are well-suited to the world we live in. The more fully our representational system is developed, the more able we are to transcend the present—to reconstruct past experiences, to think about the future, and to think hypothetically about imaginary and real-life situations. The ability to reexamine past experiences is crucial if we are to apply what we already know to new problems. For example, suppose I am home alone and must move an extremely heavy package to the car. Searching my mind for various things that would help me, I think of my son's wagon. Thanks to my ability to call on internal representations of past experiences, I do not have to reinvent the wheel!

This ability to reflect on past experiences is also needed in reflecting on the future. I must draw on what I know of the world to anticipate future events and act accordingly. Suppose I am faced with the task of telling my employer of my vacation plans. I make a prediction about the best way to do this based on my internal representation of his reaction when I mentioned my last vacation, which was already planned, versus the previous set of plans, which I had told him was tentative. (Recalling his reactions, I opt for presenting him with a *fait accompli!*) Representational thinking, then, does more than help the individual organize realities, reflect on experiences, and come to understand his world. It also helps in adapting to that world.

The understanding of pictures, models, music, gestures, and words enables us to acquire knowledge from others. The broader our ability to comprehend messages as expressed in any or all of these, the more extensive will be our knowledge, and our enjoyment as well. To the degree that we can express our own ideas in one or more of these ways we can be more effective communicators.

2. Representational competence develops in an orderly sequence.

Children are not born with well-developed representational systems. In the beginning, the infant apparently has no lasting representations of objects or events. One important source of our recognition of this point is Piaget's (1952) careful observations of how children react when an object is removed from sight. It is not until about six months that the child will search for the object or give evidence of believing that the object still exists.

Another evidence of the infant's increasing ability to represent is in his or her imitation of another person's actions, which was also observed over time by Piaget (1952). At first the child only imitates actions while they are taking place or directly afterwards. By the time the child is around eighteen months, he or she will sometimes be observed to imitate an action witnessed several days before, which Piaget calls deferred imitation. Such delayed imitation suggests that the child has formed some sort of internal representation of the event and that this representation was stored.

Compared with the infant, the child of four or five has vast representational abilities. But these abilities are still in the process of being developed and extended. For example, though the child can think in terms of past events, notions of duration and temporal sequence are crude. She has some representation of the interior of her house, but she has difficulty putting the parts she remembers together in a coherent way; she would have even more difficulty putting this into the two-dimensional form of a picture.

The development of representational competence is very gradual, with each day's changes based on yesterday's. As with all areas of development, the child must crawl before she can walk. For the teacher, this is a major reason why it is so important to try to know as much as possible about the individual child's thinking and representational abilities at any point in time. This awareness is crucial in guiding decisions about what materials, activities, and questions, are appropriate for the next step.

3. Representational competence develops fully only in response to interactions with the appropriate physical and social environments.

Development occurs in poor as well as good environments, but, as with nutrition, the better the quality of the food, the better the quality of the growth. A central concern of this book is to aid teachers in making decisions about providing a good environment for the full development of representational competence, along with the problem-solving abilities that depend on it. From the standpoint of the developmental principles that we have been listing, two general points about this decision-making are clear. First, it is obvious that as the child changes, the environment (the materials, activities, interactions) cannot be static. To be appropriate to the child's changing needs, the environment must change. Second, the child and the teacher must be collaborators in arriving at decisions for the learning environment. Good decisions cannot be made unless the teacher is in close communication with the child's thoughts and needs. And the decisions must always leave ample room for the child to choose, to accept or reject, to follow the line of his interest and find his own opportunities for growth.

So far, we have been speaking in general terms arguing for the role of the environment in promoting cognitive development in general and representational competence in particular. We shall now describe our theoretical perspective on the critical elements of the environment for such development.

Development of Representational Competence: The Distancing Concept

Think of Sarah and Jamie and the various manifestations of representational competence which they showed. How did they reach that point? Human beings have the inherent capacity to represent but, to return to our analogy of nutrition, what is the experiential diet which is required for this capacity to be actualized?

We suggest that the common ingredient in the various encounters which serve this purpose is that the child is required to deal with objects, actions, or events that are separate in time and/or space from the immediate present. We call circumstances or behaviors which create such mental demands *distancing* events. Such events begin at the start of life when a desirable object, e.g., the mother, goes out of the child's sight. Just by the fact that people come and go and time passes, each child growing up is presented with numerous occasions when he needs to represent the nonpresent, and every normal child achieves this basic ability to represent. But beyond this minimum there are considerable differences in the degree to which children have such mental demands made on them by the various environments in which they live. Parents, for example, vary greatly in the degree to which they talk with children about nonpresent events, people, places, or things. Some parents stick much more to the here and now. Other parents involve children in planning, anticipating future events, reconstructing the past, translating ideas from one mode to another. There is evidence that this kind of interaction is less common among lower-class families, but middle-class families also vary considerably in the degree to which they engage children in conversation about nonpresent aspects versus concrete, here-and-now aspects (McGillicuddy-DeLisi, Sigel, and Johnson, 1979).

With external representation as well, differences in experience seem to make a difference in children's competence. For example, children from varying backgrounds seem to differ in the way in which they interpret pictures (Sigel and McBane, 1967; Sigel, 1978). Again, the difference would seem to be linked to differences in the environment, in the materials the child has access to, but primarily in the interactions about these materials.

We have sought to apply this *distancing hypothesis* (Sigel, 1970; Sigel and Cocking, 1977, 1978) to the classroom by developing teaching strategies which incorporate this characteristic of requiring children to deal with the nonpresent. One cannot simply give a list of particular teacher behaviors which together make up the set of distancing acts. For one thing, whether or not a particular utterance or material has the dimension we call distancing depends on its effect on the person to whom it is directed. But we can state several features which characterize many interactions which are effective in expanding the child's ability to think and to represent. They are, of course, the natural outgrowth of the points we have been making in this chapter. Teacher behaviors would be likely to be effective if they have one or more of the following features:

—Placing the cognitive demand on the child: for this purpose a question is often more effective than a statement.
—Drawing the child's attention to a discrepancy, a contradiction, or inconsistency.
—Involving the child in mental activity which requires going beyond the

concrete. As we will see, this does not mean that the more abstract the mental demand the better—preschool children, on the contrary, learn most readily from involvement with concrete experience. What it means is that the teacher should understand the importance of "re-presenting" these concrete experiences: reconstructing them mentally, describing them, communicating aspects of them across time and space and through diverse means. As George Forman has written, "Knowing is not just doing; knowing is also reflecting on how the doing was done" (1977, p. vii).

Summary

We began the chapter by identifying our perspective with one of three major streams of educational thought; we take an interactionist perspective. Having broadly located our point of view within the universe of beliefs on educating children, we further defined our perspective in two ways: (1) We take a constructivist perspective on the child's development of knowledge, and (2) we stress the importance of the development of representational compe-tence. In explaining these fundamental "planks of our platform," we stated six principles:

1. The individual develops by actively constructing his reality.
2. Development takes place through a process of discrepancy resolution.
3. Discrepancies are only perceived in relation to an individual's current expectations or knowledge.
4. Human beings understand their world through representations of it.
5. Representational competence develops in an orderly sequence.
6. Representational competence develops fully only in response to inte-ractions with the appropriate physical and social environments.

These principles describe the core set of beliefs which guide the classroom strategies which you will be learning about in this book.

Looking Ahead

In the next chapter, Chapter 3, we will be looking at a classroom in which the teachers are trying to put these beliefs into action. We will highlight some of the points at which the teachers make the decision to pursue a particular objective. We hope that this will help to give you a sense of how our perspective functions as a guide to teacher goals as well as teacher practices. The teacher's understanding of what she is trying to facilitate is the indispensable foundation of good teaching. The strategies which she chooses are important, but they can only follow from this understanding, and they will vary a great deal with the child, the context, and the activity.

In the next five chapters we will describe the application of the perspective and the teaching strategies to particular areas of curriculum: art and construction (Chapter 4), movement and music (Chapter 5), science (Chapter 6), the social-affective domain (Chapter 7), and imaginative play (Chapter 8). Having taken a look at the application of our perspective to these areas, we will in the last chapter be able to draw together what we have seen about the relation of teacher goals to teacher strategies. At this point you will be ready to think about where you would begin in actually shaping your classroom and planning your first ventures with the children.

In Chapter 1 we saw the teachers involved in some tough classroom decision-making. We have attempted in this chapter to describe our framework for classroom decision-making. With this perspective in mind, let's return to the classroom and watch how this perspective is reflected in a day in the lives of two teachers and their class.

3

A Day in the Preschool

Now let's turn to watching the teachers in action. We will focus on the teachers' attempts to use the various activities of the day in ways that promote growth in representational competence and in problem-solving. There are other aspects of the children's development with which teachers are concerned that are not directly reflected here. The teacher is concerned with Elizabeth's development of the ability to walk on the balance beam. She watches for signs that Jason is more comfortable speaking up at circle time, and she notices how much time Ted spends watching the children in the block corner. She wonders why Mandy never wants to take pictures home and plans to observe Mandy with her mother at the end of the day. Although in dealing with these concerns the approach to working with young children which is being articulated in this book can be useful, these types of problems and goals will not be our primary focus. Our interest will center on how the teachers use the activities of this particular preschool day in working on three objectives: (1) increasing children's acquaintance with objects and events in the world and awareness of their reactions to them; (2) developing competence in the representational modes; and (3) increasing problem-solving abilities.

First Circle

When we enter the nursery school about half the class has arrived and is seated on the circle with Jeanne and Denise. They are discussing aspects of their rides to school on this day, a topic initiated by the children themselves. At the moment individual children are telling about their car pools. As this topic runs its course, Jeanne says, "Well, suppose you couldn't come to school in a car. What are some other ways you could get from home to school?" The children call to mind other means of transportation, sharing them with the group. At this point Jeanne is listening to all the ideas without getting the children to evaluate answers.

The children's ideas include walking, riding a bike or a horse, taking a train or plane, etc. Some children begin to give personal experiences with transportation and Jeanne notices that a few show a particular interest in talking about airplanes. DECISION: TO ENCOURAGE CHILDREN TO ELABORATE AND REFINE THEIR INTERNAL REPRESENTATION OF A SITUATION. She elicits elaboration of the airplane idea by introducing a question:

Jeanne: Well, suppose you did decide to take an airplane to school. What would you have to do?
Mandy: Just jump in and fly away!
Jeanne   (to group): You could just go right out your front door and it would be there?
Peter, Molly, and others: No! No! You go to the airport.
Jeanne: Oh yeah? Do you always have to go to the airport to get an airplane?

Sam:	Once on TV I saw a helicopter that landed right by the people's house and they got in and flew away.
Jeanne	(to group): What about that?
Peter:	But planes are too big.They wouldn't fit in your yard.
Jeanne:	Planes would be too big?
Laurie:	Some planes are little. Daddy goes in a plane only two people can fit into.
Jeannie:	So if you had a small plane you might be able to bring it into your yard? (Laurie nods.) Well, who here has had a ride in a plane?
Children:	Me! Me! I went to Disney World . . . I went on a real big one. . . . DECISION: TO HELP CHILDREN REFINE THEIR REPRESENTATIONS OF A SPECIFIC ASPECT OF A SITUATION IN ORDER TO BE ABLE TO IDENTIFY A PROBLEM.
Jeanne:	OK, think about when you rode on that plane. When it went from the ground to the air, did it just go straight up like this? (uses hand to demonstrate absolutely vertical lift-off).

The discussion continues. As the children, with Jeanne's encouragement, bring up various experiences and ideas related to airplanes, members of the group are confronted with information or perspectives inconsistent with their previous knowledge. For example, several children initially asserted that no aircraft could land in a yard and then the helicopter idea was introduced.

Soon, almost all the children have arrived. Jeanne wants to plant a seed for the children using ideas from the airplane discussion in their activities. DECISION: TO ENCOURAGE CHILDREN TO USE VARIOUS MEDIA TO REPRESENT OBJECTS AND EVENTS WHICH THEY HAVE BEEN MENTALLY RECONSTRUCTING. She says, "We need to do some other things now, but you've all had lots of good ideas here. When you're playing in the block corner, in the art area, wherever you decide to play—you'll have some ideas about planes and landing that you'll want to use."

Before beginning the free play time, to get the group together, Jeanne starts a movement activity. She uses the Eensy-Weensy Spider, a favorite finger play the children have already learned in the usual way. But now there will be a slightly different twist. The group sings it through once in the traditional way. DECISION: TO ENCOURAGE CHILDREN TO THINK OF HOW A FAMILIAR WAY OF DEPICTING SOMETHING CAN BE CHANGED TO EXPRESS A TRANSFORMATION OF IT. Jeanne says, "OK, now imagine a very, very, sleepy spider. Think about how the spider would look, how his legs would feel. How would he hold his head, legs? . . . How does your body move when you're tired? . . . Show me with your body how you look when you're tired. OK, now use your hand and fingers to show how that very, very sleepy spider would look on the bottom of the water spout. OK, when we sing make your voice sound like a very tired voice and your spider fingers move like a sleepy spider."

Again, in this exercise, Jeanne is not looking for a right way of showing a sleepy spider. She encourages each child to think of his own experiences with sleepiness and spiders and portray them in his own way.

The group repeats the song again, now with an angry spider. Jeanne comments on how they're using their faces and bodies to show sleepiness or anger (e.g., "Sam, you're making a fist. Without even looking at your face, I can tell you're angry").

First Free Play

The children are free to select any of about eight play areas, for the most part those found typically in early childhood settings: large wooden blocks, small blocks and other manipulative toys, water table, easel painting, "dry" art area (crayons, felt-tipped pens, scissors, glue), books and clay. DECISION: TO ENGAGE CHILDREN IN REPRESENTING POSSIBLE CHOICES OF ACTIVITIES AND ENCOURAGE THEIR TENDENCY TO PLAN REFLECTIVELY. Jeanne asks the children to think of where they would like to play. She may or may not ask more specific follow-up questions depending on her knowledge of the child. Michael, for example, is not yet very verbal, and Jeanne accepts his pointing to the easel and saying he wants to "make a picture for my Mom." On the other hand, she may ask Tricia, who is ready for developing more elaborated plans, what she plans to do with the building blocks she expresses an intention of playing with. Or she may inquire how Marci will go about dressing up to be a fireperson.

Four of the children select the large block area and Jeanne decides to go with them to observe and watch for good opportunities to work with the process of planning. Interactions within the block area can often be quite complex. Since it is midway through the year, Jeanne has to provide less direct support of the informal planning process she has encouraged the children to engage in. Now they often spontaneously sit down to discuss basic decisions among themselves. Jeanne sits nearby and observes the children playing to get a feel for the children's interests, as well as the level of the play and the nature of the group interaction.

Careful, focused observation is an essential teacher strategy. Jeff and Tricia are building a doghouse. They are barking, but their primary attention is on two construction problems, balancing the roof and creating windows. It is important that the teacher not attempt to shift the children's activity into other directions. The barking dogs may mislead the nonobservant teacher into thinking that the focus of the children's interest is in being dogs. Close watching will reveal that the dog noises are only an accompaniment to their major interest, which is in the problems they face in constructing the doghouse. Jeff and Tricia are not likely to be receptive to teacher comments if their building activity is interrupted by the teacher's attempt to discuss what they as dogs might eat, or how the dog catcher will be kept away. There is likely to be more impact when the activation and expansion of thinking processes take place within the context of what the children are actually involved in, what really matters to them.

The area where dramatic play props are available is adjacent to the block area. DECISION: TO ARRANGE AREAS SO THAT THE INTEGRATION OF MATERIALS AND ACTIVITIES FROM THE AREAS WILL BE FACILITATED BY THEIR PROXIMITY. Two children in the block area have taken "pilot hats" and decided to make an airplane-boat, and Jason decides that he will make a fireplace. At this point Jeanne sees a potential problem situation with space in which there may be an opportunity to help the children expand their problem-solving skills. DECISION: TO HELP CHILDREN TO DEVELOP ABILITY TO IDENTIFY PROBLEMS BY ANTICIPATING OUTCOMES. She says, "Hmmm. Are you going to have enough room for both an airplane-boat and a fireplace?" Jason, who often does things on a grand scale, shows Jeanne how his fireplace will cover a large part of the block area. The airplane-boat construction crew immediately jump to their own defense. "No! No! We won't have room!"

This is a problem which concerns the children directly. Jeanne has discovered that using problems as they arise in context of daily living is perhaps the most effective way of fostering children's skills in working through situations on their own. Although it would initially be more efficient for the teacher to take control of the space problem at this point, the children would not have the opportunity to engage in active construction of solutions to problems. DECISION: TO ASSIST CHILDREN'S REFLECTIVE EVALUATION OF ALTERNATIVES BY HELPING THEM BRING TO MIND RELEVANT CRITERIA FOR SOLVING THE PROBLEM. Jeanne and the group discuss such points as the fact that the airplane-boat needs to seat at least three people, and the fact that Jason's blocks will not stand on any uneven surface. The children finally decide on an arrangement in which the rug which borders the block area can be put to use as the bed area of the airplane-boat. This leaves sufficient room for Jason's fireplace to be on the kind of surface it requires.

The construction process begins. DECISION: ENCOURAGE CHILDREN TO REFINE AND ELABORATE THEIR INTERNAL REPRESENTATIONS OF OBJECT THEY WISH TO CONSTRUCT. Jeanne works with the children to clarify their image of what an "airplane-boat" would be like. She makes comments such as, "I've never seen an airplane-boat before. What's it like? . . . How would it be different from a regular boat . . . Oh, Peter's the pilot. What part of the airplane-boat will he sit in?" and so forth (depending on what the children get interested in). Jeanne avoids pushing too hard for a follow-through on the questions, particularly in the free-play situation. She is there, not to take over the play, but to act as a catalyst. She supports the children's activity, while at the same time stimulating inventions, evaluations, and expansion of their own ideas. Jeanne's intent is to help the children progess toward making decisions themselves as to what they want to create and how.

The children complete the airplane-boat fairly quickly and then begin using it for make-believe play. Up until this point, in addition to encouraging the development of the construction, the teacher continues to observe, looking for new directions in which the children's interest turns. If their activities turn to flying the vehicle, or watching out for sharks, the teacher should be able to shift accordingly—helping to expand the children's efforts in their chosen direction.

The flying begins! One child sits in front as pilot, and the others sit in the back munching peanut butter and jelly sandwiches and pizza, represented by appropriately shaped blocks. The pilot makes a landing, but then Jeanne notices that the play doesn't seem to go further. Realizing that several members of this group haven't engaged in any but the simplest sorts of dramatic play, she decides to introduce a new element to encourage them further. DECISION: TO ASSIST CHILDREN IN SUSTAINING DRAMATIC PLAY BY PROVIDING AN OPEN-ENDED STIMULUS TO BUILD ON. Suddenly she whispers, "Wait! What's that noise? . . . Listen to the banging . . . What do you think it is? . . ." One child suggests that the ominous banging noises are elephants who have escaped from the zoo and are on the runway. The children and Jeanne discuss methods of catching them. Michelle pretends to be one of the elephants, representing them with her body position, her way of moving, and the sounds she makes. As we will discuss at length in Chapter 8 on Imaginative Play, how and when to get involved in the children's play is an issue which demands thoughtful consideration. Here Jeanne avoids a heavy-handed approach like taking a major role or leading the children in a specific direction for what happens next.

As Denise moves around the room, she notices it has started to rain and sees Molly looking out and complaining to Tim that they won't be able to go outside. DECISION: TO INCREASE CHILDREN'S AWARENESS OF THINGS IN THE WORLD AND THEIR REACTIONS TO THEM. Denise goes over and watches with them for a while. Opening the window a crack she says to them, "You know even when I have my back to the window, I can usually tell if it's raining. Has that ever happened to you? (pause) Like at night when you're lying in bed, maybe?" "Yeah," Tim says. "You can hear the thunder." (Denise might explore whether there can be rain without thunder, or thunder without rain, but it's not her objective at the moment to explore how children understand these natural events. DECISION: TO REMAIN WITH THE FOCUS WHICH IS GUIDING HER INQUIRY. For the present she directs her inquiry toward the children's awareness of their sensory experiences.)

Denise says, "That's one way, Tim, but without thunder, I wonder how we'd do. Let's turn around and try it." Molly exclaims, "I hear it!" Denise talks to them about how it sounds—whether it always sounds the same, whether they have ever heard the rain on the roof, whether snow sounds like that. DECISION: TO INCREASE CHILDREN'S AWARENESS OF METHODS FOR FINDING OUT ABOUT EXTERNAL STIMULI. Denise inquires, "What about if we couldn't hear it? Suppose we had the record player on and couldn't hear the rain? Is there any other way we could tell it was raining?" The children mention the weather report (modern souls that they are) and Denise accepts these ideas, but poses her question again stipulating "without TV."

Molly and Tim seem to be at a loss, so Denise adds, "I think there's something else when I'm close to the window like this (drawing in a breath)." Tim draws in a breath too and they talk about the "clean smell" as he calls it. Denise says she thinks she smells the earth, the ground. Tim and Molly sniff like crazy and Molly ventures to stick her hand out the window. Denise asks Molly, "Can you tell it's raining with no sound, no smell, and even with your eyes shut?" Tim speaks up, "She can feel it (sticking his hand out too). It sort of tickles." They go on to talk about how rain feels.

When Denise first started drawing Molly and Tim into experiencing the rain at the window, she was thinking for the moment of providing the opportunity for them to become more aware of the sight, the sounds, and the touch of rain and of the sensations and feelings these evoked. Her objective was developing the children's awareness of events in the world and of their reactions to them. Denise values this awareness for its own sake. In some cases the experience will go no further, at least within the classroom. But the child will have had the experience, both with the rain and with the *noticing* of the rain and the sensations it evokes.

But today, for Molly, the noticing of the way the rain felt and sounded will lead to a spontaneous attempt to express something about the experience, to "re-present" it through a rain song on the xylophone. The desire to represent an experience can occur with or without the teacher having been involved in that experience. Children are sometimes struck by things they encounter without anyone else becoming part of the experience—without anyone highlighting or expanding it. But Molly had encountered rain all her life without ever noticing it much—it was just something that meant you couldn't go out to play.

The spontaneity of Molly's subsequent attempt to use music to express or represent rain may appear too good to be true. But such desires are more common that one might think. There does seem to be something characteristically human about wanting to find a way of capturing in a representational medium an experience, a message, an emotion. And Molly has been in a classroom where a variety of modes of expressions and communication are continually used and encouraged.

Molly is now in the music area. Picking up the sticks of the xylophone, she begins to experiment. The teacher refrains from immediately smothering her with praise or with questions. Intrigued by Molly's activity, she watches for several minutes and notices that Molly seems to be playing with a purpose.

Inviting Molly to describe her activity, but not wanting to lead her, Denise says, "You seem to be playing the xylophone in a special way." "This is raindrops," Molly comments. "Oh, I hear them," Denise says. DECISION: TO EN-COURAGE CHILD TO THINK OF HOW HER MUSICAL REPRESENTA-TION OF SOMETHING CAN BE CHANGED TO EXPRESS A TRANS-FORMATION OF IT. She watches a few minutes more before saying, "I wonder if it would sound the same in a heavy rain or a light drizzling rain? What do you think?" They explore this idea for a while and then Molly says, "What about thunder? We need thunder!" Denise asks, "Can you think of anything here we can use?" "The drum!" Molly replies. Denise inquires as to why the drum and so on.

Later in the day Denise spots the other participant in the rain experience, Tim, over at the sink washing his hands. This time she takes the initiative, "Tim, does that feel the same way on your hand that the rain felt?" "No!" says Tim. "But they're both water," Denise comments. Tim says, "I don't know but they're different." Denise says, "They're both water but they feel different? Hmm."

Denise has drawn attention to the discrepancy. It may or may not engage Tim's interest. If it doesn't, there's no point in Denise's pushing it further—following her interest instead of Tim's. But now he seems to be musing over what she's said as he continues running water over his hand. Denise says, "Let's try something, Tim." (She goes and gets the colander from the water table). "Now, close your eyes." She lets him feel the new sensation and then the old. His eyes pop open, of course, but he has felt the difference. Denise and Tim go on to talk about the colander and notice how the drops look coming through. Tim runs back to the window and extends his hand again.

Second Circle

Now it's time for the teachers to get the class together for a large group activity. In the past few weeks the children have been doing a great deal of exploring at the water table where funnels, colanders, sieves, etc., have been available. The children have had lots of time to mess about with the wondrous workings of these materials. DECISION: TO FOLLOW "HANDS-ON" EX-PERIENCE WITH AN ACTIVITY INVOLVING PICTORIAL REPRESEN-TATION OF ASPECTS OF THE EXPERIENCE. Now the teachers devise an activity intended to activate the children's internal representations of a specific aspect of what they had experienced at the water table and to focus their attention on the cause-effect relationship between the sort of implement and the water which comes through it. A guessing game is presented to the group. Pictures of water flowing through a funnel, a colander, or an eyedropper, for example, are shown to children with the teacher covering the pictured implement. Judging by the appearance of the water in each picture, children guess which implement is covered. The main focus here is for children to relate their water play experiences to pictorial representations. Particularly emphasized are the cause-effect relations between the size and number of openings and the form taken by water flowing through. After the group comes to a conclusion about each picture, they test it out with actual materials which Denise has made available to them. This actual experience is essential, especially for those children who were unsure about what object was hidden. The guessing game has focused their attention on the different forms taken by water. Now that they're tuned in to differences in form, they'll be watching for similarities and differences in how water looks when poured through different implements. Particularly with young children, hands-on experiences are crucial both *before* and *after* activities of a representational nature.

Second Free Play

After the short group activity the class disperses for free play. They again engage in planning; the teachers ask children if there is anything they want to make sure to do, or any activities they want to complete, etc.

Small Group Session

Denise invites Laurie, Sam, and Amy to participate in the day's small group activity, which is held in a quiet, isolated part of the room. During the week the class has been discussing the outside play yard—its materials, rules, and activities. The previous day in circle time the children were asked to give ideas of what would be good things to have on a playground, either from things they remembered seeing on other playgrounds or things they thought would be fun to have. DECISION: TO USE A SMALL GROUP FORMAT TO EVALUATE SUGGESTIONS MADE BY CLASS IN LARGE GROUP. Now they will follow up in a group of two or three. The teachers usually find large groups to be well suited to activities which involve supplying ideas and small groups good for careful evaluation of ideas or other more intense mental demands. The smaller group also allows the teacher to work with children who are not vastly different in developmental level. A large group of children can "brainstorm," and learn from the diverse ideas their classmates provide. When it is a matter of examining these ideas more carefully or solving problems requiring more sustained thought, the teachers have found it is usually more fruitful to follow up with a small (two to three children) group or an individual child.

Today Denise is using a flat cardboard piece cut to scaled dimensions of the playground. Several trees in the right locations have been added to give the children the idea of a model. Denise begins, "In group time you and the others gave lots of ideas of what should go in a playground and I was writing them all down. These were some of the ones that would be important to have. (Denise has chosen some of the named things which are on the current playground and some which are not: a climbing structure, tires, a sandbox, a path for tricycles, and a place to put the trikes out of the rain.) DECISION: TO EXPAND CHILDREN'S ACQUAINTANCE WITH THE USES OF A REPRESENTATIONAL SYSTEM IN SOLVING PRACTICAL PROBLEMS. "Now we're going to do some thinking about where these things could go so that they would fit and so that the playground would be a good place to play in."

Denise has a variety of cut-out shapes. Asking what should be used to show where the sandbox would be, she brings out a few possibilities. One is a circle of approximately the right scale for the sandbox and one is a very large square about half the size of the playground. Two of the children want to use the square since "sandboxes are square." Sam wants to use the circle because it is the right size. Denise says, "Is it OK to use a round piece to mark where a sandbox would be?" Sam is the only one who seems ready for this concept and argues that it really doesn't matter. The others are too literal. But after some questions from Denise and some manipulation of the materials, Laurie and Amy do see the problem with the huge square.

Laurie: Can we cut this big one so that it's the right size? DECISION: TO ENCOURAGE CHILDREN TO GENERATE ALTERNATIVE SOLUTIONS TO A PROBLEM.
Denise: We don't have any scissors here. Can you think of any way we could do it?
Laurie: We could tear it.
Sam: We could just fold it back!

Folding is agreed upon because the other children buy Sam's argument that the piece could then be unfolded later and used again if needed.

Laurie: But a sandbox isn't purple!
Denise: (in an open, noncommittal tone): Does that mean we shouldn't use this piece to be the sandbox, Laurie? What do you think, Amy? Laurie says this piece isn't the color of a sandbox.
Susan and Amy (at once): That don't matter! A sandbox could be purple.

The discussion continues as to what elements do and don't matter for the model of the playground. DECISION: TO CONFRONT CHILDREN WITH THE PERSPECTIVE OF OTHER PERSONS WITH RESPECT TO THEIR REPRESENTATIONS. Denise raises the question of what will happen when we take the model back to the other children. Will they know which piece is what? The children suggest telling them, writing the names of things on them (Denise: "But they can't all read"), drawing some sand and sand toys on the square, etc.

A little bit of planning begins for where things will go, with the children trying out different arrangements. DECISION: TO MAKE A MODIFICATION IN ORIGINAL FOCUS AS CHILDREN BECOME INTERESTED IN AN ASPECT NOT PLANNED AS CENTRAL. Denise will wait until the next time with these children to begin more evaluation of different arrangments in terms of the practicality, safety, and appearance of the alternatives. For now Denise is excited to see the children grappling with issues involved in using these representational tools in creating a model. That they had different points of view on which elements "mattered" and tried to persuade each other of their points was something she could not have been sure would happen. Since it did, she wanted to maximize the potential of that experience.

Outdoor Play

Transition to Outdoors

Now let's move to Jeanne and the children preparing to go outside to the playground. As she calls the names of the children one by one to go into the hall for their coats, Jeanne reminds them of the "no running" rule. DECISION: TO ENCOURAGE CHILDREN TO GENERATE MULTIPLE SOLUTIONS TO A PROBLEM. She suggests that they try to invent as many ways as they can of getting outside without running. The children skip, hop, move like various animals, etc. Instead of providing one solution—"You must walk"—Jeanne has encouraged them to think of different acceptable (and fun) alternatives for achieving a goal.

Outdoor Activities

All week several children have been excited about constructing an obstacle course on the playground. Provided with a selection of versatile materials such as tires, variously shaped boards, boxes, and aluminum ladders, they have been constructing long, winding pathways across an imaginary desert. It is absolutely essential to construct the pathway so that a traveler's feet will not touch the sand ("third-degree burns" will result immediately). Randy, one of the primary designers, is attempting to make a bridge using a board placed over two supports consisting of a tire each. This is, however, easier said than done, and Randy finds himself faced with problems concerning the sturdiness of the bridge. When the two tires are placed in such a way that they will reach the train (several boxes and the next step on the path) he discovers that if a person steps on one end of the board, the other end tips up dangerously. Jeanne comes over to Randy and remarks on the fact that he seems to have a problem. "Yeah," he says, "someone might fall onto the sand if the board went up." Jeanne agrees as to the importance of this problem and asks what can be done. Initially Randy seems stymied. DECISION: TO HELP CHILD TO IDENTIFY OR CLARIFY THE PROBLEM. Jeanne asks if he has checked to see if the results are the same no matter where someone steps on the board. He tests out the situation and discovers that the board flips when either end is stepped on, but not when the middle is. Randy now has a clearer conception of the problem. Jeanne remarks on how important it is for the travelers that this problem is resolved. Randy studies for a minute then shouts, "I know!" and runs to the back of the yard returning with one large, heavy rock, and one cardboard block of smaller size. "These will hold it down!" he announces triumphantly. The block is first placed on one end of the board, then the rock on the other, at which point the board tips and the lighter block falls. "Oh, no!" says Jeanne, "What's wrong?" Randy seem surprised and checks out the event by replacing the lighter block to no avail. When he removes the rock, he sees the board go back to its horizontal position. DECISION: TO CONTINUE EFFORT TO HELP CHILD IDENTIFY THE PROBLEM. Jeanne says, "Well, Randy. What do you suppose is different about the rock and the block that one will hold down the board and one won't?" At this point Jeanne is hoping to focus Randy's attentions on a specific analysis of his problem. He first experiments with adding an extra cardboard block. This is not effective. He works through the same process with one smaller rock, then a pile of small rocks, finally discovering the last to be effective. Randy tries walking across the board and has no accidents. Success! Randy has worked out his own solution. The teacher has supported him, without providing answers. Randy feels good about his own capabilities and next time may be able to incorporate some of these strategies on his own. He also has probably learned something about relationships between size and weight. Although these haven't been verbalized, inner constructions have been formed or rearranged, giving Randy more to call on in future situations.

A Note on Problem-Solving: The Teacher's Role

We have seen Jeanne and Denise working with the children in a number of different instances of problem-solving. Sometimes the teachers have engaged the children in problems, sometimes when the children have gotten involved in problems of their own they have been around to encourage and elaborate the use of problem-solving processes.

In the case of the obstacle course, Randy was very much concerned with making something work and was thus strongly motivated to find a solution. Jeanne could easily have solved Randy's problem for him, carefully explaining the principle by which the solution worked. Jeanne would have a number of reasons for not doing it this way. Can you, by this point, anticipate what they might be?

Why is it important who solves the problem as long as Randy understands how and why the solution worked? The response the teachers would give is that without the experience of working it through on his own, Randy would have been less likely to really understand how and why the solution worked. Randy is likelier to know what objects could be substituted for the rock (weighing down one side of the board) because he was the one who tried various objects and saw which ones were no good.

The child had to actively use mental representation at a number of points, such as in anticipating what might happen if one side of the board flipped up, etc. Being involved in identifying the problem, in generating alternative solutions and evaluating them, gives Randy experience with these components of problem-solving which he can apply in new situations.

We see these parts of the problem-solving process in Denise's small group working on the model playground as well. In this case the children become involved in doing some problem-solving about representation itself: How do you show in two dimensions a thing like a playground? What characteristics do the representational tools need to have and what can be dispensed with (e.g., color, shape)? What do you need to take into account in using a two-dimensional representation to communicate ideas or information to someone else? The skills in problem-solving which are being developed are the same as in the obstacle course.

The children in either case also gain in their sense of mastery and their confidence in having the ability to tackle problems. The teachers are providing a model only of the *process* of problem-solving, of the ways you can approach problems, not solving them for the children. Some encouragement to think through problems logically is given but the children must do the thinking on their own.

Objectives for the Child

In following Jeanne and Denise through a preschool day, we got a glimpse of the kinds of things they might try to do and some of their thoughts as to what they were trying to achieve. Now let's look at those objectives directly and you can think about how your objectives would compare. Is there anything you would add or change? Different teachers value different things, but clarifying what you do value is an important process for teachers to go through. Jeanne's and Denise's objectives (coincidentally not unlike our own) will be reflected in the following chapters; we will be examining the kinds of learning encounters through which the teacher could work toward these objectives.

1. Developing acquaintance with objects and events in the world and awareness of their reaction to them.

Why do Jeanne and Denise wish to achieve this objective? What values do they have that motivate such an objective? First, they value *heightened sensitivity* to things in the world and to our own reactions to them for the pleasure and self-awareness that such sensitivity affords the individual. Second, in their concern with the developing children's ability to understand and work with the various modes of expression and communication, they realize the value of giving the children *experiences they will want to re-present*. These encounters with interesting things in the world, things that provoke the senses, etc., can provide the motivation as well as the raw materials for using a representational mode to express the experience.

2. Developing competence in the representational modes.

If the teachers were to explicitly list their reasons for having this objective, there would be three: (1) the *enjoyment* of creating within the mode and of appreciating what others have created within the mode, (2) the *ability to receive and send messages* through the representational modes, which is important in dealing with the world, in sharing information, and in sharing experiences, and (3) the growing in the *capacity to process information through additional modes.* With regard to this last reason, the mental tasks confronting the human being are quite diverse in nature and for some of those one representational mode is better than another; e.g., the pictorial mode is suited to working out spatial problems. So not only can we receive information more efficiently as we grow in competence in the representational modes, but presumably our mental ability to function within the given mode should increase as well.

3.   Activating problem-solving processes and increasing problem-solving skills.

It almost goes without saying that the primary reason why the teacher has this objective is the *adaptiveness* of problem-solving abilities. The individual who grows in the ability to deal effectively with problems will reap the benefits across a wide array of real-life problems, employing the strategies to find solutions which will help him get what he wants. For society too, of course, this is adaptive, particularly in an era of rapid change and constantly changing problems. In addition, the child grows in *independence,* gaining the skills, the responsibility, and the confidence to assume the initiative in dealing with the environment. With this independence and the experiences in problem-solving comes a sense of *competence and achievement* which is so important to the developing child.

It is worth asking yourself not only what are my objectives as a teacher for the preschool program in general (e.g., the children learn to think more divergently, gain an excitement about exploring and learning, etc.) but also what are my objectives more specifically for various curriculum areas. Why am I including science in the program and what am I expecting to accomplish through it? What are the objectives for my art program? and so on. In the next five chapters we will be looking at these questions and at the kind of program plans that have emerged from one way of answering them.

4

Art and Construction

A good way for a teacher to begin thinking about the objectives and educational strategies in a curriculum area is to think of what the child's spontaneous engagement in the activity is like. Both art and construction (building of various kinds) are activities that children engage in eagerly and naturally. What are they getting out of this involvement? Although adult praise for the product may be an inducement or a nice bonus for some creations, children's desire to draw, paint, and build does not depend on such motivations. Clearly there is intrinsic motivation to engage in activities of these kinds. In what does this motivation lie?

Let's consider the child's art endeavors and describe why the child will seek out and persist in this activity. First, children enjoy the act of making marks on a page or other surface. Second, children have a tendency to exercise those skills they are in the process of acquiring. Third, there seems to be a natural desire to represent or express aspects of the world or one's experience of them. To describe each point somewhat more fully:

1. Children enjoy the act of making marks on a page or other surface.

Since the first child scribbled in the dust with his finger, there has probably been a curious adult who has wondered whether the fun was in the motion itself or in the scribbled marks in the dirt. Is it a case like crawling, walking, or running in which the child simply enjoys performing newly acquired motor skills? Gibson and Yonas (1968) found the answer to this question in a simple way by providing children early in the scribbling stage with two different writing implements. One made marks and one didn't. Children who had the nonmarking stylus quickly abandoned it. The fun seems to lie primarily in what has been called "the feeling of efficacy" (White, 1959) or "the joy of being a cause" (Groos, 1901). We will come upon this kind of enjoyment—pleasure in noting the effects of one's behavior—in many activities of the child's day. We will call activities which allow one to actually *see* the effects of one's own behavior "visible thinking"[1] activities. In the family of "visible thinking" activities which are the concern of this chapter, this pleasure is especially evident. When the child has scribbled, drawn, molded clay, built with blocks, etc., the visible products of action remain for the child and others to see; the motion of the child's hand provides immediate results before his very eyes.

2. Children have a tendency to exercise those skills which they are in the process of acquiring.

A child is learning to walk. She falls; she gets up again. Again she falls; again she struggles up. She continues the activity for hours on end. Once she

---

[1]The term "visible thinking" is from Jacqueline Goodnow's *Children Drawing*, J. Bruner, M. Cole, B. Lloyd. eds., *The Developing Child Series* Cambridge, Mass.: Harvard University Press, 1977.

can walk without falling she tries out new refinements of the activity. She practices her skill until her actions are automatic and easy. It is similar with any emerging capacity. And it is the same with graphic skills. The child keeps practicing old skills and trying out new modifications. This tendency, which White (1959) has called competence motivation, can be seen in every area of the child's development.

3. Children have a desire to represent or express aspects of the world or their experience of them.

The child does not have to have adults show him that he can draw things in the world around him, though they may have some influence. But the tendency is there to attempt to create a resemblance through one's marks to something one knows in the world.

Let's take the case of Mary Ann's dog, Maxwell (Figure 4-1). You may not be able to tell this beast from a cow, a cat, or an armadillo, but let's look at the bright side: you *can* tell it from a Christmas tree, a bridge table, and even from a meat loaf. We've all seen and enjoyed children's drawings, but it is easy to overlook the astonishing accomplishments that they represent. Mary Ann has pulled off some remarkable feats (at least they're better than the ears!).

Let's assume that Mary Ann is drawing a particular dog, her own beloved terrier, Maxwell. In the task of representing Maxwell, consider the fact that Mary Ann has seen him from countless different angles and in an infinite number of different positions. Maxwell's body is a complex combination of parts, usually in motion. Mary Ann must transform her experiences with three-dimensional Maxwell into a simple two-dimensional representation.

FIGURE 4-1. Mary Ann's drawing of Maxwell.

Notice the analyses and inventions on which Mary Ann's drawing is based. She has employed her limited repertoire of shapes to create something which is recognizably a picture of an animal—if not so recognizably a picture of Maxwell. She has used a horizontal rectangle for Max's body, vertical rectangles for his legs, a circle for his head, and lines for his tail and ears. As Golomb (1974) has written: "The child, as well as the adult, does not attempt to copy reality; his task is to invent structurally adequate forms which can stand for the complex object" (p. ix).

To understand this aspect of children's graphic work is to realize that the paper and crayon, the lump of clay, the collage materials, etc., are the scene of much challenging problem-solving. And if we look more carefully at children's artwork, we find, as Goodnow (1977) has pointed out, that the features which characterize children's art activities are the features of all problem-solving. A child will employ a unit or routine which he has mastered to solve a variety of representational problems. The circle, for example, will be put to use, not for the person's head, but for the trunk, the hands and feet, the eyes and nose.

Regarding this feature of children's drawing from one point of view, it is a case of solving diverse problems with a limited set of tools, somewhat like using a screwdriver, not only to screw and unscrew, but also to tap in nails in the absence of a hammer and to exert pressure in the absence of a lever. Such a making-do-with-what's-available requires a mental process on the part of the child or the one-tool-do-it-yourselfer. For the child who makes wide use of the circle, it is a matter of "discovering similarities and realizing that many separate items may be represented by a single symbol" (Goodnow, 1977, p. 145).

Piaget would look at this behavior as an example of *assimilation*. The child wants to draw a hand. It is true that she does not have a great deal of skill at drawing, but even more important she does not have a large repertoire of forms in terms of which she can analyze the hand. Piaget refers to these available routines as *schemata*; in the case of the hand, the child's schema of a circle and of a line might be most relevant. She *assimilates* the hand into her schemata as a circle with several lines appended. All problem-solving has this element of assimilation to some degree. The way we see a new problem is a function of other situations we have faced, and thus we think in terms of solving it in some related way.

But assimilation is not the whole story. We also *accommodate* to what is new about a situation. We adjust our available routines or solutions to the unique qualities of the new problem. As the child becomes more solidly comfortable with her current repertoire of forms and as new representational tasks present themselves, the child may be confronted by the discrepancy between the object and what she can produce with only her familiar routines. Marie wants to draw herself in her Halloween costume, which includes a witch's hat. A circle will not do; nor will a square. She must invent a way of achieving some

resemblance to the cone-shaped hat. She uses lines to create a very crude triangle; in the next days and weeks she will probably try this new form again and again. Virtually every problem is dealt with by a combination of some *assimilation* and some *accommodation*. The individual uses familiar strategies insofar as they will work. At the same time the strategies have to be adjusted, however slightly, to the new situation. The combination of these two mechanisms of development is easy to see in the child's drawing (indeed, "visible thinking") as the child invents ways of representing her world.

We have deliberately begun our discussion with a look at the child's spontaneous art and construction because a major part of the teacher's role is to create an environment where these valuable spontaneous activities can take place. The environment must contain the materials, the time, the opportunity, the encouragement, etc., so that the child will promote his *own* growth in these ways. Teachers have additional roles to play and we will be seeing more of these as we proceed. But before we do let's look at a wider range of "visible thinking" activities. We have dwelt primarily on children's drawing as the prototype of these activities, largely because it has been the most widely researched. But where do building and other construction activities come in? Why does "visible thinking" refer to the building activities as well? To answer these questions we will have to see what features characterize "visible thinking" activities.

"Visible Thinking"

Similarities in Art and Construction Activities

Block-building is not usually included in discussions of art, but there are a number of reasons why it should be. Whether a child is drawing an airplane, forming the plane from clay, or constructing one with blocks, she is involved in undertakings with much in common.

1. In all these tasks, the child is working with media in which there is a *visible product of her actions*, a product which remains after the activity is completed (in contrast, for example, with the musical or gestural modes).
2. With any of these media, the child is *searching for and trying to invent adequate forms to stand for the complex object*, e.g., to find the forms and ways of combining parts which will adequately portray the airplane (how to show the wings, etc.)
3. At first glance it may seem that art activities are of an aesthetic nature and building activities have a more utilitarian or functional focus. From the point of view of what the *child* is doing, this is an oversimplification; each activity has both an *aesthetic dimension and a "utilitarian" dimension*. The relative importance of each dimension varies, not with the materials chosen (e.g., blocks vs. paint and paper), but with the particular purposes for which the child engages in the activity and the use to which the materials are put.

Let us expand briefly on each of these points. First, let's think about some of the implications of there being a visible product of the child's actions which is present throughout the process of creation and remains when the child or artist is through.[2] The fact that the child has her work before her as it emerges is a very important characteristic. She looks at what she's got so far for her airplane. She likes the place the wings are but somehow they don't look quite right. Oh, they're too short . . . one more block on each side. . . . She adds, modifies, and in some cases "erases," that is, removes or eliminates part or all—and has another go at it. She decides when the plane can be considered finished. This is a fundamentally different kind of constructing and struggling to represent than the kind the child engages in with movement or music where the product *is* the performance. In music and movement changes are made by repeating the performance. One cannot stand back, notice a discrepancy, and then change the product as needed the way one can in what are traditionally called art and construction activities.

These features of the art and construction modes also mean that these systems can be used to represent or communicate very different *kinds* of information. The spatial layout of a building, the appearance of a household object or a family member that your friend has not seen, the route to Sarah's house—these are communicated in a very different way, usually more efficient and descriptive, through the two-dimensional and three-dimensional modes (pictures, sculpture, and three-dimensional models, diagrams, etc.—some better than others) than through the modes such as gesture, music, or even language.

The child is doing many things when he engages in any of the art/construction activities. Once the child is capable of depicting things in his art, the main point of his action is often representation. As mentioned above, viewing art activities as aesthetic and building activities as utilitarian overlooks what the activities are *for the child*. In a picture there is information to be represented and/or communicated. In representing a dog most young children are primarily concerned with "utilitarian" aims—how to convey dogness. Their primary interest is not in aesthetics. Choosing pleasing colors, spatial arrangements, etc., may be part of the task, but the job at hand is basically to invent ways of translating living, breathing, squirming Maxwell onto the flat white page. In building a boat of blocks or a walkie-talkie by connecting plastic pieces, the child is also searching for ways of making his creations look like the real thing. This does not discount the child's awareness of the aesthetic appeal of the work. Adults often see evidence of this awareness in children's explicit comments such as "isn't this a pretty boat?" and in children's use of symmetry, color contrasts, etc. So, whether the child is making a collage, a painting, or a building, both "aesthetic" and "utilitarian" concerns are involved.

---

[2]The possibility of a record, tape, or film remaining after performances in the other modes is clearly a very different matter since it too is not a static product visible in its entirety.

The similarities we have discussed between art activities and construction activities are important for more than providing a justification for a chapter grouping. An awareness of the similarities is helpful to teachers in two ways: (1) it provides them with a way to evaluate the way they handle the "art area" and the "block area"—a way to decide what it is important to put there, and a way to understand what the children are up to, and (2) it gives teachers a basis for deciding how to integrate these activities more meaningfully with each other and with the total curriculum.

Differences within "Visible Thinking" Activities

You may have already anticipated our next point, which is to look *within* this large group of materials and activities—blocks, clay, paper, felt-tipped pens, etc.—and note that there are also very big differences among them. There are differences in what individuals engaging in these various activities do and in what potentials for creating or representing the materials allow. The child in the photograph on p.53 has obviously been involved in a representational endeavor, but in this case she has not created the forms from which the trees are composed. She has the units provided to her and her job has been to decide which combination of component forms would best capture the appearance of a tree. An even more difficult task would be to create an ostrich from these geometric shapes. Here the child must use some problem-solving skills to find a way to represent the long fluid forms of an ostrich with the unyielding triangles and squares provided. Think of how much simpler her task would be if her provisions included a long piece, an oval, etc. Activities where the units are available to the child rather than created by her can be either two-dimensional or three-dimensional, as Box 4-1 indicates.

One point we are making with this illustration and this chart is that providing variety in an art program is not just a matter of expanding materials from crayons and felt-tipped pens to charcoal, finger paint, and water colors. One of the most important ways to vary the program is to include materials from each of the various categories shown in Box 4-1. This division may also help teachers to plan sequences of materials. The different categories of materials present different problems. For example, when the units are available, the hard part is the job of *analyzing* the object to be made into those units, e.g., seeing an ostrich in terms of squares and triangles.

The distinctions shown in Box 4-1 can also help a teacher formulate fruitful questions about the child's abilities in art and construction activities, questions which will help her discover the child's developmental level. For example, she sees that Jason rarely draws and is at the scribbling stage in the drawings he does produce. Since Jason is a little older than most children who are scribbling, the teacher would like to understand more fully what is involved. Is it immaturity of Jason's fine motor skills? Or is it his inability to invent ways of representing objects? The teacher knows that he builds elaborate and accurate representational structures in the block corner. She

decides to see how he does with a fine motor three-dimensional "creation by assembly" task (using small plastic blocks) and with a two-dimensional "creation by assembly" task like a collage of a motorcycle (his passion in the block corner). Watching Jason as he engages in these activities can help the teacher understand which developmental processes are involved in the fact that Jason is still at the scribbling stage. She may conclude that he has been so much more engrossed in three-dimensional building activities (where, given the level of his fine motor skills, he is more comfortable) that he hasn't begun to invent ways of representing in drawing. Thus the four-way grouping of activities in Box 4-1 has diagnostic uses as well as program-planning functions for the teacher as she thinks about the growth of the children in art and construction.

Box 4-1.

	Materials where parts/units are available ("pre-fabricated"); [creation by assembly]	Materials where parts/units are not available: [creation "from scratch"]
2-Dimensional	Feltboard Collage (with precut elements e.g., pieces of paper, pieces of fabric) Printing (with "plates" already made)	Felt-tipped pen Crayon Paint (finger paints, poster paint, water colors, etc.) Chalk, charcoal Etching on clay, sand, etc.
3-D materials used in 2-D way	Parquetry blocks Beads (for stringing in patterns)	
3-Dimensional	Wooden blocks Plastic interlocking blocks Boxes (for box sculpture, etc.) Stabiles (3-dimensional structures made with bits of wood, styrofoam, straws, clay, etc.)	Clay, plasticene, etc. Papier-mâché Sand, mud, snow, etc.

How does a teacher actually go about putting some of these theoretical thoughts and suggestions to work in the classroom? In an attempt to see how these ideas can be coordinated in a classroom situation, let's work through some parts of the planning, execution and evaluation of a series of activities with our hypothetical teachers, Jeanne and Denise. The teachers' initial planning session is a time when observations, evaluations, and new ideas concerning children and activities can be shared. All of these have a strong bearing on what decisions are made.

What Shall We Do Next?

Generating Ideas for New Directions

As Jeanne and Denise begin their planning session, a several-week series of activities is just ending and they are trying to decide on the next direction to take.

Denise says, "You know, our planning has been more successful since we started our plans by thinking of what the children were involved in right then. Activities seem to be extended at lot further when children are already interested in the topic. They get really excited and want to expand on things themselves. Let's brainstorm on their current passions."

Close observation and knowledge of the children is important for these teachers as they try to decide what might be currently significant to their class. The teachers throw out ideas based on things they have noticed in the classroom. Jeanne remembers, "Ever since Brian called that map on the phone book a treasure map, there's been quite a bit of searching for gold and fighting off pirates. Is there anything we'd want to pick up on from that?"

Denise jots that possibility down. She notes that several members of the class have spent a lot of time looking at some new dinosaur books and recalls the class discussion of the extinct beasts. Soon the teachers have come up with the following list of possibilities:

Treasure maps and pirates
Dinosaurs
Warm weather/outside play
The Wizard of Oz (recently on TV)
Changes in the world with springtime

Jeanne says, "OK, that seems pretty good for where they are these days in interests. Now let's think about where they are in terms of needs."

Referring again to the "treasure map" situation, Denise notes that the class as a whole hasn't had much experience in creating or understanding maps and diagrams. Given the teachers' emphasis on developing representational competence, including the ways in which information about the world is represented and communicated, they discuss how maps and diagrams might be an interesting next step. They like the idea of pursuing maps now while the children are showing a spontaneous interest in them. (Pirates may turn to cowboys in another week and the opportune moment would be lost.)

As the teachers go through the planning process, we see some of their beliefs about how children learn, about what kinds of abilities and knowledge will be most useful to them. It is important to clarify one's thoughts about these questions and to build the curriculum on the foundation such clarification provides. Teachers do not have to be theoreticians, but neither should they be merely picking from an activity book on the basis of an activity "sounding good." Thinking through the why of every activity and of every sequence of activities lies at the heart of the teacher's role.

Evaluating Ideas for New Directions

Now Denise is weighing the idea of planning activities around pirates and maps. She expresses a reservation, "You know, I think the idea of using a pirate theme could easily get out of hand. This make-believe gun thing has been such a problem lately and a pirate theme would feed right into that kind of play." Here Denise is taking one of the ideas she and Jeanne have generated and evaluating it with respect to possible consequences. This is the kind of thinking the teachers often try to encourage the children to engage in.

Jeanne agrees, "That's right. Neither pirates nor dinosaurs seem to me to have much potential for providing situations which the children can readily experience. And neither gives them much chance to call on past experiences. We've been saying we want to do more with our objective of increasing their awareness of 'things in the world.' I think for that purpose something close to their own reality, but something they ordinarily overlook, would be good."

Denise adds, "Yes, I think so too. Let's say we took some theme about the out-of-doors in springtime. Then our activities can center around greater awareness of the sensations of being outdoors which would get them started on noticing and experiencing how things look and smell, etc. They'd be having lots of outdoor experiences on their own and could notice new things, see further instances of things we'd talked about, etc."

"Yes," Jeanne comments, "there are times when something like dinosaurs can be good if only because of the incredible fascination they hold for kids. But I think they have less potential for our objective of helping the children develop awareness of things in the world and their reactions to them. For that, I think something closer to their experiences is better. Something they will be experiencing again and again on their own. . . . ."

Through this process of analysis, which would, of course, vary for each situation, the teachers decide on a direction for their planning. In this case they decide on a series of outside activities and go on to elaborate the idea to see if it really has sufficiently rich potential for their various objectives.

Generating Ideas for Activities

So Jeanne and Denise have tentatively accepted a general theme or area to explore, springtime in the out-of-doors. Now they generate specific ideas for activities. Sometimes a current need of the children to which the teacher wants to respond provides the idea for an activity. At other times the initial idea may come from the teacher's knowledge of experiences children enjoy. Starting with something she knows the children will like, she further evaluates the activity in terms of its potential contribution towards the objectives she has thought through. The activity may need to be modified, recast, or supplemented in order to maximize its potential for enhancing children's development. In either case, both the children's interest and their developmental needs play significant roles in the teacher's final decisions.

The teachers do not always do their planning in terms of a specific theme or unit, although they often find it useful for reasons that may become apparent to the reader as we go on. But they find it important to always think in terms of general directions to go in for the next few weeks or longer. As they become aware of the children's current needs to which classroom activities should be directed, they decide on priorities which direct their immediate plans. And it is advantageous for children to have some continuity among activities to facilitate their integrating one activity with another. Planning a week or so ahead enables the teachers to conceive of a related series of experiences so that children can draw on ideas or skills from one learning experience as they encounter the next.

Jeanne and Denise continue through this planning process and arrive at the series of activities described below. The reasoning behind their decision-making process is briefly described below each activity. It is at least as important as an understanding of the activities themselves. Following this section we will examine several of these ideas in more detail. We will look at what happens when the ideas and plans come off the drawing board and are put into the classroom.

Summary of Planned Activities for a Two-Week Period

Activity 1. Describing the preschool playground to a "newcomer"

Enlisting the help of Rocky, the new puppet, the teachers encourage children to call assorted playground experiences to mind. "Playing dumb," Rocky asks about activities, equipment, sensations, etc., that children associate with the nursery school playground. Then Rocky asks about other playgrounds. To encourage the children's mental reconstruction of playgrounds they have seen, he asks questions such as, "Hey, is there ever anything messy at a playground? . . . Mud? . . . Well, what kinds of things happen with that? . . . What do you remember about the way it feels? . . . Show me with your face and your fingers. . . . What special kinds of sounds might you hear in a playground? . . . Is there anything you see only in the summer? . . ."

The group will also be encouraged to extend these ideas during free-play construction activities such as building a balance beam, movement activities such as moving as though one were on a swing, a seesaw, etc., or art activities such as drawing what you like to do best on the playground.

Reasoning: A basic step in the growth of representational competence and the use of past experience to solve present problems is the calling to mind of past ideas, actions, events, etc. In devising this activity, the teachers are attempting to provoke children's mental reconstruction of places they have seen. The activity also serves as a useful basis for later activities concerning playground experiences.

Activity 2. Field trip to another playground

Jeanne and Denise decide to take the group on a field trip to a playground at another school. They select one which offers a variety of new experiences in terms of equipment and organization. The focus of their interactions is to refine children's awareness of what they see and experience. In some respects, the trip is approached like a research venture. Before the actual trip, the children are given broad suggestions about what to look for, e.g., "things you've never seen before," what the pieces of equipment are made from, things that might be different if it were winter, etc. During the visit itself, some comments and questions direct the children's attention to points of interest, others follow up on what the children spontaneously get involved in. For example, Jeanne or Denise might ask, "What things about this jungle gym are different from ours? . . . Do you see anything that is the same? . . . Are there any things that children at this school can do that we can't do at our school? . . . Are there any things we can do on our own playground that we couldn't do here? . . ." To extend the value of this last question, teachers help children explore how their action or position might have to be modified slightly to accommodate to the different equipment. Some activities would be impossible in one of the two playgrounds. For example, one may not be able to swing where there are no swings. But a more interesting challenge is presented by deciding how a given activity could be done if old equipment were arranged in a new way. For example, problem-solving about how to arrange things so children can slide may lead to the idea of placing one end of the board upon the jungle gym.

Focusing on the perceptions and sensations which a new experience brings, the teacher might ask, for example, "How does it make you feel when you're standing way up there? . . . Do the people on the ground look any different than they did when you stood on the ground? . . . If it were winter now, what different things might we see or feel? . . ."

Reasoning: The initial consideration in selecting a field trip was the desire to take full advantage of the enjoyable spring weather. After a long winter, both children and teachers needed to get outside. However, Jeanne and Denise also see potential in the experience of a playground. The children know their own playground very well, so the opportunities for comparison are fertile. When the children encounter a new piece of equipment which their playground lacks (or vice versa), this is an excellent opportunity for getting them thinking about how a given situation can be transformed to create a new effect. Such thinking about *change* is important in problem-solving.

Activity 3. Re-presenting the field trip

The teachers try to orient much of the following day around thinking about varying aspects of the trip and how they can be represented in the classroom. Rocky the puppet, who did not go on the trip, has children verbally describe experiences to him and those ideas are put into a story chart. He asks questions about aspects of the trip: the objects on the playground (things that moved, that could be climbed on, that weren't on the children's own playground, and so on), the spatial arrangements of the playground items, and the sequence of events on the trip.

During free-play time, Jeanne and Denise encourage the children to recreate various aspects of the trip with classroom materials. This will continue throughout the week if children remain interested and will be supported through teachers' comments, questions, and suggestions. A teacher might ask what crayon colors would be good to use to show the warm weather feeling, how blocks could be arranged to make an effective and safe sliding board, or how something could be designed which would spin like a merry-go-round. **Reasoning:** In keeping with their beliefs concerning the importance of using representations, Jeanne and Denise provide a variety of media through which the children may express their ideas. The less verbal children will benefit from such a diversity of means of expression. But an equally important reason for providing for multiple modes of representing experiences is simply to increase children's competence in a variety of representational systems.

The task of telling someone, in this case, Rocky, who hasn't been part of an experience, what it was like is one that demands active reconstruction of the experience (as well as taking the listener's perspective, which we will discuss in Chapter 7). Although it is difficult for the young children to see that a fuller, more coherent account is needed when the listener is entirely ignorant of the place and the events, Rocky's remarks explicitly direct their attention to this, e.g., "But how did you jump from the jungle gym to the sandbox? ... Oh, they're near each other. I didn't know that since I wasn't there." This is helpful in assisting the child progress in realizing that the perspective of the other person isn't identical to one's own. In addition, to the extent that the child grasps that Rocky needs a detailed and coherent picture of the playground, she sets for herself the task of *internally reconstructing* the playground field trip in a more exacting way. One of the major reasons for doing the activity and for having the puppet as the listener is to activate this thoroughgoing reconstruction on the part of the child.

When an activity or interaction is designed to help children reconstruct an experience, the teachers usually plan to include it as soon as possible after the experience.

Activity 4. "The Pretend Playground"

In addition to encouraging children's attempts to recreate or convey aspects of the trip in a variety of ways, Jeanne and Denise arrange a *learning center* specifically for that purpose. It consists of a table and assorted kinds of "junk" materials, such as toothpicks, popsicle sticks, paper dowels, small boxes, yarn, etc. For a week or two the activity in this center will be the construction of items which might be included in a playground of the children's design. Some children may wish to focus on the construction of individual items, while others may be more interested in working on problems in arranging the items on the playground site. **Reasoning:** The teachers have reasons for providing this activity as a *learning center*, a situation in which one of the teachers is usually in the area and children come and go as they please. This arrangement, as contrasted with the small groups in which a few children at a time are specifically invited to participate, makes it more likely that children will be engaging in the activity *when they are interested* and for as long as they are interested. (The more formal small groups in turn have their own advantages for certain kinds of activities, as we will see.) And why have the teachers decided on a learning center with a teacher present, rather than just making the materials available?

1. They would like to actively encourage the children to represent the playground which has recently been experienced and discussed. The trip to the playground was originally planned because, among other things, it offered a variety of representational problems (spatial arrangement, relative size, items of varying levels of complexity). To fulfill this potential the teachers opt for stationing Denise there to provoke investigation of these kinds of problems in three-dimensional representation.
2. They hope that by being in the activity area to observe, to raise questions, and to instigate discussions among the children, Denise can activate thinking in some directions that might have been tapped only superficially or not at all had the children been left to their own devices.

Activity 5. Creating new playground materials

Soon after the trip the teachers bring some new materials to the outdoor area. These include empty cardboard boxes and orange crates, tires, boards, rope, and pieces of canvas. Teachers give teams of children problems related to these materials, e.g., "Try to make something so that kids can give each other rides. . . . Something that you can all sit on. . . . Maybe a merry-go-round, or something that turns. . . ." Children will be put into groups of three to six and encouraged to solve these construction problems as groups. (This activity is described in fuller detail later in the chapter.)

Reasoning: The experience of working cooperatively, introduced to the children in a previous series of lessons, is included again here. As anyone who has ever been a member of a committee knows, group problem-solving is a different matter from individual problem-solving. It is quite different cognitively, particularly for the young child, as we will be discussing in Chapter 7 on social-affective development. The experience with problem-solving *per se* is important here too, of course. It is useful to have the opportunity to develop and practice problem-solving strategies with problems which are concrete and have purpose in the eyes of the children.

Activity 6. Photographs from different points on preschool playground
Finding where the photographer stood

The children are brought outside for a special activity involving photographs of the playground. These were previously taken of several areas and pieces of equipment and from varying points of view. Pairs of children are each given a photo and told to try to find the place where the photographer stood to take the picture. For example, four pictures may be easily identified as the jungle gym, but the groups must analyze the pictures to determine the angle from which they were taken. Then they must position themselves in that spot. A higher-level variation for some of the more advanced children would be for one child to verbally note what can be seen in a particular photo and have the others decide from what point this photograph was taken. Of course, there would be discussion of "what makes you think so," with children being given the chance to explain their choices.

Reasoning: The ability to conceive an object or scene from varying points of view is a difficult one for young children. In this activity the children are challenged to visualize what something looks like from positions other than their own. (There is a more extensive discussion of the cognitive demands of dealing with other perspectives in Chapter 7: The Social-Affective Domain.)

Activity 7. Creating a playground collage

As part of a large group activity, a story is told about a child exploring a new playground. The child has never been there before and is especially excited by the textures and physical sensations which she discovers. Denise and Jeanne encourage the children to remember the tactile sensations from their own playground experiences, and possibly to describe some of those verbally. The child in the story might touch such items as grass, the chains of swings, the bark of a tree, etc. After the children have been encouraged to call to mind their own sensations, they are presented with collage materials including velvet, aluminum foil, etc. After thinking about which aspects of the trip they wish to represent with these, children are given a long sheet of paper, scissors, and glue and encouraged to represent the trip through appropriate textures.

Reasoning: Providing good verbal labels for items and experiences can often be difficult for young children. One role of the preschool teacher is to supply some of these labels and thus help the children towards more differentiated ways of thinking and describing. Consequently, labels for some of these tactile sensations may be offered. Jeanne is primarily interested, however, in having the group recall the various sensations and compare how the playground things felt with how the collage materials feel. This *within-mode* type of representation (one textured material to represent another) is often enjoyable for the less verbal child.

Activity 8. Playground treasure hunt

Keeping in mind the children's interest in treasure hunts in free play, Jeanne and Denise devise an activity in which this interest is combined with map usage and the playground theme. It will continue over five or six days and involve four to six children in each small group situation. A teacher will begin by presenting two or three children with a "treasure" (perhaps a picture or the can of juice for the daily snack). She tells them where to hide it and gives the children the job of creating a map-picture which another group of two or three classmates must interpret. The first group will not be able to communicate with the second except through the map. During its design the teacher will help planners to try to understand the searcher's perspective, e.g., "*You* know it's the biggest tree because you saw us hide the juice there. How will *they* know which tree this picture is telling about?" She will also be present during the interpretation process. (A fuller description of the actual implementation of this activity is provided later in the chapter.)

Reasoning: Experience in trying to create or understand simplified depictions of a spatial arrangement—for example, a map of the guinea pig's cage—requires the children to think of how objects are spatially related to one another and how this can be shown. On the interpreting end, reading a treasure map, for example, the child sees how information can be gained from the map. Questions from teachers and peers can provoke him to think about *how* he knows where the treasure is. (How did you know it wasn't on the other side of the slide? . . . How did the makers of this map let you know it was in the same corner of the yard as the sandbox?) Having a turn both as map-maker and as map-reader puts the child on both sides of the communication task.

Now let's look at what happened with two of the activities summarized above (5 and 8) when they were introduced in the classroom.

Monday, April 9 (Creating new playground materials)

Jeanne and Denise begin the activity by saying that they have been thinking it would be good to have some new equipment in the play yard. Children are encouraged to generate some ideas about things they might like to have on the playground. The teachers inform the children that they have been able to get some materials such as boxes, tires, plastic hosing, a small pool, etc., and that these will be used in constructing some new toys and play areas. Today four specific kinds of equipment will be constructed, with the children working as teams to tackle each problem.

The group goes outside to the yard. Before actually dividing them into the four teams, the teachers give the whole group the chance to look over the new materials. Jeanne encourages them to think about how the materials look, what they might be called, and to what uses they might be put. Then each group is told its individual project and provided with a specific area in which to plan and build its creation.

The ability to work independently of the teacher, either as an individual or with a group, is being gradually developed over the course of the year. Providing opportunities such as this with interesting problems and the non-pressured exploratory atmosphere helps children build these skills. The extent to which such problems are presented to children, as well as the kinds of interaction the teacher will have with them as they work, is a function of the capabilities of the particular children.

Tim, Randy, Katy, and Laurie go with Denise to the familiar sandbox. Opposite the wall behind the sandbox is a small empty wading pool. The only accessible water comes from a spigot on that wall. The problem is to invent a system by which the water can be piped into the pool without getting the sand wet. The children have available to them pieces of plastic tubing in assorted lengths and widths, cardboard dowels and tubes, and masking tape. Katy immediately grabs a piece of the plastic tubing and inserts the end into the spigot. "The water will go through there," she says. Denise turns to the others, and asks in a genuine, noncommittal way, "Will it keep the sand dry?" Tim says, "No! It needs to be long!" He picks up several pieces of tubing and tests for appropriate length by adding them to the first piece. At this point Denise observes closely. She is allowing Tim to generate and test his own hypotheses. She values this manifestation of independence, and Tim's willingness to continue even without immediate success. In addition, peer evaluation, which is an extremely effective source of cognitive growth, is more likely to occur if she stands back. Tim is still trying individual pieces when Laurie picks up two and holds them together. Katy likes this idea and picking up the tape, attaches one of Laurie's pieces to her own original piece, which happens to be of the same width. Randy then begins on the next connection. Here, the tube he tries to add is wider and when the second is inserted in the first, there is a large gap. Denise sees a potential problem here and wants to know what the children think. "Is this setup OK?" she asks. No one appears to see any reason for concern and all are eager to turn on the water. Before doing so, Denise says, "Hmm, maybe we should think for a minute about what the water will be like coming through the tubes. Katy, show us with your hands where it will begin. OK, now pretend that your hands are the water and move them along the hose just the way it would move." Katy does so, the others watching intently. Denise is trying to get children to anticipate an outcome, which requires them to use internal representation. Katy must imagine the water as it would flow. This representation of movement is difficult and her mental imagery is inaccurate. In this case Denise thinks using a form of external representation—hand movement—will help Katy to notice a problem. When Katy reaches the point in question, Jeanne has everyone think about what part of the first piece of tubing would be filled, and where the water would go if the next addition were not there. Tracing the movement of the water with her hands, Katy now sees that without a new tube the water would flow onto the sand. She tries to solve the problem by adding a new piece. She chooses a thin tube. Tim, however, jumps in and points out a problem. "What happens to all the water here? (around the edges) . . . It will leak out and the sand will be all wet." Katy disagrees, saying, again, that the water will flow directly from tube to tube. Denise suggests actually trying it out. They do so, and Tim's prediction is verified. It is important to provide opportunities, whenever possible, for children to test their hypotheses.

"Now what?" says the teacher. Laurie looks for another tube of the appropriate width and comes upon a light cardboard one. Again, Denise asks for the group's thoughts on this idea, and all members find Laurie's suggestion acceptable.

So the four children, with support and stimulation from the teacher, continue to experiment until they have successfully completed the waterway. There are some problems concerning the strength of the cardboard tube and its attachment, but finally a workable channel has been created. The water flows over the sandbox into the wading pool and the "engineers" applaud.

Tuesday, April 10 to Tuesday, April 16 (Playground treasure hunt)

Throughout the week Jeanne and Denise are working with small groups for this activity. During free play two or three children at a time will work with a teacher on creating a diagram for a second set of two or three children. When the first group is done, their diagram will be given to the second group. Each child will get a chance to be a member of both kinds of groups in the span of six or seven days. (A possibility which may be tried with some diagram-making groups is for them to listen to the other groups trying to read their diagram. Listening in person is great if they can restrain themselves from direct help; otherwise a tape recorder can be used. A variation in which more interaction *is* allowed clearly has some advantages and some disadvantages.)

The treasure itself can be something as simple as a colorful magazine photo, a ball, or some plastic building blocks made into a "treasure box." The idea of looking for a hidden object is exciting in itself to young children. No need to supply something new each time (and certainly not something costly).

For making a diagram of the treasure's location, children are given white paper and felt-tipped pens of assorted colors.

Jeanne has selected a hiding place and takes the children out to bury the treasure near the biggest of three trees in the playground. At another time, with another focus, children might select their own hiding places. Here in the children's first experience with conveying location pictorially, Jeanne decided it was important to use a location which would lend itself more readily to some of the kinds of questions she expects to raise with the children. For example, a treasure hidden in the open spaces near no salient object would be too difficult for a first diagraming venture. And a treasure by the foot of the slide would be too easy to present interesting perspective-taking challenges.

Giving the children, Chris and Becky, the drawing materials, Jeanne says, "You need to make a picture which will help Sam and Katy figure out where today's treasure is hidden."

Becky grabs a felt-tipped pen. "I know!" she says, and draws a tree. "It's under this tree." She and Chris look at Jeanne, who studies the picture and says, "Hmm, they'll see that this is a tree, I think. I wonder if they'll find the treasure right away? (pausing to let that sink in). There are several trees on the playground. Do you think they'll know which one we hid the treasure by?" Becky points to the intended tree, "Yes!" Chris says, "Uh oh! The tree you drew looks like all the trees, Becky." Becky looks down at her picture. Jeanne says, "Could they look by any tree and find the treasure, Becky? Did we put one by each tree?" Becky says, "No, just one tree has a treasure. Those dummies might get the wrong tree." Jeanne says, "I don't think they're dummies, Becky. They just weren't there when we hid the treasure. We have to help them by drawing a diagram that shows where to look." After a minute's thought, Becky responds, "Well, if there's two trees, you can pick the one that isn't little. Pick the big one."

Jeanne goes on to encourage Becky and Chris to look at their drawing and figure out how they could help Sam and Katy to think about the biggest tree on their playground. Chris draws in two smaller trees and the two children are satisfied.

Even harder than seeing what is needed to convey a message is seeing what is redundant. For example, all the trees are green. Will it help the treasure-hunters if the green of the trees is colored in in the diagram? These kinds of issues may or may not be explored depending on the level of the children and whether it comes up in their suggestions.

Now Jeanne says that she'll pretend to be Sam or Katy to help the group see if they've got the kind of diagram they need. Picking up the map, she says, "Hmm. I see those trees. Does that mean the treasure is in a tree? I wonder which tree it's in." "No! No!" shout the children, "Under the big tree, silly!" Jeanne says she can only tell from the picture that the treasure is near a tree, but she can't tell where. She reminds them that they won't be able to tell Katy and Sam things like they told her.

Chris draws a treasure box under the big tree and Jeanne, still in the role of the "naïve hunter," says, "Oh, on the ground beside the tree." Chris adds a line to indicate the ground level and grins. Jeanne asks if they think their diagram is done now and concludes the discussion, telling them she'll let them know how it goes.

In examining what Jeanne and Denise do in their classroom with respect to art and construction, we have chosen to focus on a two-week period and only on the planned activities of that period. Please recall our lengthy introduction about the nature and value of spontaneous art and construction activity. In dwelling on planned activities in the latter part of the chapter, we do not mean to imply that this is where the most important development of the child in these domains takes place. It is just the contrary. We have given explicit attention to the planned portions of the art and construction curriculum for several reasons. One is that many potential excellent learning encounters would never take place unless teachers made plans, gathered the necessary materials, etc. In addition, this seems to be an area in which teachers feel the need of assistance. We particularly wanted to emphasize the importance of the reasoning behind an activity. Thinking of one's planned activities in this way will help the teacher to clarify her objectives and to develop her inquiry strategies since she can take the time to think through possibilities. This in turn should improve the quality of interactions with children in their spontaneous art and construction activities.

Teacher Objectives: Application in Approaching Art and Construction

Before leaving art and construction, let's look again at the three basic objectives of these teachers as outlined in Chapter 3 and at how they are applied in art and construction.

1. To develop acquaintance with objects and events in the world and awareness of reactions to them.

Do you remember any activities that were oriented towards this objective in the two weeks we have just sketched out? One example is Activity 7, in which the children's attention was drawn to the textures of things encountered on the playground. There is a representational element to this activity as well, but a central aspect is the awareness of the diverse textures of everyday things.

Among the external stimuli of which the teacher might seek to develop an awareness are the artistic and construction media themselves. For example, teachers may explore with a child the way finger paint feels and looks and smells and the child's sensations as he works in the medium.

The teacher may also get the child's reactions to his own painting (or sculpture, building, etc.), as it is being done or after it is finished. The child is not just the creator of his own picture but the perceiver or appreciator as well. Encouraging the child to think about, and perhaps communicate, his impressions of this picture—not just what he drew but what emotional or aesthetic reactions he has to the product—may heighten the child's awareness of these reactions.

Responses to artistic works differ from individual to individual. Preschool children will only be beginning their understanding of this difficult notion of individual differences. This can begin to happen through such experiences as sharing reactions to pictures—those of artists and those of group members (in the case of the latter, not evaluative comments, such as, yech!, but reactions as to "how it makes you feel," etc.) The child gradually sees that different ideas and feelings are communicated to individuals by the same "work of art."

2. To develop competence in the representational modes.

We have seen several examples of activities designed to facilitate the development of the child's "receptive" and "productive" representational competence in art and construction. Among the activities with an emphasis on these objectives were the treasure hunt activity (Activity 8) and the pretend playground (Activity 4). These activities and others in the chapter are oriented partly toward activating the child's *internal representation* of the event, the object, or the spatial arrangement in question. But getting the children engaged in mentally reconstructing how things look and where they are in relation to each other is only part of the idea. There is also concern with developing their competence with the *external system of representation*. For example, we saw examples of the teachers working with pictorial comprehension—with photographs, pictures, maps or diagrams, etc. Why do they consider these valuable foci for activities? Let's examine the values which have led them to have program objectives of this nature.

First, let's consider the teacher beliefs underlying the concern with developing the children's *receptive capabilities*—perceiving, analyzing, understanding, appreciating—in the representational modes we are concerned with in this chapter.

(1) Many of the messages we as adults encounter in our dealings with the world are in the pictorial mode. Pictures, photographs, and cartoons inform us, communicate to us, entertain us. We read maps and diagrams. Some adults have occupations which depend on the ability to visualize three-dimensional reality from two-dimensional representation, e.g., blueprints, specifications, patterns, etc., and all of us encounter tasks that demand this ability from time to time. Representations in three-dimensional media, being less portable and less reproducible than two-dimensional ones, are less pervasive in our world of communication and information transmission. But there are numerous instances in which we get messages from three-dimensional models of various kinds. Competence in getting the message easily and accurately from the various kinds of two- and three-dimensional representations is clearly a critical skill in today's world.

(2) The teachers are also concerned with the children's aesthetic development in the visual arts. Howard Gardner has written:[12]

> The arts involve a communication of subjective knowledge between individuals through the creation of nontranslatable sensuous objects, (1973, p. 36).[5]

Young children respond to the nontranslatable messages in paints, statues, photographs, etc. The teachers seek to nurture their enjoyment of this dimension, their sensitivity to the beauty and to the rich communicative power of the visual arts.

(3) It is useful to be able to receive and process information through a diversity of representational modes. The third reason for providing children with a diversity of experiences with pictures and three-dimensional materials is the premise that through such experiences children develop in the ease and proficiency with which they "think in the mode."

Up to this point we have been looking at the teachers' reasons for developing representational competence of a *receptive* nature. What about the development of the *productive* capabilities in these systems? Similar values apply when we are looking at the child as the sender of messages and as the creator of artistic works. By producing in these modes, as well as receiving, the child increases in the ease, flexibility, etc., with which she thinks in the mode. There are few individuals who would need to be convinced of the enormous

satisfaction from being able to create—to express thoughts, feelings, perceptions of reality in visible products of one's own devising, to originate pleasing
or striking visual effects—these are joys we all understand. And for the child in
particular, finding ways of representing is important and fascinating work.

3.To activate problem-solving processes and increase problem-solving skills.

In art and construction, as in all domains of the preschool program, there
is much fertile territory for problem-solving. There are problems involving the
physical aspect of the materials and those involving their message aspect
(problems in representation/communication). Examples of the former are
trying to build a bridge that will stand, trying to make the red paint pink, or
figuring out which side of a picture to put glue on so that the picture shows. The
latter type of problem is different, e.g., how can we make sure people can tell
it's a helicopter instead of a regular plane? How can you tell this is the older
brother from the picture? etc. In some cases the child finds her own problem
and the teacher's role is to pose questions which will activate or extend one or
more of the problem-solving processes (observing; identifying the problem;
generating, evaluating, or elaborating solutions). There are also times when the
teacher takes a more active role in bringing a problem to the child's attention.
She may do this through the materials she presents or the way they are
arranged. She may create a situation which has the problem built in, or she may
present the problem verbally. These more active teacher strategies of engaging
children in interaction (with you the teacher, with peers, or with materials)
through which they will become interested in new problems is not at all at odds
with viewing the child as an active learner. The teacher simply recognizes that
not all interesting problems jump right out at children, that part of the role of
any good learning environment is helping the child see and become intrigued
by various kinds of problems.

The active role of the teacher in the stirring up of interesting problems is
frequent for the type we have called the *message* problems. Our example of the
treasure map shows how a teacher-provoked problem—how can we let Katy
and Sam know where the treasure is, etc.—led to absorbed thinking about
various problems that would have been unlikely to occur to the children
spontaneously. The child is still the one who must do the inventing. And if the
problem doesn't seem like a problem to him the teacher will learn a great deal
from that and work with the child only on aspects he *does* perceive as
problematic.

The teacher takes an active role at times in the physical aspects of
problems as well, though these more often have a way of "asking themselves."
Three-dimensional materials such as blocks are particularly rich in potential
because the physical problems are direct, observable, and often of great
interest and importance to children. For example, we have described an activity
in which the children tried to build a means of getting water across the sandbox

without spilling. They could see when they had a problem—after the fact if not before—and were eager to correct it. Working with the two-dimensional media also presents problems of this nature. In gluing, cutting, painting, etc., there is a thicket of problems to be dealt with in making things do what you want (and the "joy of being a cause," the excitement of mastery to fuel the effort).

Summary

Children have a spontaneous enjoyment of drawing and building and a tendency to seek out these activities. Three reasons why children seek out and persist in art activities were described. First, children enjoy having an effect and making marks or building things bring immediate visible results. Second, children have a tendency to exercise those skills they are in the process of acquiring; they will work at an emerging skill until they master it (and in art as the child improves at one skill, new possibilities emerge which in turn need to be mastered). Third, there seems to be a natural desire to represent aspects of the world and one's experience of them. This desire involves the child in the struggle to invent forms for representing, a struggle which is a form of problem-solving. The child has a limited repertoire of forms he can produce at any point and attempts to draw new objects must rely on these possibilities. The child assimilates the new object into his existing routines, but he also accommodates, that is, he makes some changes in his routines, as he is confronted with new representational tasks (Sigel, 1978).

We have discussed art and construction in the same chapter because they have several significant characteristics in common. The term "visible thinking" captures the first of these common features, the fact that in activities of either art or construction the child is working with media in which there is a visible product of one's actions, a product which remains after the activity is completed. Inventing forms for representing things is central in the young child's art and building activities alike. In addition, there is not a real difference between art and construction, as is sometimes assumed, in terms of the "aesthetic" vs. "utilitarian" nature of the activities. In both we see the desire to accomplish a purpose, often representational, and the desire to create eye-pleasing effects.

The "visible thinking" activities of art and construction have these significant characteristics in common, but this does not mean the whole family of activities is quite homogeneous. There are significant differences within these type of activities which teachers need to be aware of and take into account in their program. In the case of some materials, there is "creation by assembly;" the forms or units are provided and the task of the "artist" is to arrange them. This is in contrast with materials/activities which involve "creation from scratch;" in these the forms themselves are produced by the individual. Drawing is a case of two-dimensional "creation from scratch," modeling with clay three-dimensional example of this sort of production. Examples of two-dimensional "creation by assembly" are collage and feltboard activities. "Creation by assembly" with three-dimensional units is exemplified by all forms of block-building. When the child is working with materials of this kind, the job is not necessarily easier. The representational problem is largely one of analysis. The child must consider how the object which he is trying to represent can be shown with the kinds of forms available—a task which varies greatly in difficulty as a function of how well-suited the units are to what is being represented (e.g., squares and triangles to produce a house vs. the same forms to represent an ostrich). When the child is the producer of the forms "from scratch" his difficulties are somewhat different. In these cases, he isn't bound by the limitations of the available units, but he must do the creating of the forms themselves. This involves invention and analysis of a somewhat different sort, as well as a degree of fine motor skill which usually is more demanding than that needed to arrange prefabricated units.

These categories are suggested to the teacher as being useful in providing a range of different representational challenges. They may also suggest some interesting combinations and sequences in what is introduced into art and construction areas. With these categories in mind, the teacher is also in a better position to identify the individual child's abilities and limitations in art and construction.

The second portion of the chapter describes the classroom implementation of the theoretical points which have been made in this and previous chapters. We witness the teachers' planning of several weeks of activities concerned with art and construction, from the generation of new directions and ideas through the evaluation of specific ideas. The teachers (Jeanne and Denise) arrive at a series of eight activities planned for the two-week period. A summary of these is given, including the reasoning which underlies each activity. Two activities are then described more fully as they were carried out. What teachers were thinking and deciding is described, as well as what was said and done.

Finally, the chapter is summarized in terms of where each of the three objectives outlined in Chapter 3 was manifested in the activities of this two-week period. We descibe how the areas of art and construction are used to (1) develop children's acquaintance with objects and events in the world and awareness of their reactions to them, (2) develop competence in the representational modes, and (3) develop problem-solving skills.

Suggested Resources

Arnheim, R. *Art and Visual Perception: A Psychology of the Creative Eye* (Berkeley, Calif.: University of California Press, 1967).

Bland, J. C. *Art of the Young Child* (New York: Doubleday, 1957).

Croft, D. J., and Hess, R. D. Part 3: "Exploring the Arts." In *An Activities Handbook for Teachers of Young Children.* 2nd ed. (Boston: Houghton Mifflin, 1975).

Gardner, H. *The Arts and Human Development: A Psychological Study of the Artistic Process* (New York: John Wiley and Sons, 1973).

Goodnow, J. *Children Drawing.* In *The Developing Child Series,* edited by J. Bruner, M. Cole, B. Lloyd (Cambridge, Mass.: Harvard University Press, 1977).

Hartley, R. E., Frank, L. K., and Goldenson, R. M. *Understanding Children's Play* (New York: Columbia University Press, 1952).

Hess, R. D., and Croft, D. J. "Versatility of the Arts in a Preschool Program." In *Teachers of Young Children* (Boston: Houghton Mifflin, 1972).

Hirsch, E. S., ed. *The Block Book* (Washington, D.C.: National Association for the Education of Young Children, 1974).

Johnson, H. M. *The Art of Block Building* (New York: Bankstreet Publications, 1945).

Lorton, J. W., and Walley, B. L. "Art." In *Introduction to Early Childhood Education* (New York: D. Van Nostrand Co, 1979).

Lowenfeld, V., and Brittain, W. L. *Creative and Mental Growth* (New York: Macmillan, 1964).

NAEYC Publications, *Water, Sand and Mud as Play Materials* (Washington, D.C.: National Association for the Education of Young Children, 1959).

Pluckrose, H. *Art,* Informal Schools in Britain Today series (New York: Citation Press, 1972).

Sigel, I. E. "The Development of Pictorial Comprehension." In *Visual Learning, Thinking, and Communication,* edited by B. S. Randhawa and W. E. Coffman (New York: Academic, 1978).

Starks, E. B. *Block Building* (Washington, D.C.: Department of Elementary, Kindergarten, Nursery, National Education Association, 1965).

5

Music and Movement

Movement permeates human activity—we move when we work and when we play. In numerous *occupations* the speed, balance, precision, and efficiency of movement play a life-and-death role. (In others it is more a matter of "hire-or-fire.") These are among the qualities of movement which determine *athletic prowess*—which people will beat us at tennis, which ones we will beat, and which ones we will all pay to watch.

There are also the movements which convey meaning—both the *social-gestural system* with its conventional actions such as waves, shrugs, winks, and handshakes, and the less deliberate but equally meaningful movements like the trembling of a hand, the yawn, the contorting of a face in pain. In acting (both professional and the kind we all do) both kinds of movement may be used deliberately to convey meaning. In *mime*, for example, the performer takes natural human movements, facial expressions, etc., as well as the functional movements of everyday activity and presents them out of context. In this way the mime conveys to the audience what he is doing and feeling—impatiently trying to put up an umbrella, contentedly petting a dog, and so on. Movement communicates events, situations, and emotions.

In some forms of human activity, it is not a matter of a goal or a message. There is pleasure in moving in certain ways and pleasure in watching others do so. There are activities in which the achievement of excellence lies not in a goal attained through movement (scoring a point, arriving at the finish line first), but rather almost entirely on the beauty of precision or movement itself. Some sports are this sort—figure skating, diving, or gymnastics—in these sports champions are judged by the faultless precision and grace of the movement itself. *Dance* is also an activity of this type. Whether or not a dance also conveys a message—a story, an era, a feeling—the essence of the dance is in the pleasing quality, the aesthetics, of the movement itself.

Movement has had, on the whole, a place of much respect in preschool education. Teachers from a variety of approaches seem to find movement of great appeal to the young child and to recognize that it is useful in many ways in the classroom. Why is it that body movement is such an undisputed cornerstone of nursey and kindergarten classrooms? We have mentioned how fundamental movement is in life as we know it. In fact, the centrality of movement is evident from the earliest days in the life of the child.

From infancy, movement outside the child affects him. Some body positions and some kinds of motion may excite or disturb the child, while others may comfort him. During the first year of life the child employs movement to gain satisfaction of his needs as well as for the sheer pleasure. Increasingly he repeats and modifies movements that are stimulating, actions that produce desired effects and interesting events. Well before any meaningful sounds are uttered, the child is beginning to organize his movements to fulfill his needs. As each new motor activity is added to the child's repertoire, the action begins haltingly and as discrete steps. Gradually these separate movements are coordinated.

Movement is one important way for the child to gather impressions of the world. He constructs his ideas about what the world is like from the results of his actions. For example, seated in his high chair, he strikes the rattle on the tray before him. It falls. He strikes his mother's arm. It moves but returns to place. From such encounters, he forms differentiated expectations for animate and inanimate objects. As Piaget (1952) has outlined, in the infant's early interactions with the world—in the *sensorimotor period* (0-eighteen months of age)—it is through action on objects that the child constructs his knowledge of the world.

The infant's movements have effects not only directly on physical objects; they also operate communicatively on the human environment. The child moves in a certain way and mother adjusts his position. He tries to reach his teddy bear and it is brought within his grasp. Just as crying naturally accompanies the child's distress and also communicates distress to the adult, so the early gestures of the child, though they are not intended to communicate, do convey messages to those around the child. As the child develops and a movement—reaching, for example—is interpreted by others—as desire for the object—the child begins to use the motion with a more deliberate intent of communication. Many of the movements of the adult social-gestural system are of this nature, such as facial expressions. They can be employed by adults with more or less deliberate communicative intent. In early childhood they are more reflexive but are gradually coming to be used purposefully as well.

Some gestures are acquired by children in a different way—through social learning. Peek-a-boo, waving good-bye, putting a finger to the lips are gestures that are learned much as the first words are, by association with a context. Originally, the child had no tendency to wave on seeing someone leave. Adults wave to him when leaving. After a while, he comes to associate leaving with waving, and he may wave even when someone puts on a hat. We will be seeing more in this chapter of these two overlapping but differing categories of gesture—those that are socially learned nonverbal means of communication and those that seem to originate as natural concomitants of the emotion, the intent, or the meaning they convey.

In the beginning, actions of either kind are closely linked to the context within which they occur. By about twelve months the infant reaches what Piaget (1952) calls the tertiary circular reaction in which she begins to use actions more deliberately. Before, she has accidentally produced an effect and merely repeated the action that yielded the sensory goody. Now the infant has a goal and invents a means to achieve it, often combining old movements in a new way. This is the final achievement of the sensorimotor period, but action is still bound to the immediate situation. For Piaget, the dawn of representation can be seen when the child begins to do such things as imitating on Wednesday movements she saw on Tuesday (as in the famous tantrum Piaget's daughter reenacted).

By the time the child is two, her movements are less tied to the immediate stimulus or state that produces them. She can move in ways that represent meanings and she understands something of the representational dimension in the movements of others. For example, if she lacks the word for a new toy she wants mother to get for her, she may show the movement involved in using it (such as banging her hand up and down to show she wants the toy hammer). This new capacity does not diminish the fact that movement remains a way of responding to emotion and sound and a way of finding out about the world and solving problems. All of these aspects of movement are important: the child spontaneously moving in response to music, emotion, or mood; her moving to achieve results, or solve problems; her use and understanding of the representational possibilities of movement.

The first of these aspects, movement in response to music or mood, has probably been the strongest element within the traditional preschool's approach to movement. Among the suggested resources at the end of this chapter we cite some helpful resources for activities, materials, and strategies in movement. Included are a number with good suggestions for this expressive—affective response through movement.

We will be focusing our attention primarily on the other two aspects: (1) the role of movement in the child's *problem-solving* and *construction* of *knowledge* and (2) movement as a developing *representational system*. We will first consider movement in relation to problem-solving and learning about the world.

The Basic Movement Approach

There is a body of interesting work in what is called the basic movement approach to physical education. The work of Rudolf Laban (e.g., 1948) has been influential in setting new directions in physical education. The Laban-influenced curricula place less emphasis on games and specific skills and more on acquainting children with the diverse potentials in the movement of the body. Instead of giving children directions to move in a particular way, teachers give them problems to respond to. The problems are open-ended with many alternative solutions and no one "right way," e.g., "What are some ways you can think of to get on and off this box?" Follow-up questions would attempt to get children to explore more alternatives or notice something about their movements ("What were your legs like when you jumped off? Were they different than when you stepped off?")

The basic movement approach attempts to lay the foundation for physical education both in terms of *structure* and *process*. One of the ways in which Laban has had a major impact in physical education, as well as dance and gymnastics, is in his analysis of the elements of human movement. His work provides an understanding of the *structure of how we move*. A number of current educators have developed curricula which are indebted to Laban's analysis. Bonnie Gilliom (1970), for example, examines the structure of how man moves and selects "themes" of movement which are applicable to specific skills, games, dances, and sports, as well as the movements of everyday life.

She has developed curricula around the following themes: *Where can you move?* (space), *What can you move?* (body awareness), *How do you move?* (force, balance, weight transfer), and *How can you move better?* (time, flow). The possibilities within each of these questions are further spelled out, as can be seen in Box 5-1. Gilliom's curricula are for beginning grades through upper grades. Thinking about the young child in particular, we have simplified and adapted Gilliom's movement chart, which is one of several based on Laban's principles of human movement. A simple way of describing the contents of this chart would be to say that it specifies what there is to movement. In other words, with respect to movement, this is the lay of the land. It is useful in thinking through a curriculum area for the teacher to think about the "nature of the beast" she is confronting. What are the characteristics of movement as compared with other modes? What are the basic elements of movement, the ways in which one movement differs from another? Laban's analysis provides considerable help in responding to these questions. Basic movement education operates from this foundation in describing its objectives for the learner. There are three types: *knowledge, skill,* and *attitude* objectives.

Let us look at a specific example of each of these three types of objectives, again from Gilliom, within the theme "moving at different speeds." Within this theme, Gilliom defines such *knowledge objectives* as understanding that movements vary in speed from very slow to very fast and that one way to vary a movement is to change the amount of time it takes to do the movement (1970, p. 182). *Skill objectives* for the theme of moving at different speeds would include learning how to vary the speed of movements, to accelerate and decelerate slowly and quickly, and to consciously control the speed of body movement (1970, p. 182). *Attitude objectives* are not specific to a theme or unit, and they are achieved gradually over the years in school. For those in basic movement education, as for us, the development of these attitudes is perhaps the most crucial set of objectives of all. It is important for the children to become "willing to listen to problems, to think about them, and to seek increasingly more skillful, thoughtful, and original ways of solving them through movement" (Gilliom, 1970, p. 182). Stress is also placed on appreciation of individual differences, task persistence, self-motivation, self-esteem, and enjoyment of movement.

To this point, we have been looking at the kinds of goals the basic movement teacher wants to achieve with children and, before that, at the elements of movement and their relationship to one another. This might have seemed to be a big buildup (or even, heaven forbid, a digression) before directly considering the problem-solving aspect of movement curricula as we mentioned we would. But this is an important preamble. A consideration of the basic elements or dimensions of movement and the relationships among them, in other words, of the *structure* of movement, can help the teacher in several ways: (1) in indicating the *kinds of problems and activities* to plan for children, as well as suggesting the natural links and sequences among them, (2) in creating *a compass for focused inquiry* by providing ideas of profitable directions in which

Box 5-1. How Do We Move?

| | | | | Movement: | | |
The Body	Body Relationships/Actions		In Space	In Time	With Force	With Flow
Body parts	*Relationships of body part to body part*	*Actions*	*Divisions of space*	*Speed*	*Degrees of force*	*Dimensions of flow*
Head, neck	Near to each other (curled)	Balancing	Self space	Slow	Strong	Free, ongoing
Shoulders, arms	Far from each other (stretched)	Crawling	General space	Medium	Medium	Bound, controlled, restrained
Elbows, hands	Rotated with one part fixed (twisted)	Stepping	*Dimensions of space*	Fast	Weak	
Back, spine	*Relationships of body parts to objects: on, off, over, around, to, far from*	Rocking	Directions	Accelerating	*Qualities of force*	
Chest	Walls, floor	Rolling	Forward	Decelerating	Sudden, explosive	
Waist	Boxes, benches	Sliding	Backward	Sustained, sudden	Sustained, smooth	
Hips, legs	Beams	Climbing	To one side	(also qualities of force)		
Knees, feet	*Relationships of one person to another*	Flight	To the other side	*Rhythm*		
Body surfaces	Near to	(etc.—these could be described and broken down in various ways)	Up	To pulse beats		
Front	Far from		Down	To phrases and rhythmic patterns		
Back			Levels			
Sides			High			
Body shapes			Medium			
Symmetrical-asymmetrical			Low			
Curved			Ranges			
Straight and narrow						

Straight and
wide
Twisted

Meeting
Parting
Facing
Side-by-side
Shadowing
Mirroring
Leading
Following

Large
Medium
Small
Planes
Pathways
(floor or air)
Straight
Curved
Zigzag

Adapted from "Movement Chart III: How Do I Move?" In *Basic Movement Education For Children: Rationale and Teaching Units* by Bonnie C. Gilliom (Reading, Mass.: Addison-Wesley Publishing Company, 1970), pp. 212–213.

to carry exploration with the child (which will increase understanding of important dimensions, relationships, etc.), and (3) in increasing the *coherence of evaluation* of the child's understanding and skill by making explicit what there is to be understood and how it interrelates. We will be seeing examples throughout the chapter of each of these ways in which understanding the structure of movement serves a useful function for the teacher.

We have been making the point that it is important to our approach and to the basic movement education approach to plan a curriculum on the basis of a solid analysis of the *structure* of human movement. It is just as important to us and to the basic movement approach to emphasize the *processes* through which children most effectively develop. And again, there is much common ground. We would be in close agreement with educators of the basic movement approach in our view of the *processes* through which children acquire knowledge, skills, and attitudes and of many of the *educational strategies* which are consequently employed.

As we mentioned briefly above, basic movement teachers seek to facilitate development in movement through strategies which differ from the typical explanation-demonstration-practice cycle used in physical education in particular and education in general. Instead, children are presented with open-ended problems and challenged to discover their own alternative solutions. The teacher does not require the children to respond verbally, although in some instances they may wish to do so. But the problems should require reasoning and imagination on the part of the child. If they only direct him to move in ways that do not challenge him to think, they have failed in their purpose. In all these respects, we have found the basic movement approach to be a "soul-mate" of our own.

Let's turn to some specific activities which our hypothetical teachers Jeanne and Denise might plan for movement. They can determine how closely spaced in time these activities will be only as they see how each successive activity goes. Based on the difficulty children have with an activity, their involvement in a given type of activity, etc., the teachers may conclude that the children would benefit from additional exploration of one problem or aspect of movement before preceeding to the next. Another possibility is that the teachers may feel that the particular way an activity was done (e.g., the manner in which the problem was presented, the follow-up questions, the materials) was not successful in activating exploration of that dimension of movement. From a partial failure the teachers can learn about what the children have difficulty perceiving or doing, where they seem to get stuck in a rut, needing new problems, questions or in some cases, materials, to get them thinking. So, it should be understood that this series is not laid out on an unchangeable syllabus, with dates planned for each activity. Rather, the teachers evolve a general plan in terms of direction and in terms of key steps along the way. In the example we are considering here the class has explored a number of aspects of body movement in the following sequence:

—body parts and shapes
—the range of possible movements at different joints
—the various ways you can get from one place to another
—the directions you can move in space

Now speed of the movement, and later rhythm, will be the focus. These dimensions will not be explored in isolation, but in the context of what the children have already done with movement. It should also be noted that the same basic problems or themes of movement will be returned to again and again. Each time new facets, or subproblems as Gilliom (1970) calls them, can be explored. Early in the school year the notion of moving in different directions may be new and engagingly difficult. A month or two later, this concept is well understood on a certain level (not due to maturation alone, but to the occasions on which the children have explored the possibilities, sometimes with teacher interaction and sometimes without it, varying their actions and consolidating their initial understanding). Now it is time to seek a higher or broader understanding or to tackle a related problem. The model is a spiral of increasing breadth.

Let's have a look at a series of three activities which the teachers have planned to spark some exploration of the dimension of speed in movement.

Activity 1: Moving fast, moving slowly

At the beginning of the outdoor period, the children are gathered at one end of the playground in a line. Jeanne says to them, "What is one way you can get to the other end of the playground *fast?*" The children mostly suggest running, and Jeanne says, "OK, why don't you show me? Run down there fast and back fast." After this she goes on to inquire about other ways to get there fast and gives the children the opportunity to explore ways, commenting here and there on new ways she sees being tried. From observing the children, Jeanne sees that a few of them have discovered that the same movement, in this case walking, can be done at different speeds. Now Jeanne introduces a new element to the game—the use of the SLOW traffic sign, a conventional representation of speed change with which the children are familiar from a discussion of road signs. Pointing out the different speeds at which various children are walking, she assembles the scattered class for a new game. The children are told that they are to begin walking toward Jeanne as fast as they can, but when they see the SLOW sign, they must slow down. This game is played for awhile, with occasional questions or comments such as, "Who's walking more slowly, Bob or Marie? Yes, they're both walking slowly, but

Marie is walking even more slowly than Bob—oh, now Bob has slowed down . . . " "Would the person who's walking the slowest get here first?" "What do your arms do when you're walking fast?" etc.

Now free play will begin. Jeanne tells the children that the signs will be put near the tricycle path and that they may want to take turns being the police officer. During the outdoor period, both in the tricycle area and elsewhere, the teachers watch for opportunities to extend the children's investigation of speed differences or to introduce the idea of the speed dimension into their ongoing play.

Reasoning: Children have some notion of "fast" and "slow." They often link the terms with certain kinds of movement in an all-or-none way, e.g., running is fast. This activity and later ones will give the children an opportunity to construct a more elaborated and multidimensional idea of the relationship of speed to movement.

In addition, the experience of consciously controlling one's own speed is a demanding one for young children. They will succeed at various levels. Some will slow down immediately on seeing the signal and in the course of the activity only improve from good to better in the immediacy of their response. Some will respond promptly but by stopping and then starting up again at a slower pace. Some will not respond until they are aware of the rest of the group going slowly. All of these children are benefiting from the experience at their own developmental levels.

After the brief activity, as they play on their own, the children may continue to explore speed differences. The teachers occasionally draw their attention to some aspect of their movement or ask a question which raises a discrepancy to be resolved. The activity and the free exploration provide (1) problem-solving experiences with speed and (2) the opportunity to try controlling speed deliberately.

Activity 2: What Am I? (with speed variations)

At circle time in the classroom, Denise plays a "What Am I?" game with the children—with a new twist. She represents things which move in distinctive ways and which can move at different speeds. In each case she performs the action first. When children guess what she is—windshield wipers, for example—she engages them in the action and then introduces a change in speed (a transformation within the mode to express a transformation within the actual event). "Now it's raining harder and we need to turn them up to fast. OK?"

The game can include a variety of types of problems, each with a different mental demand. Sometimes the questions will focus on the *reason* for moving at a given speed. For example, "When do you think a rabbit might move like that? That could be one reason, can you think of any other reason? . . . When might he hop more slowly?" etc. In other instances the child is the one to show how one would move differently if some condition were different ("Let's pretend we're raking leaves . . . OK, now it's about to rain and we have to finish in a hurry. Would we rake any differently? Show me . . ."). At another point the children are shown an action performed at an inappropriate speed (e.g., feeding a baby from a spoon at a very rapid pace) and asked, "What's wrong?" . . . "Well, what would be a better way? Why do you think that would be better?"

Reasoning: To increase the children's awareness of the dimension of speed in movement, Activity 2 builds on Activity 1 in several respects. Activity 1 did not deal with body movement as a representational system; nor was it concerned with any cause-effect relationships of movement speed to situation. Activity 2 does both. Varying degrees of representation are involved. In some cases, an action is performed more or less as it would be in the actual situation, simply removed from context. The child has to deal with imagining the missing aspects of the situation—the rake, the baby, etc. In other cases, a different kind of representation is involved, as an object or animal is conveyed—windshield wipers, a rabbit, etc. As can be seen in Box 5-2, one way in which representations through use of the body vary is the degree to which representation is through a *dynamic quality*, or quality of motion (a bird's flight or a rabbit's hopping) or through a *static quality*, or quality of appearance (a bird's wings or a rabbit's long ears). In the case of this activity, the children and teacher are imitating the motion. Rather simple movements are selected, so that the primary focus can remain on varying the speed of each.

A second aspect which is explored is the relationship of the speed of movement to various outcomes. The teachers think through examples which will be meaningful to young children and in which certain basic ideas about time/speed of movement are illustrated. For example, in the case of leaf-raking, the idea is that movement would be speeded up when something needs to get done in a hurry—that when things are done quickly they take less time. Children are given problem situations which are intended to activate the construction of relationships of space, time, and movement. Further impetus to mentally explore these relationships should be provided by Activity 3.

Activity 3: Film of movement (with slow motion and regular speed)

The teachers have obtained a film of various kinds of movement in regular and slow motion. Before showing the movie, they ask the children to help think of some ways we can move which are fast. The children suggest running, riding a bike, riding a roller coaster, etc. (Jeanne recollects with them some of the ways they moved fast in Activity 1.) For slow, they suggest walking, crawling, and tiptoeing. Then the teachers run the first part of the film, which is a normal-speed segment showing a runner. The fact that he's moving very fast is acknowledged. Then a segment with a runner in slow motion is shown. This involves a discrepancy, which Jeanne attempts to draw attention to. "Is this fast or slow? Is he walking or crawling then if it's slow? He's running? But I thought you said running was fast . . . How do you know he's running? How is he moving differently from someone walking?"

The various sections of the film (running, pole-vaulting, and broad-jumping) are shown. In watching the film the children will have the opportunity to notice things about the movements that they have never noticed. Only occasional comments and questions will be offered by the teachers as they and the children share the pleasure of watching the slowed movement. With a question here, a comment there, they will be spurring the children to think about the speed/movement discrepancy and notice the distinctive features of various kinds of movement.

Reasoning: As we mentioned in discussing Activity 1, children have a tendency to have rather undifferentiated notions of the relationship of speed and kind of movement. For example, running is slow, walking is fast. Although the children would recognize walking versus running, their mental representations of each are not likely to be well developed. They will have a tendency to center on a single aspect, such as speed, to the exclusion of others. This activity is intended to focus the child's attention on other aspects of running, etc., and thus provoke him to construct fuller and more accurate notions of the time/space/movement relationship.

At the same time, a greater awareness of how we move is facilitated. It is not important *per se* for children to know that in running the legs are more bent than in walking. What is important is the mental process of elaborating and using an internal representation of action.

While the class is exploring the *speed* dimension of movement, it seems natural to next incorporate the related dimension of rhythm. Rhythmic movements have often been used during the various speed-related activities and in the children's free explorations. Now the time seems ripe for a greater focus on rhythm. Activities which involve music along with movement are naturals here. (One example of such activity will be described in the music section of this chapter. Teacher source books are full of them.) Before turning to music, let's look more fully at the representational use of movement.

How Do We Represent Through Movement?

At the beginning of the chapter we suggested that movement has both communicative and aesthetic functions. We noted that in some cases, such as pantomime, the communication function has major importance, while in others, such as dance, what is primary is the aesthetic quality of the movement and the patterns of movement. In still other activities, only what is achieved through movement counts and "form" is of secondary importance, e.g., climbing a ladder, scoring a touchdown. The *elements* of movement are the same in any case. We have certain body parts. They can be in various relationships to each other and to objects (near, far; on, around, under). There are a finite number of actions (stepping, balancing, crawling, etc.), although they can be varied in a seemingly infinite number of ways. Our movement in space can be in various directions, at various levels, along pathways of certain kinds (straight, curved, zigzag), and with ranges of movement from large to small. Speed and rhythm further define our movement. In Addition, the force of the movement can vary in degree (from strong to weak) and quality (sudden or sustained). And the flow of the movement can vary in the degree to which it is free rather than restrained.

These aspects of movement were presented in Box 5-1, "How Do We Move?" Now we see them again in Box 5-2, "How Do We Represent Through Movement?" It is through these aspects that we are able to convey various kinds of meaning with our bodies. If I am portraying an elephant, I may use my arm to show the trunk; I may portray his four-leggedness by getting down on all fours, etc. These would be ways of showing what the elephant looks like, of capturing his static *qualities of appearance.* Alternatively (or in addition), I might choose to convey the elephant's slow, lumbering gait, perhaps with a trunk slowly swinging back and forth. Here I would be representing the dynamic *qualities of movement* of the elephant.

Another point the teacher will find helpful in working with movement as a representational system can be illustrated by this observation: the ballerinas in *Swan Lake* do not flap their arms. Arm-flapping does not appear to be highly honored in the world of ballet. So the clever ballerinas and their choreographers use less direct, less imitative ways of conveying swanness. The effortless, graceful motion of the swan is shown through smooth, fluid movement.

In contrast, take a mime who is portraying a man striking out in a baseball game. For the most part, he is directly *replicating* the body position and the movements of face and body which we would be seeing if this were really taking place. He does, of course, do some exaggerating and he makes selective use of distinctive details, but in its essentials the movements of the mime are close to those of the batter. What we are seeing is the movement *removed from context.* There is no pitcher or catcher, no umpire or fans. The mime is not actually holding a bat. But through careful mimicry of what the body would look like in the situation, the mime conveys a message.

Let's think briefly about the various cognitive demands involved in understanding or using movement of these kinds. No matter which kind of representation of movement we are discussing (whatever aspect of the body's potentials, whether in direct or more abstract representing of the movement), the child must call to mind her *internal representation* of such movement. The process of trying to convey the movements (in *external representation*) presses the child to a more refined mental representation, whatever form this may take. In trying to walk like a chicken that was seen the day before a field trip, the child must think carefully about how the chicken looked when it walked. If the child were instead drawing the chicken, it is likely that her focus would be on the features of the chicken, its color, etc. An activity or question that activates the

Box 5-2.   **How Do We Represent With Movement?**

Features, dimensions of movement	Aspects of referent which may be represented
ARRANGEMENT OF BODY: STATIC	CHARACTERISTICS OF APPEARANCE: STATIC

Body parts: their shapes, their relationship to each other and to objects	*Body position, orientation of:*
e.g., on hands and knees ————————>	cow (representing what X is)
prone ————————>	sleeping (representing what X is doing)
e.g., extended index fingers (pointing up) held on top of head ————————>	*Features of:* rabbit (representing what X is)
eyes closed ————————>	sleeping (representing what X is doing)
	Pose of:
e.g., arms crooked in front of body ————————>	mother (representing what X is)
arm bent back at shoulder joint and at elbow ————————>	throwing (representing what X is doing)

MOVEMENT OF BODY: DYNAMIC	CHARACTERISTICS OF MOVEMENT: DYNAMIC
Basic actions (or ways of moving from place to place)	*Action of:*
e.g., sliding ————————>	ice skater (representing what X is)
stepping ————————>	mounting stairs (representing what X is doing)
Directions, levels, ranges, planes, pathways	*Direction, etc., of:*
e.g., circular pathway ————————>	hawk (representing what X is)

backward direction	———————>	fear reaction [backing away] (representing what X is doing)
Speed		*Speed of:*
e.g., slow	———————>	elderly person (representing what X is)
fast	———————>	hurrying (representing what X is doing)
decelerating	———————>	coming to a stop [of a train, for example] (represent- ing what X is doing)
Rhythm		*Rhythm of:*
e.g., short-long beat	———————>	horse (representing what X is)
regular	———————>	marching (representing what X is doing)
Degrees of force/ qualities of force		*Degree and/or quality of force of:*
e.g., strong, explosive	———————>	volcano (representing what X is)
medium, sustained	———————>	pushing a heavy object (representing what X is doing)
Quality of flow		*Quality of flow:*
e.g., controlled	———————>	robot (representing what X is)
controlled (restrained at one leg joint)	———————>	leg in cast (representing X's condition)

---

child's internal representation of the chicken moving (poultry in motion, one might say) contributes to the development of mental representation in a different modality.

Often when one is representing through body movement, one is not doing an instant replay of movement just as it was. For example, suppose I am trying to portray the movement of a fish. I must represent the movement of a legless, armless, creature propelling itself through water. I'm on dry land, I can't float, I have arms and legs and no fins—and I must work with what I have. I must do some mental work to analyze the movement of the fish to come up with features of movement which I can in some way produce. One child might use his hand as the fish, moving it with a fluid motion in a rhythmic wiggle. Another child may walk in a wiggly pathway. Another may think of using his arms as the fins of the fish, and so on. All of these, from a cognitive standpoint, involve *active analysis* and *mental transformation* of the movement of the fish to enable the child to show the fish when the possibility of direct imitation is absent. Becoming more capable of such analysis and mental manipulation or transformation is important in a great many ways, not the least of which is the role such ability plays in effective problem-solving. In much of problem-solving an individual must think through how a thing can be changed to produce a desired effect.

The familiarity and relative ease of movement for the young child (in contrast, for example, with the struggles involved in the newer task of making a crayon do what one wants it to do) are part of the reason that movement is such a fertile area for mental exploration and problem-solving. Since the behavior itself is not too troublesome for the children, their minds can engage without constraint in dealing with the cognitive demands of activities. And since the children are physically active while they're being challenged to think, even the child who is not inclined to sit still long to draw or do a puzzle can remain with such a learning encounter for an extended period of time.

Teachers' questions can play an important role in increasing and focusing what a child learns through exploration of the representational aspects of movement. Perhaps an opportunity occurs when a few children are preparing a short "dramatic sequence" for the rest of the group or when the class is playing a sort of charades at circle time. Or a teacher may see a good chance to find out what a child is trying to convey as she imitates a policeman's signals in "directing traffic." These are a few examples of the kinds of questions a teacher could ask in these contexts:

How does X look/move? How can you show the way X moves?

"Oh, you are elephants (on being informed to that effect) and this is your jungle. I see you're four-legged like elephants. Is there anything else about the way an elephant moves that's special—different from a dog or a cat? . . . Oh, I see some trunks swinging back and forth now on these elephants . . . They move slow, Laurie?"

"Think about the chicken we saw yesterday at the farm. How are you going to show the other children that's the animal you are? . . . Is there anything else about the way the chicken moved that you remember? . . . Anything else he did?"

The cognitive demands of such questions are twofold. By being asked to think about how the animal (or person, machine, etc.) moved, the child is encouraged to sharpen his internal representation(s) of the movement. There is an additional cognitive demand in trying to think of effective ways to convey the message to others. The child must reflect on which features of appearance (e.g., body position) or movement (e.g., speed, rhythm, quality of force) will get the message across. Feedback from peers such as wrong guesses or blank looks can play a role in provoking less egocentric enactments and more reflection on the *distinctive features* of the movement which will best express the identity, the situation, or the emotion the child is trying to convey.

How can you tell? Why do you think so?

"What made you guess Mary was a robot?"

"Why do you think Jay is climbing a ladder? Why not a stairway?"

"What was it about the way Tim moved that made you think he was an iceskater?" And if there's no response, "Can you try to move that way? Hmm, what are you doing that's different from regular walking?"

"Jane says she knew the little boy was scared even before she saw the witch. How could you tell he was afraid, Jane?"

These questions are addressed to the "audience" or observer of representational movement rather than the "actor." Questions of this type draw children's attention to considering what features of movement or appearance they have based their conclusions on. It is often relatively easy for children to make good guesses as to what is being depicted. It is far more intellectually demanding for children to try to identify what it was that made them think so. For example, in the case of Mary's robot, children may pick up on a general resemblance but not at first be able to think in terms of the jerkiness or stiffness of Mary's movement (even Mary herself may not have been consciously aware of what feature of movement she was using). When children don't move beyond their intuitive "gut-reaction" (e.g., "She just looked like a robot"), follow-up questions can help. For example, the teacher might say, "Would you have thought she was a robot if she moved like this?" (using smooth movements). "Well, what's different? . . . Hmm, you're doing a robot walk like Mary's. Can you show me how *I* would move like a robot? . . . What should I do?"

It is not important to the teacher that the children know the elements or characteristics of movement by name. She hopes to get them thinking about how movements vary and how we get messages of different kinds from these variations. Her questions may provoke some children's thoughts about a particular element of movement, such as smoothness vs. jerkiness, and further spontaneous exploration of variations along this dimension may follow. In addition, questions of the how-can-you-tell variety are a reflection of the goal (across all curriculum areas) of increasing children's tendency to reflect on their own mental processes and the cues they have used to arrive at conclusions. In other words, the objective is to engage the child in considering "how one knows what one knows."

Can you tell _____from what you see? (Characteristics of movement as a representational system)

"You all think Molly is a rabbit hopping along? Is she in a hurry, do you think? (Why? etc.) Can you tell what color she is? (What would we have to do if we needed to show her color? . . . What else could we do?)"

"If we just had a picture of Marci combing her hair, how would we know if she was doing it fast or slow? Yes, Todd, we could tell from a movie, but what about a picture in a book?"

Questions such as these direct children's attention to the characteristics of the representational systems themselves. Can color be shown through movement? Can speed be conveyed in music? In a picture? If so, how? Thinking about such issues can be helpful in (1) solving problems of representation *within* a particular mode, such as movement, (2) choosing the most effective mode for a given kind of message, and (3) translating a message from one mode to another with awareness of what is "lost in translation."

Summary

We began by discussing the variety of human activities based on movement of the body: occupations and everyday functioning in the world, sports, arts (such as mime and dance), and gestures. Movement has several facets. It is the means of accomplishing physical goals (getting upstairs, digging a well, making a touchdown), it conveys meaning, and it is pleasurable to engage in and observe. Each of these facets has greater or lesser importance in a given activity; for example, in dance, it is the aesthetic quality of the movement which is central.

The importance of movement is evident from the earliest days in the life of the child. Three aspects of movement were noted with respect to the child's early development: movement in response to music, emotion, or mood; movement to achieve results, solve problems, learn about the world; and use and understanding of the representational possibilities of movement. Our focus in the chapter is on the latter two aspects.

First, we examined some implications for movement curriculum in relation to problem-solving and constructing knowledge about the world. We presented the basic elements of movement, based on the work of R. Laban (1948). A central teacher strategy is to present children with open-ended problems which encourage exploration of these elements and thus increase understanding of what one can move, where one can move, and how one can move. As an example we looked at how teachers might work out activities to encourage children's thought and exploration in relation to a given element, speed of movement.

The second aspect of movement considered in relation to curriculum was the representational potential of movement. The elements of body movement articulated by Laban again form the basis for increasing the child's understanding of the possibilities of movement, here with respect to representation. There are features in the arrangement of the body which convey how something looks (which we call "characteristics of appearance: static") and features of movement which convey how something moves or what someone is doing (which we term "characteristics of movement: dynamic").

There is often a considerable degree of mental transformation involved in translating into body movement the actions and/or appearance of that which is being represented. This transformation is minimal when movement closely imitates human action (as in replicating the movements of a batter striking out); it is greater when the movement cannot be directly imitated either because it is impossible (as with the fish) or artistically undesirable (as in the ballet rendition of a swan). These considerations should assist the teacher in designing activities around representational use of movement and in capitalizing on children's spontaneous use of movement to imitate and represent. Questions and comments by teachers can further extend the children's thought about and exploration of the representational possibilities of movement. Three types of questions are suggested: (1) How does X look/move? How can you show the way X moves? (2) How can you tell_____? Why do you think so? and (3) Can you tell_____from what you see? The cognitive benefits of each type of question were discussed.

Now we will turn to the frequent partner of movement—whether in the military march, on the disco floor, or in the early childhood classroom: music.

Music

From infancy the child is surrounded with sound—the vacuum cleaner, the airplane overhead, the dog, the doorbell, the thunder and the rain, and most pervasively, the human voice. The sound of human speech accompanies the most interesting and satisfying events of the infant's day—feeding, being held, watching faces and bodies moving. There is evidence that from a very early age infants are particularly receptive to the human voice. As types of auditory stimuli go, speech is varied and complex. With much change of rhythm, tempo, pitch, and volume but with a certain regularity of cadence, speech is more like music than any of the other sounds in the child's environment. Long before the child can understand language, he responds to these sound qualities of speech. Differences in volume, rhythm, tempo, and pitch, whether in speech or in music, are within the young infant's capacity to distinguish. One group of researchers found that even newborns, while they were still residing in the hospital nursery, would modify their rate of sucking pacifiers in order to obtain piped-in music of their own preference—classical, popular, or vocal (Butterfield, 1968).

In the baby's own producing of sound, at least by the time he is babbling, we hear him playing with many elements of sound—loudness, duration, pitch, and so forth. Babbling begins to sound more and more like speech with the

rising and falling intonation of adult conversation. Later when the child is beginning to learn words and then put them to use in short utterances, his halting speech will not so noticeably be characterized by these "musical" qualities. But at the same time, the child will be heard engaging in chanting and playing with rhythmic patterns of various kinds, often accompanying movements. This playing with sound and rhythm continues in one form or another throughout childhood. Meanwhile another important development has taken place.

By the time the child is three, he is dealing with numerous representations of the world as well as with the world itself. There are a variety of modes within which the child represents and comprehends the representations of others. He is quite competent with his native language. He is drawing, painting, and building things he sees. In creating things in these modes, the child often reflects what he has felt as well as what he has seen. In movement—gestures, body movement, dance—messages and modes are conveyed, sometimes not deliberately but increasingly in conscious communication or for controlled effect. With music that the child hears or makes, he can find reflections of what he has seen, done, or felt. The child responds to two aspects of music which are referred to as *formal* and *referential* (e.g., in Gardner, 1973). There are the *formal* relationships that elements (rhythm, tone, tempo, etc.) have to one another independent of any symbolic or expressive aspects the music may have, and music may have *reference* to events, experiences, or objects. Let us look first at this referential aspect of music.

There are several different ways in which music can be *referential* or representational. Gardner points out two of these: the first is in the "widely sensed relationship between musical patterns and the emotional-feeling life of the individual" and the second is in the way in which a tune is linked with the context in which it is typically heard (1973, p.130). For example, Brahms' "Lullaby" comes to mean "good-night" or "it's time for bed." We'll return to look more at each of these.

A third way in which music is referential is through correspondence with what is being represented. The most obvious and direct case is musical representation of sound. In a picture portraying an object there is correspondence between the representation and the real thing—in outline, in distinctive features, in spatial arrangement. Likewise with music and sound. The sound of a rainstorm, a galloping horse, or a locomotive can be fairly precisely simulated, a technology which sound effects experts have evolved. Somewhat less directly, the distinctive features of a sound or sound pattern can be captured in characteristics of music such as tempo or rhythm.

When a musical piece conveys some object (or event) from another mode (not auditory), such as the feel of velvet, or the appearance of lofty mountains, what is probably happening is that the listener is responding to properties which are not specific to one sense only. For example, music that has a "velvet sound" would have a smooth, rich quality. Music representing a sprightly dance of a fairy queen would have light, quick notes while the music to represent flying would contain, perhaps, "gliding" notes, with gradual transitions from one note to the next.

Returning to the first referential aspect of music which we mentioned, the link of certain music with certain emotions, we can see that this link could be formed either through association of the piece with a context or by the correspondence of properties in the music with an event or emotion. A familiar funeral dirge and the wedding march are both stately tunes performed at a pace which has some correspondence with the slow walking of persons in the respective rituals and with the dignity and importance of the occasions. But that one is for the listener mourning music, conveying grief, while the other is linked with joyous and hopeful thoughts is largely a function of the listener having heard them in their respective contexts. So there is some *correspondence* between the stateliness of the music and the type of occasion and the accompanying emotion, but the role of *context* is also involved. (It could also be noted that this example helps us distinguish conventionalized meaning from personal meaning. Not everyone who is familiar with The Wedding March is filled with joyous feelings on hearing it, though they do know that this is music which conventionally accompanies a happy occasion. And this personal emotional reaction often varies from one listening experience to another.)

Children do not have to be of advanced age or training before music "speaks to them" in these various ways. From infancy, certain songs, like lullabies, go along with certain globally experienced contexts—the comfort, security, and closeness of being held and rocked by mother is then evoked by the crooning sound of the lullaby. If a parent wants to let a toddler know that it's time for "Sesame Street," he has only to hum the theme song and the child will go and install herself comfortably in front of the TV set.

As for music "referring to" or evoking impressions of nonmusical things, sensations, or experiences, the child seems to very naturally find such links. Some would contend that the child's impressions of the world are less differentiated, less divided into sight, sound, touch categories. For children, then, music may evoke other affective and sensory experiences even more than it does for adults. There is some research to support this notion. Pflederer and Sechrest (1968) collected young children's verbal responses to music and found they did report sensory impressions from other modalities, as when some music sounded "sort of hazy."

It seems clear from teachers' and parents' reports, as well as from research, that young children do "think of things" when they hear music—sights, sounds, feelings. However, the children are usually not aware of what characteristics of the music they are responding to as the basis of these linkages. We shall see that heightening this awareness is one of the many ways through which the teacher can facilitate the growth of the child's musical intelligence and enjoyment.

Now let us turn to the *formal* aspect of music. We have seen that music can represent or express meanings. At the same time, music is a system. The elements of rhythm, pitch, beat, accent, volume, etc., reside in a systematic organization. In this book we are looking at the *external representational systems*, language, art (both two- and three-dimensional), movement, and music. These various systems are not all representational to the same extent; neither are they all equally systematic. Gardner has made this point:

Music is highly organized and systematized, but has only limited reference (though these referential aspects may be important); alternatively, paintings are clearly referential but lack systematically related components (1973, p. 128).

Thus music is a system in which the *formal relationship of elements* is quite structured. In the music curriculum for the young child (barring the precocious musical genius) these formal elements are not taught explicitly; nor is the

Box 5-3.   **The Elements of Music[1]**

Rhythm refers to a regulated pattern formed by long or short notes. Subelements of rhythm include *beat, accent,* and *pattern.* A piece of music is divided into measures. *Beat* is a regular and rhythmical unit of time; the rhythm is a product of the number of beats in the measure and the time value assigned to each beat. *Accent* indicates a special stress given to a musical note within a phrase. In clapping the beat of a piece of music, one would clap harder on some beats than others, the beats with accent. *Pattern,* as the name suggests, refers to the design of the rhythm, e.g., long-long-short long-long-short or long-short-long long-short-long. As we all recall from high-school English, rhythm is characteristic not only of music but of poetry, prose, and natural speech as well. (Children are often struck by the rhythm of words and phrases far more than we meaning-bound adults.) In seeking to enhance children's awareness of rhythm, teachers often encourage them to clap or move with it.

Tempo indicates the relative speed of a piece of music, simply how fast or slow it is to be played. This is another element for which the coordination of movement with music is a natural way to increase awareness and enjoyment of varying tempos.

Melody is the succession or arrangement of notes. Its subelements are *pitch, direction,* and *shape. Pitch,* which in physical terms is the sound frequency of the tone, is to the ear the feature of how high or low a note is. *Direction* refers to whether a melody goes up, down, or stays level. *Shape* is the characteristic way a melody goes up, or down. An awareness of melody can be fostered by having children show with their hands when the music goes up or down.

Tone Quality (or *Timbre*) is the distinctive characteristic of a sound that sets it apart from other sounds identical in pitch and volume. The most noticeable tone differences would be between various instruments; for example, a piano, a flute, and an oboe may play the same note and the sound quality will be very different. Children are quite capable of distinguishing the instruments with respect to tone quality, though describing their differences is obviously more difficult. *Dynamics* is the variation in force or intensity in music, the loudness-softness and the suddenness or gradualness of changes in loudness. This is a salient element for young children.

[1] The descriptions of the elements of music are based on the definitions of the terms by Barbara Vance in *Teaching the Kindergarten Child: Instructional Design and Curriculum* (Monterey; California: Brooks/Cole, 1973).

notational system for representing them. It seems probable that such instruction would be premature. But the child is already experiencing and reacting to the elements and patterns of music, to its melody, beat, volume, and so on. As in all areas of the young child's daily adventures in the world, in his encounters with music and other sound he learns actively. He doesn't passively take in all musical stimuli. He notices, compares, and remembers selectively. He assimilates new stimuli into his present system.

The Teacher's Role in Shaping the Musical Environment

Not considering for the moment what happens in the teacher's interaction with the child, her decisions shape the musical environment in several important respects: (1) in the *selections* provided for listening and for group singing; (2) in the music-making *materials* made available for exploration; (3) in the *opportunities* given in the course of the day for listening to and exploring music; and (4) in the *experiences* included in the program—planned and spontaneous—which the child wants to "make music about."

In thinking about the selections to include in creating a rich and developmentally appropriate musical environment for children, teachers can benefit from reminding themselves of the elements of music/sound. In Box 5-3, a brief definition of each of the elements of music is provided. We emphasize that the elements are not explicitly "taught" and need not even be mentioned by name. Rather, they would be part of the musical experience of the child. Keeping these elements in mind, the teacher seeks to provide the necessary experiences for growth of the children's awareness of these variations as they listen and as they create within the musical mode.

The goal is not to teach children how to read music or to provide the kind of knowledge that would allow them to define or discuss the elements *per se*. The aim rather is to promote growth of the ability to notice and enjoy these aspects in the music. It is appropriate, however, to gradually give the children a music vocabulary as they are ready. The availability of words to describe different musical qualities may even help in noticing the qualities and can certainly play a role in consolidating and communicating an awareness of musical characteristics.

Turning to the next of the teacher's roles, that of providing music-making *materials*, there are two points to be made about the choosing of instruments and materials. First, it is obvious but important to teachers' choices of musical materials to note that the diverse instruments and sound-producing media (such as wooden and metal objects of various kinds; jars containing buttons, rice, metal pellets) lend themselves most easily to exploring and learning about different musical aspects. The instruments are analogous to the diverse art materials. Just as the textures and colors and the nature of what can be done with various art materials provoke ideas and explorations of various kinds, similarly the presence of instruments and other sound-producing materials, with their diverse potentials, serves a function in the birth of musical ideas. For example, the succession of notes from high to low can be far more successfully explored with a xylophone than with a drum.

Often conventional instruments, especially the more elaborate ones such as pianos, only allow the child to hear the end result. One key is struck, a note is heard; a different key is struck, a different note is heard, but where is the relationship? The two keys look the same. In contrast, suppose the teacher places in the music areas jars with different amounts of water in them. The child investigating the varying sounds can see some relationship between the amount of liquid in the jar and the pitch and can test his tentative theories and generate new possibilities by modifying the amount of water.

A second point is that for the young child there are coordination demands involved in making the instruments and other materials do what he wants. Taking this into account, teachers often provide only a few instruments such as blocks, sticks, tambourines, and perhaps triangles or cymbals. However, a music area of this sort would limit the musical potentials to simple percussion. Exploring such aspects as tone and pitch would be constricted. The task, then, is for the teacher to find ways that a broad range of music-making potentials can be provided through materials children can handle. It often seems to be the case that a wider range of sound-producing media, including the improvised ones like the jars-with-water mentioned above, also makes for richer problem-solving possibilities. For example, the teacher may provide the materials for making drums. On experimenting with bases of differing depth and diameter the child is likely to get involved in a variety of problems with creating desired effects and noting the relation to drum appearance. This is less likely when drums are merely provided, especially if they are uniform in size and sound.

The third way through which the teacher plays a role in the musical environment of the child is in *providing opportunities for listening to and making music*. The importance of free-play periods in this respect is clear. (We have seen the critical value of free play in one after another of the areas of the young child's development and we meet it again here.) To be able to listen to music when one wants to, not always when someone else determines, is important—almost an inalienable right! Also valuable in the development of sensitivity to one's own affective states and aesthetic preferences is being able to make some choices in what music to listen to. A growing awareness of various types of music, of what one likes and how one's preferences vary with mood is not fostered in an environment in which music is only provided at specified times and by teacher fiat. With the advent of tape recorders and earphones it is much easier within the busy preschool classroom to provide children with the option of listening and to make a variety of selections available from which the children themselves can choose.

We have looked at three of the four aspects of the teacher's role in shaping the musical environment of the child: providing the *music,* the *materials,* and the *opportunity* to listen and play. The fourth is harder to define but equally important: *providing experiences which are exciting to "make music about."* What makes a person, adult or child, want to make music is so individual and difficult to specify that we cannot describe in detail what kinds of experiences will be most likely to provide this urge and the raw material for musical production. But several ingredients seem promising.

The physical environment and the experiences which make up the child's day should be a rich palette for the senses—colors, textures, sounds, interesting sights, tastes, and smells. However, the environment should not bombard the child with too much at the same time. The effect is better when there is not such a deluge that the child "tunes out" and misses the vividness of novel sensations and experiences. The auditory environment is of particular interest for the stimulation of musical creation. In the first three chapters of her book, *Children Discover Music and Dance,* Emma Sheehy (1968) writes about the kind of environment of sound which stimulates children to want to create in the musical mode. We cannot be as abundant in our comments here, but will simply give a few examples of the kinds of things the teacher can do to add sound-wealth to the classroom. These would fall into two main categories: bringing things in and sharing with children what is already there. A teacher might want to bring in a tape of bird calls before the group goes for a walk in the woods. During the children's making of popcorn, she can use the tape recorder, starting with the sizzle of the oil and continuing through the rapid popping stage. And of course there are endless possibilities for sound-production among physical materials.

Young children like to play with the sounds of words. As Sheehy urges, teachers should "play with children as they play with words, give them stories and verse to stimulate their imaginations, and especially, let them enjoy it all" (1968, p. 11). Such writers as Edward Lear, Dr. Seuss, and Laura E. Richards are delightful resources in this kind of sound and word play—not to mention the Mother Goose nursery rhymes themselves. But perhaps the most influential ingredient is the teacher's own sensitivity to sound, as well as to other interesting or beautiful events around her. You may recall the listening experience Denise, Tim, and Molly shared in Chapter 3 when Denise opened the window during a rainstorm. The enjoyment of these experiences in their own right is the main point. But an additional fruit can often be the musical exploration of an experience and/or the emotional reaction it evoked.

Developing the Child's Musical Intelligence Through Planned Activities

We have looked at four teacher roles in creating an environment conducive to musical development. There will also be times when the teacher will want to plan music-related activities for the involvement of the entire class or of small groups of children. We will look at a few of these. A great number of excellent activities for the enjoyment of music and awareness of its elements have been suggested over the years by music and early childhood teachers. Consequently, following our general strategy in this book, we will look at examples which are less likely to have been a part of preschool programs (except by accident), explaining why we think they would be of special value.

As we saw in the previous chapter, Jeanne and Denise, the two teachers in whose heads and classrooms we are snooping, sometimes find it useful to work with a theme or topic through which they integrate a variety of activities, both within and across curriculum areas. A series of sound/music activities, part of which we will be looking at now, was planned when the class was exploring aspects of transportation (starting from an interest a number of children were showing in building cars and motorcycles in the block area).

On Monday, Denise shows a film of various forms of transportation to the group as a whole. She runs it a second time through without the picture. It is easy on the whole for the children to identify the modes of transportation after just seeing the movie, though there were a few interesting confusions. The game was fun with the mystery and challenge it offered, and taking away the picture seemed to achieve the objective of increasing the children's awareness of the sounds that vehicles make. By questions and comments, in fact by the nature of the game itself, the teachers draw attention to the fact that one can identify something by the sound that it makes. The ability to do this is something that preschool children clearly have, but often without the notion that they are doing it. Encouraging them to think about how they are doing this increases their observing and their awareness of the nature of the sound. As we saw with movement, the children are encouraged to think about "how they know what they know," and to reflect on what cues they base their inferences on.

Stopping the film after the sound of the helicopter, Denise asks, "What was that one?" Some children shout immediately, "A plane!" and others, "A helicopter!"

Feeling that for some of them "plane" may encompass helicopter, Denise tries to clarify what they are thinking. "Some of you said a helicopter and some a plane. Mark, did you mean any special kind of plane or a regular jet plane, or what?" Mark replies, "A jet." Several other children changing or clarifying their original statement of "plane" say, "A helicopter! A chopper."

Denise notes, "Some of you thought you were hearing a jet and some a helicopter. Would they sound the same, do you think? Maybe they make the same noise? Would you like to hear this one again? Get your ears ready to listen—here it comes."

Mark and some other children now exclaim, "It *is* a helicopter," while a chorus of mostly younger children are still saying "a plane," "a jet," or changing to imitate the others. (One feature of large group sessions is the difficulty of determining who really thinks what and why. The teacher is able to engage in more follow-up and thus learn more about the thinking of the individual child in learning encounters with small numbers of children.)

Denise asks one of the helicopter identifiers, "Laurie, what makes you think we're hearing a helicopter?" Mark breaks in, "I hear the 'pellor." Denise sees a nod from Laurie and says. "Laurie, you heard the propellor?" (Another nod.) To try to see if Laurie is really understanding, she asks, "What part of the helicopter is the propellor?" and Laurie makes a circular motion with her hand.

The focus of this activity is not on distinctive features of different planes and vehicles nor on the cause-effect relationship behind the sounds, i.e., *why* the propellor makes a certain sound, so Denise does not stop to pursue Laurie's concepts of these aspects. Instead, she proceeds, "But before when some of you said it was a jet and some said a helicopter, *nobody* said it was a rowboat. How come? There was a rowboat in the film. How did you know that wasn't what we were hearing?"

The discussion goes on for a few minutes, centering around motor sounds and "water sounds" and touching on the things that sound fast or slow. Now in concluding the circle, Denise plays one more segment to give the children a brief introduction to identifying transportation sounds in *music* rather than *direct replay of the sounds* themselves. She and Jeanne will be following up on this in the more focused way that small groups allow. For now Denise is concerned with opening up the idea of being able to hear transportation sounds in music and with concluding the circle at a point of high involvement. She plays a brief segment of the "Cannonball Express," a tune (instrumental only) in which the fiddle not only simulates the building speed of the locomotive but does a very realistic train whistle as well. This is a good place to stop. When the children identify the song as a train song, Denise asks only one question, "Do you think we were listening to a train that time? Did someone tape-record a train, do you think?" The fact that this was music in which someone was playing to sound like a train is discussed. Denise asks if the children woul like to form a train. They will drop off each passenger in the place where he or she has chosen to play.

The teachers are tentatively planning to move from this direct, nonmusical representation of sound first to the musical representations which are most direct (as with "Cannonball Express") and then to music in which the subject is evoked in a more abstract way rather than by close replication of sound. For example, the teacher might choose a segment in which a slow, steady rhythm suggests the rowing of a boat or one in which accelerating tempo conveys increasing speed. (These would be likely choices during the period in which the children are exploring rhythm and speed in movement activities.) The teachers would be likely to engage the children in tapping out the quickening beat or in moving around in a circle, changing their pace as the music changes. During this activity the teachers ask questions such as, "What does this sound like? What does the music tell us is happening?" or make comments such as "Jon is slowing down. Oh, I see several people slowing down. Why are you doing that?" The child's own change in pace can play a role in heightening his awareness of the changes in the music.

Summary

Sounds are a part of the child's life from birth. The infant shows special interest in sounds such as human speech and music and can distinguish differences in volume, rhythm, tempo, pitch, etc., long before she makes any sense of the meaning of what she hears. In her own babbling the infant plays with these elements of sound. Indeed, sound play continues throughout childhood. The child is also gaining in representational ability, which plays a role in her musical development. Interest in variations and patterns of sound provides the basis for the child's response to *formal* aspects of music, while the child's ability to deal with representation makes it possible for the child to respond to music on a *referential* level as well.

Looking first at the referential or representational aspect of music, we noted two major ways in which music can come to have reference beyond itself: through some similarity or correspondence with that which it represents (e.g., the rhythm of hoofbeats conveys running horses) or through association with a context (e.g., the "Happy Birthday" song). Children experience music as meaningful in both these ways.

Apart from what music may mean to them, children also experience its "formal" characteristics—pattern, beat, rhythm, tempo, etc. These elements should be considered in the teacher's music planning, though not directly taught. Rather, the teacher takes into account how she may make the child more aware of the elements through decisions made about the musical environment and through interactions with the child about musical experiences. Without her even interacting with the children, the teacher's decisions shape the musical environment in four ways: (1) in the *selections* provided for listening and singing; (2) in the *music-making materials* made available for exploration; (3) in the *opportunities* provided in the course of the day for listening to and exploring music; and (4) in the *experiences* included in the program which children will want to "make music about."

The teacher also interacts with the children about music, both in spontaneous encounters throughout the day and in planned activities with the class and with smaller groups. The first example is a large group activity in which sound conveys a message directly. The children hear the sounds of various vehicles and discussion centers around how they can identify the vehicle from the sound, i.e., what features are giving them the idea. The activity is concluded with a musical selection with a clear representational dimension, the sound of a train. In the small group activity that follows the teacher pursues with the children the representational qualities of the music: What does this sound like? What does the music tell us is happening (e.g., speeding up, slowing down, hitting bumps)? What about the music made you change the way you moved? Children's movement to music can play a role in heightening their awareness of changes in the music.

Suggested Resources

Barlin, A., and Berlin, P. *The Art of Learning Through Movement: A Teacher's Manual for Students of All Ages* (Los Angeles: Ward Ritchie Press, 1971).

Bentley, A. *Musical Ability in Children* (New York: October House, 1966).

Cherry, C. *Creative Movement for the Developing Child* (Belmont, Calif.: Fearon Publishers, 1968).

Croft, D. J., and Hess, R. D. "Exploring the Arts." In *An Activities Handbook for Teachers of Young Children*. 2nd ed. (Boston: Houghton Mifflin, 1975).

Ets, M. H. *Talking without Words* (New York: Viking, 1968).

Gardner, H. *The Arts and Human Development: A Psychological Study of the Artistic Process* (New York: John Wiley and Sons, 1973).

Gerhardt, L. *Moving and Knowing: The Young Child Orients Himself in Space* (Englewood Cliffs, N.J.: Prentice-Hall, 1973).

Gilliom, B. C. *Basic Movement Education for Children: Rationale and Teaching Units* (Reading, Mass.: Addison-Wesley, 1970).

Gray, V. and Percival, R. *Music, Movement, and Mime for Children* (London: Oxford University Press, 1962).

Hackett, L. C., and Jenson, R. G. *A Guide to Movement Exploration* (Palo Alto, Calif.: Peek Publications, 1966).

Horton, J. *Music*. In Informal Schools in Britain Today series (New York: Citation Press, 1972).

Johnson, H., ed. *The Complete Nonsense of Edward Lear* (New York: Dover, 1951).

Lorton, J. W., and Walley, B. L. "Music." In *Introduction to Early Childhood Education* (New York: D. Van Nostrand Co., 1979).

Rasmus, C. J., and Fowler, J., eds. *Movement Activities for Places and Spaces* (Washington, D.C.: American Alliance for Health, Physical Education, and Recreation, 1977).

Richards, L. E. *Tirra Lirra: Rhymes Old and New* (Boston: Little, Brown, 1932).

Sheehy, E. D. *Children Discover Music and Dance* (New York: Teachers College Press, 1968).

Shelly, S. J. "Music." In *Curriculum for the Preschool-Primary Child, A Review of the Research*, edited by C. Seefeldt (Columbus, Ohio: Charles E. Merrill, 1976).

Vance, B. "Movement: The Child's Natural Language," and "Music: The Universal Language." In *Teaching the Prekindergarten Child: Instructional Design and Curriculum* (Monterey, Calif.: Brooks/Cole, 1973.

Zimmerman, M.P. *From Research to the Music Classroom, Number 1: Musical Characteristics of Children* (Reston, Va.: Music Educators National Conference, 1971).

Science

Enter any preschool classroom and the chances are very good that you will see plants growing, or animals in small cages (maybe a hamster or a guinea pig), and perhaps a table in the corner with rocks. Ask yourself why these things are in the preschool classroom. What is the educational value of such materials? By the time you reach this point of the book, you will have begun to realize that everything in the classroom is there for a reason. As you ask yourself why such materials are in the classroom and as you continue to scan the room, you notice there are books with interesting and dramatic covers, with pictures of rocks, animals, or clouds. Again you ask yourself why these kinds of books are there. Of course, everything looks interesting and appealing. Your first thoughts are that nature study is a traditional part of the early childhood curriculum, but why? As you reflect further on what "nature study" is and on why it would be included in the program, and think back on your reading of this book, a new set of issues comes to light—namely, how can these materials be used to contribute to the growth of the children's problem-solving strategies?

"Nature study," we believe, should be in the classroom, not to make children naturalists or just because materials are interesting and familiar aspects of the child's world, but because nature study provides a way for introducing children to the wonders of the world of science and scientific thinking.

We identify science with water tables and balance beams, the study of plants, animals, or rocks. Let us not be beguiled by these materials and this content and equate them with science. Science is more than such content; science also refers to a particular way of acquiring and organizing knowledge. Science involves *content, methods,* and *organization.*

In this chapter we will (1) present a conceptualization of how and why science is highly important for early education, as well as what intellectual and social characteristics of young children should be considered to construct appropriate science programs, (2) identify criteria for selecting materials and tasks, and (3) conclude with some sample learning encounters.

What Is Science?

Before justifying the why's and wherefore's of science education for the preschool, it would be helpful to clarify what we mean by science. The term *science* may mean different things to different people. For some, science is often closely identified with technology; for others, science is the man or woman in the white coat seeking to unlock the mysteries of the universe in a lonely laboratory; to still others it is a body of knowledge that is esoteric and technical; and to some it is just a way of thinking and problem-solving. Each of these is an accurate portrayal of aspects of science and the scientific enterprise. A formal definition of science is as follows: "1. Any department of knowledge in which the results of investigation have been logically arrayed and systematized. 2. Knowledge of facts, phenomena, laws and proximate causes, gained and verified by exact observation, organized experiment, and ordered thinking" (Funk & Wagnalls, 1977). Essentially, this conception of science describes the processes by which the secrets of nature can be penetrated and understood. The outcome of scientific investigations is a body of knowledge which is often used as the basis for producing products, such as television, radio, synthetic fabrics, etc.

For our purposes, the conception of science will focus on the *processes* of science because, as Bess-Gene Holt (1977) writes, "investigating, discovering, experimenting, observing, defining, comparing, relating, inferring, classifying, communicating, to name a few–these are what the growth of the mind is all about. The products of science (for us), the known and the unknown, are some of the elements of cognition" (p. 6). While we encourage the use of these processes is general, our scope in this chapter is the fostering of these thinking skills in relation to physical phenomena.

Traditionally, the preschool curriculum included materials familiar to young children, nature study, mechanics, etc., enabling the child to get to know about the physical world. We believe that in addition to the content, emphasis on the processes of scientific thinking and problem-solving "contributes greatly to the development of reasoning and reasonable human beings" (Holt, 1977, p. 5).

Let us turn now to answer the question "Why are science experiences relevant for early childhood education?"

Why Science in the Preschool?

There are at least three reasons why a science program is appropriate for preschool and early elementary school children. The first reason is that children do seem to have a natural curiosity about their physical environment. Second, there is natural compatibility between scientific reasoning and problem-solving and the child's fundamental search for answers. Third, preschool children can acquire knowledge about their physical world for its own sake.

Children are natural explorers: Children from earliest infancy explore their environment. Watch any young infant and you will notice how she looks around, picks up all kinds of objects, mouths them, handles them, visually examines them. The young infant running her hands over an adult's face, the preschooler staring at novel events or manipulating objects—these are exploratory behaviors. Psychologists contend that in this way children get to know their environment, and by so doing, reduce the strangeness and the uncertainty of the world of objects or events.

Exploratory behavior can be broken down into two phases: phase one, in which the child asks what the object does (curiosity about properties of materials), and phase two, in which she asks what she can do with the object (personal sense of mastery and control) (Berlyne, 1970).

Exploratory behavior is motivated by the child's curiosity. This behavior is usually stimulated by novel, surprising, and/or ambiguous situations.

Active exploration is the way children get to know the attributes of objects, how they function, what can be done with them. Rolling a ball, throwing it, bouncing it, feeling it, squeezing it—each of these actions helps to increase their knowledge of "ball." The children's subsequent play with these objects indicates how they have integrated this knowledge into a concept. Observing children engage in such activities provides a good example of the construction of knowledge. It is as if the children are building the concept "ball."

Once children come into contact with many diverse objects and events, and they develop their understandings of what they can do with objects, they begin to show how they can work with them. Now the child is in control of the object. Of course, there are times when the answers to the novelties and the surprises are not forthcoming, as when a ball which the child expects to bounce does not bounce or when a piece of play dough is not malleable as usual. For these unexpected situations, children tend to invent answers—inventions based on their limited experience, knowledge, and cognitive developmental status. Since the need to resolve these uncertainties is strong, children tend to create their own notions rather than seek answers as adults might, using logic, for example. This is due not only to the child not having developed consistent and logical strategies for solving problems, but also to the child's lack of awareness that he does not know. According to Piaget, children think they know things that are in fact not true. This is the children's way of coming to terms with the mysterious, the unknown, and the unpredictable.

Piaget provides many examples of how children seemingly invent answers to questions they have, about their bodies, their dreams, how weather is generated, etc. For instance, he reports an example of the child's understanding of how one thinks. The child asserts that he thinks with his brains. When asked, "Who told you?" the child answers, "No one." He is then asked where he learned the word "brain." The child answers, "I have always known it." The information is not attributed to anyone. It is as if the child has discovered the answers to these questions on his own. In this way the child has reduced uncertainty and provided answers which have resolved the mystery (Piaget, 1959). These inventions are not deliberate and planned, but rather they appear as natural outgrowths of the child's efforts to make the unknown known; the uncertain, certain. We shall have occasion to return to this question of how children think and reason in relation to physical phenomena when we discuss the thinking and reasoning characteristics of young children in the context of science curricula.

Children as scientists: The second reason that science and its relevant processes are appropriate for early childhood education is that young children in their exploration of the environment behave *as if* they are scientists. In the engagements with objects and events, they exhibit what Susan Isaacs (1966) refers to as *proto scientific behavior,* where *proto* refers to the primitive nature of their scientific approach. Neumann (1972) provides a vivid description of how children engaging in what he calls science are like the adult scientist:

sciencing are given a chance to observe and manipulate a variety of man-made and natural objects in ways that help them to recognize similarities, differences, and relationships among objects and pheonomena. They sniff, look at, listen to, feel, pinch, and if possible taste a variety of materials in order to develop and extend their ability to make careful and accurate observations" (pp. 137–138). Observations of children in free-play situations without adult guidance will confirm this description.

Let's look at an example of this kind of behavior in the classroom. Mary is standing by a record player watching the record spin round and round. For no apparent reason Mary takes a tiny car and places it on the record. The car spins off. Mary proceeds to replace the car, suggesting that she wants the car to spin on the record. After many trials, Mary finally gets the car to spin with the record. Now we can come to understand what Mary was trying to do. She was *not* interested in the music, but rather was interested in the physical event of the spinning record. Mary was involved in exploring the material visually, and she persisted in trying to reach her goal. This activity is what Berlyne would call *directed thinking,* where the child seems to work from some kind of plan, as if she knew what she wanted to do and made many persistent efforts to achieve that goal. It was when the car spun on the record that she left the task and went on to something else.

Events of this type of spontaneous exploratory behavior abound in the classroom and provide the children with innumerable opportunities to express their exploratory and investigatory interests and by so doing have the chance to enhance their problem-solving skills. The teacher can provide such opportunities by having materials available for the children and also by allowing freedom for such exploration (including quiet, solitary exploration).

Recall what we described at the opening of the chapter when we suggested that you reflect on the materials in the classroom. Now you can see how materials become the grist for the child's exploratory mill and for the teacher's aiding and abetting this process. The child, oriented to explore, manipulate, and experiment with the array of materials the teacher provides as part of the classroom environment, now has a rich opportunity to do what is natural for him and compatible with his interests.

Gaining knowledge of the world through science: Both the scientist and the proto-scientist in the course of their explorations come to know more about the materials they are working with and come to understand how some things work and how other things do not. In effect, they come to know about the properties of objects and materials. Similarly, children acquire knowledge of objects. Some of this newly acquired knowledge can easily be articulated and shared with others, e.g., labeling properties of objects or demonstrating how a record player works; while some of it cannot be easily expressed. We refer to this as *intuitive understanding.*

Knowledge of properties of materials and functions acquired through exploration can form a basis for subsequent problem-solving activities. In our example of Mary and the record player, Mary not only got to know something about the properties of the car, the record, and the record player, but she used this knowledge to solve her problem. Further, she may now be in a position to relate this knowledge to other things. For example, it is possible that the idea of objects rotating will or can be related at some time to her body rotating or to the playground merry-go-round. The relationship involved in Mary's problem happens to be a complex one; she will not understand the relationships between speed of rotation and finding the appropriate spot for the car on the rotating disc in anything but an intuitive way. Nonetheless, even this intuitive knowledge may be useful later.

When we say the child has intuitive knowledge or understanding we mean she has a sense of something. She is able to act *as if* she knows, yet she cannot spell out what she knows or how she came to know it. It must be kept in mind that children possess much knowledge that is intuitive. Perhaps an example in a more simple context will help. Children often know how to find their way from one place to another or they are able to sense when their parents are upset or disturbed about something. Yet if children were asked to describe how they came to know that their parents were upset or how they managed to get some place, they would not be able to put it into words. They may not be aware of themselves as "knowers," as possessors of knowledge. Our point, then, is that in the course of children's explorative behavior, they accumulate much information about objects, events, people. This knowledge is not consciously acquired, as is typically associated with school learning. It is almost like what some psychologists call incidental learning. It is knowledge acquired in the process sometimes of working on other objectives. If you think of all the things the child learns while building with blocks, or painting, or working with wood, or watching a butterfly, you will come to appreciate that knowledge is gained over and above the primary purpose of those activities. Thus you should keep in mind that every activity by virtue of its inherent complexity allows for such kinds of knowledge gain. While the scientist learns more about his world through the experiments that work and do not work, so the child learns much about its world through interaction with physical materials.

What is the rationale for viewing science experience in a developmental context? Science is appropriate in the early childhood classroom because of the children's natural tendency to investigate their physical world, because it is there to explore, and because of its intrinsic interest. These activities are analogous to those of the adult scientist. This is the child's way of gaining knowledge of the physical world. But, as we made clear, the child is not an adult and must be viewed as an adult thinker. He is the *proto-scientist* just beginning to master some of the most elemental cognitive processes that are also employed in science. The place of science in the preschool must be viewed from the developmental perspective. To think in developmental terms means to realize that the child is an ever-changing individual who is not a miniature adult, but is qualitatively different from an adult. The child is not merely less experienced and less knowledgeable, but less equipped to employ those cognitive processes involved in science at the logical, rational level possible for the adult.

When we speak of the difference between the child and the adult in quality of thinking skills and thinking patterns, we mean that the child thinks but thinks differently. His reasoning is different. For example, children do not proceed step-by-step in their logical reasoning the way adults do; rather, children may connect two seemingly unrelated ideas of illogical connections. An array of beautiful examples of children's reasoning is given in Susan Isaacs' work (1966). We present them here to give a flavor of the quality of children's thinking:

> Harold (5;3) and Paul brought some shells which they had gathered at the sea-side during the holiday. They were put into a large bowl with water. There was also some seaweed, which, Harold said, "will tell you when it's going to rain, and will tell you the time." When he had put it into the water, Harold said, "Now it will rain—the seaweed is wet" (p. 112).
>
> Several of the children talked about "the war." Christopher (5;6) said, "My daddy fighted, but he wasn't hurt, because he's alive now" (p. 147).

These examples are instances of differences in how the child thinks. The kinds of answers and explanations adults would offer might also be incorrect but they would be based on a qualitatively different kind of reasoning.

Let us now turn to a discussion of the characteristics of children's thinking and reasoning as a framework within which to develop a science program. After all, the intent of the program is to fit with the children's interests and capabilities as active thinkers coming to terms with an exciting, mysterious, and ever-expanding environment.

Cognitive Characteristics of the Preschool Child Relevant to Science Problem-Solving

We can only sketch briefly the characteristics of the thinking of the preschool and early elementary-aged child. There is a body of research which provides the specifics (Elkind, 1967; Inhelder and Piaget, 1969; Inhelder, Sinclair, and Bovet, 1974; Sigel and Cocking, 1977). These authors provide descriptions of how children of this age level typically think and reason. Any such characterization, however, should serve only as a general guideline since wide individual differences exist. For example, some children are precocious in their ability to represent and deal with representational material, while others of the same age are less sophisticated (Sigel and Olmsted, 1969). Such individual differences do exist and may become important factors to be considered in interacting with the child. This is one reason why the strategies we have been discussing throughout this volume are significant teaching tools. Through appropriate inquiry it becomes possible to gauge where the child is at. The characteristics of young children in general which we will be mentioning are only a starting point for the teacher in planning and arranging activities.

To determine what particular types of mental processes are involved in solving science problems, let us first discuss the ideal model of scientific reasoning. Using this model as a base, we can then identify the mental activities involved. In Table 6-1, the major processes involved in scientific thinking are listed. These processes do not necessarily take place in any given sequence in the thinking of the scientist. Chances are, however, that during the solving of a problem each of these processes is used. Let us now turn to a discussion of each process in terms of the capability of preoperational children.

Table 6-1   **Steps in Sciencing**

Identify Problems
Observe Discrepancies
Infer
Generate Hypotheses
Test Hypotheses
Interpret Results
Draw Conclusions and Generalizations

Problem Identification and Observation

When is a problem a problem for the young child? Does the concept of *problem* exist for young children? What does exist is the simple fact that something does not work: e.g., the wheels of a car do not turn; or the bridge the child builds does not stand up under the weight of the truck; or the plants don't grow as expected. In Webster's Dictionary "problem" is defined as "a perplexing question or situation, especially when difficult or uncertain of solution." A problem is, in fact, a type of *discrepancy*—the discrepancy between the expected or desired and the outcome (see Chapter 2). The implication of the definition of the concept "problem" is that a solution is possible and that the individual is aware that a solution is possible. Such an awareness requires anticipation of an outcome. The problem-solver has to be aware of the discrepancy and of a potential solution. The awareness of a solution requires that the individual be able to represent a possible solution through anticipation of it. For the child, awareness of a problem may be evidenced when the child asks a question. It is doubtful if the child at this age anticipates novel solutions or outcomes. However, when the problems are related to the child's previous experience, he is more likely to reconstruct (represent the solution) because he had that experience.

Imagine a young boy trying to fix a broken toy or trying to open a container. He is trying to solve a problem. It appears as though he is aware that something is wrong, and that persistent effort may perhaps result in a solution. He says to his teacher, "I can't get these blocks to stand" or "The paint keeps dripping" or "The clay is too hard" or "The phonograph does not work." For these types of problems, the child knows what outcome he wants—the blocks to stand, the paint not to drip, the clay to be soft. The child has experienced in the past the situations he now wishes to achieve; at some prior time the block stood, the clay was soft, the paint didn't drip. What the child does not know is the means to arrive at the end-state. He does not know, for example, *how* to stop the paint from dripping.

The child's persistence in the struggle to solve problems implies that he is aware that something is wrong and wants it righted, or he sees something puzzling and wants to figure it out. In a child's daily routine he frequently encounters such problems—conditions that are perplexing and need solution. For example, during a situation in which cooking is involved the teacher might ask, "What happens to the egg we put in the cake?" or "How could we tell what color the cake will be?" For the child these questions may not arise as problems. Often what is a problem or a discrepancy to an adult is not so for the child. Although children often do not infer or note discrepancies, they may come to realize a problem is present with guidance from the teacher. For example, the teacher presents a glass of water and a piece of sugar to the child. The sugar is placed in the water and the child sees the sugar dissolve before his eyes. The teacher asks where the sugar is or what happened to the sugar. The child may not perceive this as a problem to be solved; the sugar is gone and that is that. There is no reason for problem-solving on this matter. He does not think to ask, "Where is the sugar?" The child may not seek explanations to the question "Why can I not see the sugar?" or "Where did the sugar go?" He tends to accept what he sees as the reality. Since the sugar is not visible, there is no sugar. Observation confirms his belief that in fact there is no sugar—it is gone. He does not see this as something puzzling or that something is to be discovered.

Let us examine a problem where the change is visible. We turn to the classical problem of conservation of number. The problem presented to the child is as follows: eight egg cups and eight eggs are lined up as follows before the child, where o represents the egg cups, and 0 represents the eggs:

Figure 6-1

```
o  o  o  o  o  o  o  o
0  0  0  0  0  0  0  0
```

The child is shown that for every egg cup there is an egg. He is asked, "Do I have as many egg cups as eggs?" The child answers, "Yes." The examiner then changes the alignment as follows:

Figure 6-2

o   o   o   o   o   o   o   o
    o o o o o o o o

Now the child is asked, "Do I still have as many eggs as egg cups?" The typical answer of the preschool child is, "No, you have more egg cups than eggs." The examiner lines up the egg cups and the eggs again in the presence of the child as in Figure 6-1. Again, the question is asked, "Do I have as many eggs as egg cups?" Again, the child says, "You have an egg cup for every egg." "OK," says the teacher, "Now watch what I do." For a second time the eggs are bunched up and the inquiry is repeated. The child answers in a similar vein: "You have more eggs." When asked to justify the answer, the child might say, "You have more because there are more," or "because you have bunched them together." While observing that nothing was added or taken away, the child centers only on the mass and not on the discrete elements. He does not grasp that the number is conserved, i.e., remains the same in spite of the rearrangement. By focusing on the actions of the experimenter, the child does not "abstract" the basic fact that nothing has changed. The child is not able to keep the original configuration in mind when he observes the new pattern. The observable overpowers or cancels out the child's earlier acknowledgment of *equality*. Since the child *centers*, i.e., focuses on a particular aspect, in this case the action, the child fails to understand that the spatial arrangement is irrelevant; the critical factor is that the number of items has not changed. The child does not *decenter*; he does not seek or take more than one aspect (length *and* density) into account. Not considering the discrepancy between his first assertion that the number of eggs is equal to the number of egg cups and his second assertion that there are more eggs than egg cups, the child does not perceive a problem—even when the change is visible.

This example illustrates how the child may not perceive an inconsistency or discrepancy and thus not see a problem. Until the child does see the inconsistency, there is no cognitive growth.

Children, however, might discover problems themselves by observing discrepancies. Noticing that the guinea pig sniffs in his cage, or the hamster burrows under a pile of wood chips, the child asks, "Why is the guinea pig sniffing? or "Why is the hamster burrowing?"

These types of inquiries are reflections of the child's "natural interest in question-asking, exploring and finding out" (N. Isaacs, 1974, p. 89). Children scan, search, and examine objects and events with all the senses. Manual manipulation and visual exploration are among the chief modalities the normal child uses in his building a repertoire of knowledge. What children will find of particular interest and what will arouse their curiosity varies with individual backgrounds. Generally of interest will be objects and events which can be acted upon, modified, molded, and changed as the child wishes.

In the course of these engagements, the unexpected or the novel will occur. The child will see discrepancies and problems; it is, as we indicated

earlier, these unexpected events that motivate the child to seek answers. It is these types of experiences which stimulate the critical "why" questions. The children need to know, as Nathan Isaacs explains:
". . . These questions should lead the child from his first crude methods of associative belief to the increasing discovery of a specially valuable type of controlling knowledge, which offers the most direct and assured access *to security and to practical ability of every kind"* [italics ours], (Isaacs, 1974, p. 50). Questions may be answered in at least two ways: the child discovers his own solutions through a variety of cognitive activities or through appeal to the adult for answers.

It is the former activity which we shall focus on in this chapter. This emphasis is consistent with the point of view expressed throughout this volume that *activity,* actions on and with objects, provides critical experiences for the development of thought. A second and equally important way for the child to come to discover answers to *his* questions and to grow cognitively, is through guided inquiry, which we will continue to discuss throughout this volume.

Let us return now to a discussion of some other relevant cognitive processes involved in the children's actively exploring and manipulating their physical world—their proto-scientific activities.

Generation of Hypotheses

In the course of the children's exploration and engaging with objects as well as observing many of the natural phenomena around them, they ask many questions to reduce their uncertainty. To provide what N. Isaacs called "security," they ask such questions as "Why can't I go outside?" or "Where do the birds go in the winter?" or "Why do some birds go away and others stay?" or "Why do the leaves fall off the tree?" Questions are not only posed verbally but are evident in their actions. A child is playing in the sand and then goes to the art corner and gets some paints to mix sand and paint, or she tries to mix one set of colors with another. Such activities can be interpreted as instances of hypothesis-formation.

A hypothesis is in fact a question. To be sure, hypotheses in a formal sense take a different form—usually an if. . .then type statement, for example, "If I put this object in a glass of water, then the water will rise." Basically, this statement asks the question "What will happen when I put the object in a glass of water?" In the scientific hypothesis a supposition is made, a conclusion is suggested. The question does not necessarily involve the conclusion or supposition.

The scientist making a formal hypothesis often couches it in "if . . . then" terms because he suspects a particular outcome will occur (prediction). He is able to do this because of his ability to reason logically and because of his knowledge and experience with the phenomena in question.

The child in her own way begins the long process of hypothesis-formation by first asking a question or posing a problem, but she probably will not construct it in a logical way; for example, she cannot state a logical outcome. The reason is that the child has not yet evolved the capability to think in abstract, logical ways; nor does she have the knowledge and experience necessary to conjecture a general outcome. What the child does is pose the question. She may even pose a conclusion, but the conclusion is not necessarily logically connected to the question. For example, Stacey has noticed that every time it rains the teacher closes the windows. One clear day Stacey sees the teacher closing windows and says to her, "Is it going to rain today?" This is an *inference*—a question based on previous experience, but it only involves some elements of the previous situation—the closing of a window and the rain. Stacey does not take into account the conditions that occurred at the time the teacher closed the windows in the past, nor that at this time there is no rain and she is closing windows. Rather, Stacey focuses on the similar action in the two situations and concludes it is going to rain. The child is usually certain that his or her conclusion is correct in this situation. Young children can be very dogmatic.

Let us take that situation and think of it in terms of adult scientific thought. Stacey could venture a scientific hypothesis; namely, in the past the teacher closed windows when it rained; she closes the windows now—why is she closing them? Does she close the windows *only* when it rains? What are the other weather conditions like when she closes the windows?

Posing such questions would be typical of the adult who is able to consider the generality of the teacher's behavior; is able to make appropriate causal connections; is able to think about exceptions. The preschool child asks the questions of the teacher because she focuses on the immediate action, is limited in the number of factors she can think about at one time, and makes her inferences on the basis of what she sees in relation to what she remembers of that event from the past.

The generation of a hypothesis or posing of a question are in a sense equivalent for the preschool child. It should be kept in mind the child may not verbalize his hypothesis, but rather, express it in his actions. The child moving about the room, exploring for particular objects, trying out different colors in his painting, or using various size blocks in building his construction, may well be working from a hypothesis. This leads us now to the next phase in scientific problem-solving—hypothesis-testing.

Testing of Hypotheses

Once a hypothesis has been generated, the next step in scientific problem-solving is to obtain evidence to determine whether it should be accepted or rejected. For the adult scientist a hypothesis is a proposition advanced as possibly true, but it needs more evidence before it can be substantiated. Scientists have created formal procedures for gathering such evidence. Rigorous experiments, careful observations, and organization of known information are brought to bear to test the hypothesis. An adult scientist requires painstaking preparations before he or she begins this activity. Note that these procedures involve experimentation, exploration, and incorporation of previous knowledge. Children engage in similar activities, but without the sophistication of the adult. They experiment, of course not using the formal system of the adult scientist; they explore their environment for information, and they appeal to authority—usually the teacher. They cannot "review the literature," of course, at this stage of their lives.

We shall discuss each of these activities through an example frequently observed in the preschool. As you read the example, try to think of the young proto-scientist discovering new knowledge for himself. As you imagine him searching for answers, try to figure out what cognitive operations are activated in the process.

Jerry has just noticed a new large magnet on a table with a number of other items, such as large nails, pieces of wood, glass, marbles, plastic knives and forks. Jerry picks up the magnet and begins to touch it to the various items on the table. He "discovers" the magnet attracts only the metal items. He concludes that magnets attract *only* metal and not wood, plastic, cloth, or glass. He has, on the one hand, found a potential discrepancy—magnets attract only some things and not others. For some children this discrepancy raises a question, "Why does the magnet stick only to metal things?" Other children will *conclude* that magnets stick to some things and not others and let the situation rest there.

The hypothesis-testing in the above could come from a teacher planned situation where the child is experimenting with the magnet. Hypotheses can be generated and tested in the context of a free-play situation as well. This may be the more common event where children notice something happening and proceed to experiment and–or explore as part of their ongoing activity. Susan Isaacs (1966) provides an example of such experimentation:

> [The children were playing with modelling wax near a hot water pipe.] Some modelling wax having been dropped on a hot water pipe, the children discovered that it melted, and tried some more. When they found that all the wax would melt, whatever colour it was, they went on to try other materials—plasticine, wood, chalk, and so on, talking about it together and telling Mrs. I. "Plasticine melts. Wood won't melt," and so on. The whole of this was entirely spontaneous (Ages 4; 0-5; 0) (p. 125).

The children have discovered that not all materials melt. They have discovered two classes of materials, those that will melt and those that will not melt. This is an example of children's testing their hypotheses through their own activity.

Another way to test a hypothesis is with the aid of the teacher. Children can pose questions, hypothesis-like suppositions, to the teacher, expecting the all-knowing adult to come forth with the answer. The teacher has choices: to give a didactic answer or to engage in inquiry, enabling the child to generate his or her own testing activities and eventually coming to a satisfactory solution to the problem. An example of this latter type of approach, one consistent with the orientation of this book, is as follows:

Jenny is interested in attracting insects in the playground. Every time she approaches a grasshopper or an ant, it scurries away. She is not having much luck. She knows she has a problem but does not know how to solve it. The teacher notices this and decides to help. She decides that she will first find out why Jenny thinks insects ran away. She asks Jenny what might bring insects to her. Jenny doesn't know (an example of knowing the problem but not having specific experience to go about solving it). The teacher asks Jenny if she ever attracted dogs and cats. Jenny said that sometimes she did when she had what they liked to eat, like a dog biscuit. From this developed a discussion of what insects like to eat. This led to making decisions about insect "food." Jenny did not know what insects liked to eat. The teacher told her to guess. Jenny said that maybe they would like candy since she likes candy. The teacher accepted this and they placed candy near the ant hill. Sure enough the ants climbed all over the piece of candy. Jenny had attracted her ants. This episode illustrates how a teacher can help the child to discover and solve some scientific problems.

In each case the children, through their own actions, posed a hypothesis–at times on the basis of a plan, at times in a spontaneous way–and "discovered" or identified new information. The child, having only a loosely developed view of reality, will deal with the bit of information in a fragmented way or in a global overgeneralized way. This may sound contradictory, but let us clarify it through examples.

Recall the example of wax and melting. The children "discovered" that wax, irrespective of color, melts and the other items do not. The generalization the children made from this might be that only wax melts. This generalization is clearly based on the children's having observed the wax melting and the other materials *not* melting. They did not come to a principle of the causal explanation, nor an understanding that what accounts for items melting is their melting point, for example. The children accept a fragmented bit of knowledge and may be satisfied with their answer.

On the other hand, young children still working with one aspect of a situation can overgeneralize. For example, they see mosquitoes or other insects, note that some are unpleasant, therefore *all* insects are unpleasant. The new information becomes part of the child's knowledge repertoire. Knowledge is organized into groups or classes. Let us turn now to a discussion of classes and the processes in developing them—classification.

The Role of Classification in Science

Classification refers to the process of arranging or putting objects, people, or events into a category or a class on the basis of their similar characteristic (s).

The significance of this operation for science resides in the fact that classification is a process by which diverse items (objects, events, or people) are organized and given a common label. In this way, instances in the environment are organized and complexity is reduced. These classes form the basis of our concepts. Because of the capability to generate classes and label them, we can handle our complex and highly varied environment. Just imagine what it would be like if we did not have the category "automobile." If we treated each car as an individual, with an individual name, and not as a member of a class sharing common features and a common label, we would have to learn about each *one*. Fortunately, we develop a generalized category "automobile," and so develop an understanding of the *class*, a most economical process. Thus, we can speak of characteristics of "automobiles." We know how to deal with them as a group. We use this knowledge also in working with them on an individual basis.

While this is crucial for us in our daily life, it is even more critical for the scientist. He searches for the common features among the objects and events he deals with. Such discoveries enable him to develop classes and thereby identify general principles that govern these classes. For example: in biology all creatures who have vertebra and whose female members have mammary glands to nourish their young form the class "mammals." Knowing these characteristics of this class in general helps us know something about a large group of individuals and about a particular class member. We generate rules which would govern our behavior with this class. In preschool science problem-solving activities the children expand their ideas of classes by incorporating the new information in existing classifications and/or acquiring new labels as well. For example, the child learns that a cow is an animal, but later learns it is also a mammal. This is a change in both the label and in what goes in which class.

It should be made clear that classification behavior does not emerge from nowhere at the preschool level. Quite the contrary. Classification begins with the beginning of life. Infants, as soon as they become aware of their external world, begin to organize objects, people, and events into categories. What is critical for us is that the basis of classification changes with age. From infancy to preschool, children become increasingly able to create more extensive classes. They begin to shift from using such attributes of objects as color or form to inferential categories. For examples, they will select from an array of items varying in shape (triangle, square, and circle) all the similarly shaped ones, but later classify them all as being geometric forms. Preschool children, when using toy replicas of real things, such as a hammer, saw, or screwdriver, can form categories on the basis of a concept of function—"These are things to build with"—or of class—"These are tools." While the preschool child has a limited range of things he will see as similar—because he judges on the basis of the observable, not the inferred—he will exclude items the adult might include in one class. For example, ducks, chickens, or snakes are often considered in the class "animals" by very young children. They are classified as being on a farm or not having legs (Sigel, 1972). As the child gets older and is able to infer common attributes such as "living," the duck, chicken, and snake are classed with other animals since they are all living. This achievement appears later, but its beginnings are visible in the preschool, since preschool children are generating new categories—organizing objects, events, and people.

Children, while initially focusing on one aspect of an object, can be helped to shift their perspective and take other alternatives into account. A guided inquiry strategy of the kind discussed throughout this volume can achieve that objective (Sigel, 1972; Sigel and Saunders, 1979).

Since science activity involves formulating generalizations about classes of events, children's understandings of how classes are created and how classes do, in fact, play an active role, should contribute to their scientific problem-solving, particularly by helping them to generalize.

The second operation that is crucial for scientific problem-solving, even at the preschool level, is *seriation*. "Seriation" refers to the ability to organize items in a series, varying, for example, in such features as size—big, bigger, biggest, or number—1, 2, 3, or weight—heavy, heavier, heaviest, etc. The child comes to understand that many things can be ordered in a series. Ordering in a series is a type of classification—the classification principle is a variation in a particular characteristic that increases or decreases—size, weight, height, or whatever. To understand seriation requires an understanding of relationships between units, for example, understanding that two is less than three and more than one; also, two is twice one. Understanding these relationships is important in scientific problem-solving because it involves quantification, the use of mathematics. We do not expect the children at this level to be mathematicians. They are, however, beginning to think more precisely in quantitative terms. They already have the rudiments of counting, or comparing relative quantities—e.g., more or less. These are additional attributes that can be used to organize items.

Classification and seriation, then, are two cognitive operations that are found in all phases of scientific problem-solving. Being sensitized to the role these processes play in the child's scientific thought will help the teacher formulate her teaching strategies and planning of activities.

Children's Awareness that Hypotheses Have Been Substantiated

Children usually will accept the results of a particular experiment or a discovery as in the example described. You will recall that once the children discovered that wax melts they were satisfied; they did not ask "why." Jenny was satisfied with attracting ants with candy. She did not ask "why."

There are at least three reasons why children are generally satisfied with their discovery, as when they saw that magnets attract particular metals and do not attract other items.

1. They are not oriented to the notion that causal relations have to be inferred. Causal connections are not apparent in the activity of most interactions. There is nothing observable in the magnet that will clue the child in to what makes it attract some things and not others.

2. Related to this lack of awareness of the need to make inferences is the tendency to take a subjective perspective rather than an objective perspective. They tend not to separate self from object or event.
    Young children characteristically also tend to believe that their perspective is everyone's perspective. In other words, everyone will agree with them. Young children are often surprised that an adult does not agree with them. How often has a preschool teacher heard a youngster announce, "I know, I know" in answer to a question, when there is every indication that the child does not know. Children believe not only that they know, but that others know just like they do. This is called egocentrism—a term Piaget has suggested to characterize young children's thought where the child has "an implicit belief in his own ideas, and no need of proof. His questions are largely rhetorical, not genuinely inquiring. He assumes others understand what he says without effort on his part, and that they believe as he does" (S. Isaacs, 1966, p. 73).
    Although much research on egocentrism in the past few years has investigated the validity of this early idea of Piaget's, the results still support in general terms the idea that children do tend to think egocentrically. For example, the young child may mumble something and expect another to understand him, or a child may draw a picture and scribble over it and be surprised that a second person, who did not observe the drawing, does not know there is another larger drawing on the paper.

3. The child, not having established an objective view of the world, tends to reason about causality in terms of his previous experience. Thus he has come to learn by this time that many things happen because of adult intervention, or that the understanding of causal relations comes from asking his parents or other authority figures. Piaget suggests that this type of experience leads the child to believe that things happen for the sake of people or are "caused" by some superior force, for example, God. The child has not come to realize that things can happen independently of individuals (Piaget, 1930; 1959).

Thus the level of the child's acceptance of evidence that he has answered his question is a function of his experiential level (state of knowledge and social background) as well as the cognitive level from which he is operating (an egocentric perspective). While the child is acquiring new knowledge and experiences, he tends to tie these new experiences to his existing view of physical reality. Of course, not all children are satisfied with the immediate or the first answer. Some children continue to be curious about the "why" of their experimental findings and persist in trying to go beyond the given. They are not satisfied with the answers they have received, either from their own activities or from the teachers. Thus, some children notice that some metals are attracted to a magnet and may persist in inquiring further, as if they realize that the answer is not complete. In the magnet example these curious children may persist in posing the question, "Why are some things attracted to magnets and not others?"

Some children accept the obvious, while others continue to generate new questions or hypotheses. This type of curiosity may be due to a complex of personality and cognitive factors. A variety of complex reasons, seemingly from the child's social background, emotional make-up, and cognitive level, underlie the level of curiosity and exploratory activity (Berlyne, 1970; Sigel, 1972). From the point of view of the child's intellectual level of development, to move beyond the obvious, that is, to seek further explanations of observed phenomena, necessitates the ability to assume an abstract attitude. This means that the children are able to be aware that actions of physical phenomena have an explanation—a cause—and that a cause has to be inferred. Children can be helped to increase their probing or question-asking by becoming "liberated" or "freed" from their egocentric view, as we have indicated. This can come about through challenges to the perspective the child works from. These challenges can occur in at least two ways: one, the child encounters surprises and unexpected occurrences which involve discrepancies. For example, the play dough cannot be molded or the color expected to appear on the paper does not. Such happenings are very frequent. Yet, it should be kept in mind that resolutions of such discrepancies may not always occur—the child may give up because the problem is too complex, or the child is not ready to probe further, for reasons we discussed earlier in this chapter. The child may not be motivated to persist. A second source of challenge can come about through the teacher's activity—posing appropriate questions which take into account the child's emotional and intellectual level. "Liberating" the child from his egocentric perspective is central to the developing of science problem-solving skills.

Summary

In sum, then, the child is a problem-solver by natural inclination. Teachers can build on this and provide the educational experiences to enhance problem-solving activities. Since it is very important to understand how children at this developmental level think and reason, we have described some salient features of children's thought which are relevant for scientific problem-solving. By exploring those teaching strategies which encourage children to challenge their own perspective, by providing materials for exploration, and by encouraging exploratory activities, teachers are providing opportunities for growth.

A word of caution, lest you think our emphasis on exploration and discovery means a lack of structure, organization, and planning: it should be made clear that just the opposite is the case. An environment that is structured, but free, where the child's thoughts and reasoning are accepted with respect

Table 6-2

Schematic of Science Problem-Solving Tasks and Some Relevant Cognitive Processes

Science Problem-Solving Procedures	Cognitive Processes Engaged	Science Problem Tasks
Identify Problems	Notice discrepancies, inconsistencies, and incongruities	Notice that magnets do not pick up some metal-looking objects
Explore through Observation	Analyze objects visually	Inspect objects that float
	Compare and note similarities and differences	Inspect objects that float and those that do not
Manipulation	Integrate visual and motor activities	Pour fixed amount of liquid specified in recipe
Generate Hypotheses	Anticipate outcomes	Anticipate what will happen when ice is left in a warm place.
	Relate previous experience to current (re-presentation); infer relationships	Recall what happened when a structure was built with too heavy a top
Test Hypotheses; Experiment	Notice effects of different combinations	Vary amount of salt in play dough
	Plan and decide what to do next	Collect different objects before testing magnet
	Seriate	Arrange weights from increasing to decreasing
	Compare alternatives, attend to changes, and generate transformations	Use magnifier with a variety of objects
Collect Data	Attend to outcomes of manipulations	Watch to see effect of changing heat and cold on mercury thermometer
Interpret Data and Make Conclusions	Infer causality	Infer that things sink *because* they are heavy
	Generalize	Conclude *all* heavy things sink
	Classify	Create two classes: sinking things and non-sinking things

(this does not mean agreeing), and where emotional support for the search is present, is an environment conducive to the development of creative and productive scientific problem-solving.

Before going on to specific lessons, let us summarize our understanding of scientific problem-solving and children's cognitive functioning:

Table 6-2 summarizes the relationships we discussed in the preceding pages. Note that classification and seriation are not in the chart because these operations permeate the activities from the beginning to the end. Consciously or not, everyone of us, children and adults, classify. We are placing experiences into categories—a most efficient and economical way to organize experience. It is also necessary in adapting to the complex environment in which we live. The variation in quality and quantity is with age (Inhelder and Piaget, 1969; Sigel, 1972). In addition, experiences are seriated. Such a process as seriation is intrinsic to our adaptation—we order objects, people, and events on some basis (size, weight, familiarity, pleasantness, danger, etc.). Again, as with classification, the complexity changes. Nevertheless, children from early on are able to seriate in some fashion.

This chart, then, serves as a guide and a quick review of the relationships between science problem-solving tasks and the relevant cognitive processes.

Guidelines for Selecting Activities for Science

A truism in planning science activities is that they should take into account the capabilities of the child for engaging as active participants in the activity. Since we are interested in fostering particular abilities and skills, and since we contend that action is critical, selection of activities should allow for a direct "hands on" approach as much as possible. Let us turn now to these issues.

A key decision facing teachers planning science experiences in early childhood classrooms is to select activities that involve the use of those cognitive processes important in program objectives. The teachers whose decision-making we are following, Jeanne and Denise, attempt to select activities which maintain children's interest and at the same time enhance awareness of objects and events in the world, representational competence, and problem-solving skills. Choice of the type of activity and the representational demands must be tempered by an understanding of the nature of children in general and of their developmental level in particular. It is important to consider children's cognitive levels in deciding on activities and materials, particularly with respect to the types of transformations and discrepancies involved.

First, as we have noted in earlier chapters, children enjoy making things happen. In the physical phenomena of science, there are rich opportunities enabling children to "cause" something to happen. For example, a child uses a magnet to pick up steel objects. Enjoyment of this sense of "being a cause" is consistent with the child's developmental level we discussed in the previous section. It is important to work with this tremendous natural pleasure. Therefore we should minimize situations where the children are witnesses or passive participants in science activities. Whenever possible, let them act on materials directly; let them experience the joy of being the cause of an event. Second, to achieve skills in problem-solving the child must engage in "problems" wherein solutions are possible but where gradually he comes to learn that solutions can be achieved by different routes. But this is not universal—so the child has to learn to perceive and understand this fact. Third, the child will need the careful structured inquiry of the teacher to provide the guidance to evolve his strategies, to help him focus his attention, and to engage in reflective abstractions—learn the "rules" of problem identification, search for solutions and ways of generating solutions until the correct or desired one emerges.

In sum, the basic principles that should guide selection of activities and materials are as follows:

1. Choose activities that allow the child to be the cause of the action and employ a "hands on" approach.
2. Choose activities and materials that allow the teacher to employ inquiry strategies that focus attention on discrepancies and on the *actions* in the situation.
3. Choose activities that help the child focus on the transformations, on change from one state to another, rather than on the beginning and the end states.

Different science problems and experiences have different educational value in providing the child with a meaningful experience. For example, asking children to make astronomical observations and then report them would be beyond their competence. Problems such as how we digest our food, or how nutrition helps us grow, are relatively ineffective in promoting scientific investigation because they involve nonobservable changes or long-range outcomes. In either event the children cannot directly observe the transformation. Young children gain little from such problems. Taking these considerations into account leads to another important guideline:

4. Select problems where the rate of change is rapid and observable, such as water changing colors or ice melting.

Problems with relatively rapid change provide the child with an experience that is perceptible and consequently more accessible to understanding. In contrast, in an experiment with growing plants where the plants take months to grow the child does not perceive the transformation readily, and it is difficult for him to keep in mind the transformation. Further, such transformations involve inferential thinking often beyond the child's ability. Indeed, the experiment may take too long *if* the purpose is the child's understanding causal relations. The plant material might be useful if the child is prepared for long-term change. (In this case, the task would be a different one involving memory of previous events, and perhaps representation of states along the way through drawing, measurement, etc.).

Some guidelines in considering the types of transformations are as follows:

(a) **Some transformations have visibility of change;** for example, water is colored when dye is placed in the water. The child sees the transformation. This allows for different issues to be discussed. In contrast, in the boiling of an egg the change is not visible, only the outcome. The child cannot see the transformation. Another example of effects that are not directly observable is a very slow change such as human maturation. When the child is older and has increased in inferential and representational abilities, the boiling egg may be an appropriate task. He will also be better equipped to comprehend such phenomena as the fact that what he eats appeases his hunger and contributes to his growth and strength.

(b) **Some changes are reversible, while others are irreversible.** Decide which of these you want to demonstrate in a given situation. A reversible change is one in which an item or object can be changed—transformed and returned to its original state. A tray of water is put into a freezer and the water becomes transformed into ice. The tray with the ice is put into a warm room and the ice becomes water. The ice returns to its original state. In an irreversible change the item cannot return to its original state. For example, in a cooking experiment, an egg is mixed with flour. The egg is transformed and cannot be returned to its original state. We have described *reversibility* and *irreversibility* for actions of objects. When the child is confronted with a reversible transformation in the natural world, he can only understand this experience when he can mentally represent the reversal (Piaget, 1970). Another example would be the cognitive operation where an individual can describe reverse procedures. For example, you might take a tube and place a red block, a blue block, and a green block in it in order and in the presence of the child. Turn the tube over and ask the child to tell you the order in which the blocks will come out. To be able to tell the order correctly requires the child to reverse mentally.

5. *Limit the number of factors that can influence the change in the problem.*

Young children are limited in the number of things they can mentally handle at one time. Too many factors create confusion. For example, asking children to classify objects on the basis of interpreting color, form, and function would be difficult. Chances are that the children can organize a group of objects around one or two of these—all red ones, all blue ones, etc., or all that run on wheels, or all that float, but to create classes of three or more factors—large, red, round objects—would be somewhat difficult. It is critical that the teacher be alert to the number of factors the children are being asked to keep in mind as they work on a problem. Even if the teacher continually reviews what has been identified, there will be a limit to what the child can remember. Observe how many elements the children are handling with relative comfort. The problem should pose a challenge and not be beyond the reach of the child.

In incorporating these principles consider the following guide-lines for fostering interactions:

1. As you explain or ask something, watch for signs of the child's failing to understand, as in the following: Teacher: Johnny, how much water do I have to pour in here to make it the same amount as in here (teacher pouring water into a cylinder comparing it with a low flat dish)? Child: My mother has something like this (pointing to cylinder). Teacher repeats question, wording it somewhat differently. Child: See you have two jars with water. In this discussion the child does not focus on the issue. The reasons could be that (a) the question is not sufficiently clear, (b) he does not understand the task, (c) he does not find it interesting.

    The teacher then should alter the question and accompany it, if possible, by having the child perform some relevant action, such as pouring the water. This leads to the next principle.
2. Engage the child in relevant activity—this is important in the impact of the learning encounter, particularly in exploration of physical phenomena. Give the child a chance to handle material where possible.
3. Have materials which are not only safe but directly appropriate to the problem. If the children are going to cook (for real), have only the relevant material available unless you have reason to have more. Too often science tables are cluttered. Yet go into a science laboratory and clutter is a no-no!
4. Try to get the child to attend to his actions. For example, ask him to repeat some steps, if necessary.
5. Be honest in admitting when you know or do not know. This becomes relevant in science especially when new problems arise, as when a record player does not work, or a pot leaks, or something doesn't occur as expected.

Some Sample Teaching Encounters— Spontaneous and Planned

Opportunities for engaging children in scientific thinking abound in the preschool. These are two general types. First, there are the occasions when a child gets involved spontaneously in exploring some object or phenomenon. Second, there are the more structured tasks which the teacher directly initiates and guides. Let us turn first to the free-play situation.

Scientific Thinking in Free and Spontaneous Situations

Timmy is at the sink with a tin can which has a loose cover. He turns the faucet on as if to fill the can, but the stream of water hits the lid and spurts in an arc, right by Tim onto the floor. He seems gleeful about this occurrence. He takes the can away from the faucet, but this time he angles it slightly so that the water makes a bigger arc and spurts onto the floor. Jeanne notices this and approaches Tim. She has two choices: one, to point out that Tim is violating a rule of spilling water onto the floor, or two, to try to discover what Tim is trying to do and work with him on this aspect. Jeanne decides to let this situation become a problem-solving task. Consequently she asks, "What are you doing, Tim?" Tim answers, "I am making a fountain." Jeanne then asks, "Can you get the water to go into this side of the sink?" pointing to another section of the sink, "We need to keep it off the floor. Let's see if you can figure out a way to aim it." Tim apparently interprets this as a challenge rather than a reprimand. He puts the can under the faucet at the angle he used before and again the water sprays onto the floor. Jeanne still wants to avoid solving the problem for Timmy; instead she opts for encouraging him to generate alternatives to arrive at a solution himself. She asks, "What other ways could you hold the can under the faucet?" Tim shifts the angle and the teacher asks, "Where would the water go if you held it that way?" Tim does not answer but proceeds to tilt the can, placing it under the faucet. The water sprays towards the far end of the sink. Tim shouts gleefully, saying, "See, the fountain is going away." The teacher, noting Tim's interest and absorption in the idea of creating fountains, asks quietly, "Can you make the fountain go between here and here" (indicating the "safe" areas). Tim has discovered that there is a relationship between the direction of the fountain and the tilt of the can. He continues to experiment, noting excitedly each time the waters sprays in the direction he expects. The teacher has another decision to make: should she stop interacting with Tim since he is absorbed in his investigations and has discovered that he can control the direction of the spray? She decides to stop since she accomplished two objectives: she helped Tim continue his explorations constructively without getting water all over the floor and she helped him discover how to control the direction of the spray.

This example illustrates how to convert a potential disciplinary situation into a constructive science experience, here the discovery of the relationship between the direction of flow of the water and angle of the can. The alternative here was to discourage the child's exploration by focusing on the rule infraction—no water on the floor. The teacher chose the educational alternative.

Opportunities of this type occur frequently in the course of a child's free explorations. Careful observation of the child's engagement with various materials in the classroom allows for discreet teacher involvement. The principles guiding such involvement are as follows:

1. Notice how involved the child is. If he/she seems to be concentrating intensely, stay by passively but do not interrupt.
2. As you observe, try to get a sense of what the child *is* doing, rather than what you think the child *should* be doing.

3. If the child seeks to engage you in the activity, enter it in terms of what is happening. Let the child lead you.

4. If the child seems to want your participation, try to get a sense of what his or her intentions are. Ask such questions as, "Do you want to tell me what is going on?" or "I am not sure what you are planning. Would you tell me?" If you ask such questions, ask sincere ones. Thus, if the child is building a house and it is obvious, try to get elaboration on this idea by such questions as "What is the house for?" or "How do you want the house to look?" Or if the child is collecting all kinds of material from different areas of the classroom, you might say in a gentle way, "What are you up to, Mary?"

5. Try to be positive in your inquiry, using questions which would get the child to elaborate his or her explanations.

6. Be ready to withdraw if the child seems uninterested in your participation.

These guidelines are intended to help you decide on your point of entry, minimizing disruption of the child's activity. To borrow a phrase from traffic control, "Blend with traffic."

An example of working with these guidelines is illustrated by the following spontaneous activity. Josh brings the teacher into the situation and she helps him increase his understanding of the event.

Free-Play Experience: Josh and the Case
Of the Missing Sunlight

As usual, Josh had removed his shoes during free play and placed them in the middle of the rug. Jeanne had asked him to put them with his coat in the hall and now, as she helps another child put on a smock, notices that it's been several minutes since Josh left. Knowing Josh is inclined to explore, she decides to wait before going to him. When she does go out to find him, she sees him in a dark corner near the coat hooks. "Josh, what's up?" "Look!" he says, pointing excitedly at a small spot of sunlight shining on the wall from a window around the corner.

Jeanne is impressed with Josh's enthusiasm and decides this situation can be a valuable learning experience for him. "Josh, I see that spot there all by itself. I wonder what it is." Jeanne wants to find out what ideas Josh has about the sun spot. This will help her decide what to say or do to encourage Josh's own thinking processes. Josh responds definitively—"It's sunlight." Jeanne is surprised by the label Josh uses and since she has not heard this term from him, she wonders how much understanding goes along with the label. Jeanne, while accepting the answer, also asks for clarification. "Do you mean sunlight like the sunlight that comes on you outside when it's a sunny day?" "Yes," as he studies the spot.

DECISION: Jeanne has obtained some clarification and in view of his definitive answer as well as his concentration on the spot, Jeanne could stop. Should she go on? Jeanne decides to proceed because this situation is a natural one for scientific reasoning—but she must be careful and not be a distractor.

Jeanne decides to pose a problem of her own. "Well, how could that outside sunlight be here in this little dark corner?" "It's sunlight. I know it is." Josh's response indicates that the question is *not* his own problem. Ignoring Jeanne's question, he brings up his own. "Look! Now it's disappeared!" Josh evidently is not interested in Jeanne's structuring of the problem.

DECISION: Should she continue to press what she thinks is the interesting issue or should she let Josh go on in his way? Jeanne decides to keep quiet. Josh continues to study the spot of light.

After a brief pause, Josh says, "The spot of light is gone." Jeanne asks, "What happened?" "I don't know," says Josh, looking around for it. The spot reappears. Jeanne notices the reason for the change.

DECISION: Should she say anything or not? Jeanne decides to get Josh to *observe* and more specifically to clarify his problem.

"Josh! Did you see what happened?" she asks. Josh moves closer to look at the spot and suddenly the spot is gone again. Josh looks puzzled. He tries to find the spot—it reappears when he moves in a certain direction and disappears when he returns to his initial spot. It seems to Jeanne that he is starting to grasp a relationship between his body and the place of the spot, though it may be a "superstitious" idea of a connection. He moves back and forth several times, observing the effects.

"Look, I can make it change!" he says, continuing to move. "I see that you can, Josh," says Jeanne, "but, how are you doing that...? Where are you making the spot of sunlight go?"

Josh looks puzzled for a second time, and soon comes up with *several potential solutions.* "Maybe, it's behind here" and he looks behind the cubbies. No luck there, and he also checks under his body and tells the teacher to move to check under her. He is testing out ideas. These tests are analogous to hypothesis-testing, as in scientific investigation. His method of testing is observational. These observations do not substantiate his hypotheses. He shrugs his shoulders, appearing frustrated. Jeanne decides to provide a cue to guide Josh's exploration: "Wait a minute, Josh. Hold your hand over the spot. What do you see?"

"The spot! I've got it on my hand!" Jeanne asks if he can get it on other parts of his body and Josh proceeds to arrange himself so as to place the sun on his foot, leg, and then the teacher's arm and hand.

DECISION: Should she help Josh draw conclusions and create closure, or should she go on to help him understand the reason for the sun spot? In view of Josh's continued interest in exploring, Jeanne decides to continue to encourage Josh's problem-solving about the phenomenon.

Jeanne asks some questions to see what kind of ideas he can develop. "Maybe, since we can make it go onto our hands and arms, we could actually hold it on our hands and bring it back into the room. What do you think, Josh?"

Josh initially sees no reason why this wouldn't work, and tries to grasp the sunlight. He first goes for it as it shines on the wall, and finds it eludes him. "It's slippery," he says, and then, "I know," and he positions his hand in such a way that the spot is reflected on his open palm and then quickly clutches his fingers together. He notices that the sunlight is now shining on his closed fist. He turns to Jeanne and says, somewhat exasperated, "I can't catch it." "It is light," he says. "Nobody can catch it."

DECISION: Jeanne decides that this is a good time to conclude the situation as Josh's statement is accurate.

She concludes, "I guess that is the way with light. Let's come back later and see if it's still here." Josh seems satisfied. Jeanne is thinking of a follow-up science lesson for the class with light and shadows, using Josh's experience as a base.

As you reflect on Josh and the sun spot, you will notice how Josh actually followed through in this activity much as a scientist would. He observed, he generated and tested hypotheses, he came to some conclusions. The teacher played a critical role by getting into the child's perspective, engaging him in inquiry which furthered his understanding and helped him seek to verify his results. She decided to bring the situation to a close when Josh came to a conclusion. Jeanne could have carried the situation further to draw a connection between the window and the sun spot, helping Josh discover the way the spot entered the room. Jeanne's stopping when she did, however, was reasonable because she and Josh had arrived at an acceptable solution. To be sure, every problem can be pushed back to further and further causes. The sun spot problem can be examined not only from the perspective of what is it, but how it got there, why it hit that spot, will it always be there, etc. How far to attempt to extend the child's search for relationships and causes should be based on the child's interest, his level of understanding, and the teacher's knowledge of the subject matter. Josh had reached a point of satisfaction with his understanding. Since his conclusion, although limited, was accurate, it was a good time to stop.

These spontaneous interactions often arise with one or two children. On occasion, discussion of physical phenomena arise in the group context.

A Group Discussion

The children are arriving on a warm day in early spring. Jeanne and Denise are sitting on the floor and as each child enters he or she joins the group sitting on the floor. When we begin our observation of the group, a conversation about boots is already underway.

"Yeah, but my mom put my boots away in the attic," says Mary, and Michael tells the group that his boots were so full of holes that his mother put them out with the trash. Several other children talk about the present status of their boots, Jeanne and Denise listening intently. Finally Jeanne says, "I asked who wore their boots to school today, and you gave me a lot of ideas about boots. But I still don't quite understand why no one wore boots today and yet not so many days ago everyone wore boots to school."

The children reply, "It's too hot . . . ! Don't need boots in the summer . . . ! There's no more snow . . . !" Denise offers a counterargument. "Well, I don't see why you need boots only in winter time." The children join in, seemingly agreeing by pointing out the problems of wet shoes, socks, feet, and Michael remarks on the problems he had with his holey boots toward the end of the winter. This might have been about as far as the discussion would go when Brian says, "Yeah, and then it got hot and the snow melted like this." Slowly lowering his hand, he demonstrates the drop of several feet of snow to nothing. Picking up on this spontaneous employment of an external system of representation, Denise asks Brian to demonstrate again and encourages the other children to tell about what happened to the snow. Then Denise says, "Now each of you use your hands to show us how it would be when the snow had just started . . . Now, very slowly, more snow is falling . . . and a little more . . . now it's stopped! Show us!"

The children use various body parts and movements to show aspects of the increasing snowfall. Brian has added his arms and the upper part of his body to his picture of the snow depth, while Chris wriggles his fingers to show increasing amounts of snowflakes rising on the ground. Laurie's snowflakes are falling through the air with varying speeds and when Jeanne mentions the beginning of a breeze, they sway back and forth. The movement activity continues on for some time with a few children representing rain and melting snow.

Again a spontaneous comment provided an opportunity for the teachers to provoke further exploration and discussion, this time the representation of weather phenomena through body movement. Questions and comments like these were offered by the teachers.

—Pretend that there's deep snow on the ground and show me how you would walk.
—What if it were mud?

—Now, what if you were playing outside on a warm sunny day, when suddenly the sun disappeared? What might happen then . . . ? in the sky . . . ? to the way you felt?

—What if it got very cold . . . ? How might you look?

—What could you do about being cold . . . ? Show me how you would curl up . . . ? What warm clothing would you use . . . ? How would you put it on . . . ?

What other things do people and animals do to keep warm?

While these activities do provide valuable science experiences and they should not be underestimated, they still serve a different function from that of planned activities. The planned activities can and should have a continuity and follow-through not possible in the spontaneous interactions.

Our purpose is not to develop a formal science curriculum. Our examples are intended to demonstrate how planned activities can be used to contribute to thinking and problem-solving skills. You will recall that we suggested a set of guidelines for selecting activities and describing how to use them. Let us now take that list and apply it to teacher-initiated activity involving principles of *flotation*—sinking and floating objects. The choice of his activity is based on a simple observation that children enjoy water play and do experiment with sinking and floating objects. The activity further fits our guidelines of active hands-on participation, and it is simple. One drawback is that a complete understanding of the displacement principle is probably not possible. Thus, solution to the problem can only be approximate. However, chances are that the children will let you know when they have had enough. Let us now turn to an activity Jeanne and Denise are planning after they have observed the interest generated by some of the children trying to float various objects

Teacher Evaluation and Planning

"You know," Denise said to Jeanne, as they watched a small group of children at play in the water tub, "it seems as though they're really getting involved in the issue of floating and sinking. Watch them trying to figure out which things make the best boats."

As they observe, without interrupting, the teachers notice Ted's attempts to discover which of the available materials (including small blocks, plastic cups, wooden cylinders, etc.) will work for him to carry a cargo of pennies. He systematically tests each possibility for buoyancy, and if it passes, checks to see how many pennies it will support. Mandy, at the other end, is intrigued by filling floating plastic tubs with water until they sink, pouring gradually, and stopping as soon as sinking is achieved.

A few days later we find Jeanne and Denise together in another planning session. They are generating ideas for themes and activities, starting, as previously described, from interests they see in the children. Remembering Ted's exploration at the water table, they decide to try the floating-sinking activity as a basis for classifying a group of new materials relative to those that sink and those that float.

Denise: We've had some exciting sessions in doing the type of activity where a discrepancy is presented. If they've formed some kind of rule, for example, "all wooden objects floats," and then you present them with a case that doesn't fit, like a piece of heavy wood which sinks, it shakes up their ideas and makes them explore further.

Jeanne: I like that idea too. And, in addition, I wonder if we couldn't find a way to make use of one of the representation systems in an activity.

I'm sure we can find something where they can be working with a picture to implement some of their floating and sinking concepts.

Denise: OK, I think that we should talk about our objectives here. What concepts, exactly, we went to work on, and what scientific processes we will want to emphasize. . . Is our purpose to really get them understanding *why* things float? Relative density and all that?

Jeanne: No, I wouldn't really think so. I don't think that's appropriate with this age group. I would think that to start it would be important to get the children to observe—noticing that some things float and others don't. And especially that it's not specific to one situation. If it floats in the sink, it should float in the bathtub, pool, and puddle also.

Denise: Yes. That way they'd be forming some kind of mental concept . . . class . . . of floating vs. sinking things. . . And from there to see if they can abstract some attributes which seem to differentiate the two groups, maybe?

Jeanne: If we can get them to do that—construct rules for what will float—then we can plan some kind of activity where they apply those.

Jeanne and Denise continue their discussion, finally arriving at the activities described below. They attempt to incorporate the ideas mentioned earlier into activities geared to the developmental level and to the interests of individual children. Another important aspect is the sequence of presentation. The initial activities are designed to provide a common groundwork for the later ones which will elaborate on that basis. It is easy to assume certain understanding on the part of the children, such as the awareness of the floating constancy of one object. Jeanne and Denise try to avoid these assumptions whenever possible, as we see in this activity.

Activity: ''Boats and Submarines''

Materials and Teacher Organization: Children are divided into two groups of approximately ten, each going with one teacher. For each group there is a tub of water situated in the center and a tray of objects to be tested for buoyancy. These have been especially selected and are equally divided between floaters and sinkers. They are also not too "tricky," that is, it should be relatively easy for children to isolate attributes common to several of either category. A sampling of the items might include several small wooden blocks of assorted colors and shapes, some plastic and metal silverware, a wooden pencil, a pen, and a plastic cup. The total number of items is about thirty. Finally, two smaller trays with pictures representing floating or sinking.

Teacher Strategies: Jeanne introduces the activity by encouraging the group to pretend that each child has a tiny insect for a pet. Briefly, they show how they hold this tiny creature, tell what it might look like, how it might move. Then the teacher points out the water tub and indicates it is a lake for these tiny pets.

"On the tray are some things that can be used either as boats or as submarines for the pets. Our problem here is to find out which will stay up on top and be boats and which will sink underneath as submarines. Each child will get two turns to test some of these on the tray to see which they are."

Jeanne goes on to point out the other two trays and to have the children interpret the meanings of the pictures, deciding which tray is for the potential submarines and which for the boats. Then, one at a time children select an item from the large collection, test it for buoyancy, and put it on the proper tray. During this part of the activity Jeanne does not ask for much predicting on the part of the children. She spends more time encouraging specific observation and comparing, especially after the two categories have begun to grow.

"Before we try out any more, let's look at the things that have floated and have made good boats. . . What different things can you say about them?" Depending on the children's responses, Jeanne may ask such further questions as "Can you see anything that's the same about all the floating ones. . .? Or about just some of them. . .? What are they made of. . .? Shaped like. . .? How about the submarines. . . ? Are there any square ones that were submarines. . .? Any metal ones that were boats. . .? Any metal submarines?"

Jeanne won't insist on the formulating of generalizations about the categories. However, if one of the children should spontaneously mention something, such as "None of the metal ones are good boats, they all go down fast," she might point out to the entire group, "Brian had an idea that no metal ones seem to float too well. What do you all think about that. . . ? Is there anything we can do to test if that happens for other metal things. . .? Can you see any other things the same about just floaters or just sinkers?"

When each child has tested and classified one item, Jeanne tells the group that now the job is to let the tiny pet decide if it wants a boat or a submarine, and select that specifically from the items left on the original tray. Basically, in this part of the activity, the child must decide if he or she is going to go for a floater or a sinker, look at the pretested items already in that class, and try to predict which attributes would most likely help predict another member.

"Ok, Amy, does your pet want to go on a submarine or a boat. . .? A boat . . . ? Well, which tray has on it the things that were good boats. . .? OK, before you pick a boat then look at these and see if that can help you to figure out which of the others will be good floaters."

Jeanne asks all of the children to help point out attributes which might be important in this decision, and then Amy selects one item. She picks a metal spoon because "It's long and thin like the pencil and the (plastic) knife and fork that floated." Jeanne accepts the decision, pleased with the reasoning she observes, and allows Amy to try it out herself. It doesn't float!

"Oh, no, what happened!" And as Amy picks it up to try again, Brian remembers his earlier idea. "The heavy metal ones—they can't float—only splash down." After trying again herself, and hearing Brian's thought, Amy tries a plastic spoon—still long, but not made of metal—and is successful. The activity continues in this way.

Here we have seen the children incorporating past ideas and observations into a new problem-solving situation. The teachers have structured the activity in such a way that each child gets an opportunity for both aspects, and, in addition, can gain from the experiences of the others. An essential decision strategy on Jeanne's part is the follow-up questioning right after the child gives a prediction. When Amy explains that she selected the metal spoon because it shared longness and skinniness with some of the other floaters, Jeanne sees, first of all, that she used reasoning to arrive at the prediction, and secondly, what kind of an understanding existed. For example, if Amy had selected a plastic spoon for reasons of length, she would have experienced success but for the wrong reason. Keeping this in mind, Jeanne might have, later on, discovered a way to present Amy with a discrepancy— the metal knife, still long but not buoyant. This kind of follow-up not only helps children arrive at more accurate concepts, but encourages the evaluation of ideas through testing. In addition, the teachers learn about what the child is thinking.

Reviewing this planned experience, we can summarize Jeanne's and Denise's activity as follows:

1. They selected an activity which was already of interest to the children.
2. They decided what the limits of the activity would be.
3. They decided what types of material to use.
4. They arranged the situation so that each child could participate actively.
5. They planned the activity so that the children could observe the consequences of their actions.
6. They defined the problem and identified relevant observations.
7. They selected a task in which alternative solutions could be generated.
8. They decided to look for indications that the children had gone as far as they could in their understanding. The teachers realize the difficulties children have in understanding the principle of displacement.
9. The teachers assumed that learning outcomes of the task would be as follows: some objects float and others sink (classification); objects that float in one situation can float in others (generalization); certain kinds of solid heavy objects sink and certain light ones float (generalization).
10. The teachers noted individual differences among the children in formulating general rules. This helped them to know when to stop.

The critical point is knowing when to stop—when the children seem to have absorbed what they can and before interest wanes. Leave the children on a note of high interest and it is more likely that continued exploration and thinking will take place.

Summary

We have presented a rationale for science education at the preschool level and discussed the relationship between science education and children's intrinsic search for reducing uncertainty and mystery in their daily encounters.

Although we have provided guidelines and samples of spontaneous and structured activities, we did not lay out a set of detailed lessons. This is beyond the scope of this volume. (The suggested resources at the end of the chapter may be helpful for this purpose). We have stressed that encounters with any type of materials can be used for scientific inquiry. It is critical to develop a style of inquiry which extends children's thinking by focusing on interesting and relevant problems, by activating children's attention to discrepancies, by asking them to generate solutions and to discover solutions to the problem. By providing a sequence of activities, each incorporating previous experience, the teacher assists children in constructing a repertoire of strategies and knowledge. The teacher's inquiry can serve to focus children's attention, maintain interest, and thereby enhance a sense of control, of mastery, and of satisfaction in their engagement.

We have noted that children do observe and make inferences about what they do observe. One type of inference that is particularly relevant to scientific thought is that which deals with cause-effect relationships. Many hypotheses ask the question of "Why?" and a why question is often answered with a because statement. Young children do not have the ability yet to answer why questions with a logical answer.

We have discussed some of the cognitive characteristics of young children that should be taken into account as you proceed through these activities. In this way you will have a framework within which to judge the adequacy of your methods and the activities you select.

We feel by this process one contributes to the child's developing problem-solving skills. We agree with Nathan Isaacs that development of inquiry skills, especially causal inquiry, is crucial. As he so eloquently states," ... causal inquiry becomes, of course, eventually the basis for our most systematic and comprehensive investigation into the constitution and controls, the general structure, of our world; in other words, the warp and woof of science" (Isaacs, 1974, p. 50).

Suggested Resources

Butts, D. E., and Hall, G. E. *Children and Science: The Process of Teaching and Learning* (Englewood Cliffs, N.J.: Prentice-Hall, 1975).

Duckworth, E. "The Having of Wonderful Ideas." In *Piaget in the Classroom*, edited by J. Raph and M. Schwebel (New York: Basic Books, 1973).

Elkind, D. "Piaget and Science Education." *Science and Children,* 10 (1972): 9–12.

Forman, G. E., and Kuschner, D. S. *The Child's Construction of Knowledge: Piaget for Teaching children* (Monterey, Calif.: Brooks/Cole, 1977).

Harms, T. *Maximizing Learning from Cooking Experiences* (Chapel Hill, N.C.: Frank Porter Graham Child Development Center, 1977).

Hawkins, D. "Messing About in Science." *Science and Children,* 3 (1965): 5–9.

Hawkins, F. P. *The Logic of Action: Young Children at Work* (New York: Pantheon, 1974).

Holt, B. *Science with Young Children* (Washington, D.C.: National Association for the Education of Young Children, 1977).

Isaacs, I. *Children's Ways of Knowing* (New York: Teachers College Press, 1974).

Neumann, D. "Sciencing for Young Children." *Ideas that Work with Young Children,* edited by K. R. Baker (Washington, D. C.: National Association for the Education of Young Children, 1972).

Rowe, M. B. *Teaching Science as Continuous Inquiry* (New York: McGraw-Hill, 1973).

Selberg, E. M., Neal, L., and Vessel, M. F. *Discovering Science in the Elementary School* (Reading, Mass.: Addison-Wesley, 1970).

7

The Social-Affective
Domain

Traditionally, the preschool experience has been viewed as providing a significant opportunity for children to broaden their social horizons. For many children it is the first major experience outside of the family; for all it is a new social experience. But the child who walks through the door of the preschool on the first day of class is already a person with a history of living in a social context. And the child is already a thinking, problem-solving individual.

From the beginning of life, the child grows up in a social context. Other people are among the first objects the infant encounters. And compelling objects they are—moving, talking, smiling when she smiles, feeding her, holding and caressing her. A few of these objects (mother, father, etc.) appear with greater regularity and do especially important things for the infant. They feed her, change her diaper, rock her. They begin to be distinguished from the others. The child develops certain expectations. When she is hungry and a certain face appears, food is on the way. When another particular face appears (known to us as that of the babysitter), then mother, the food-face, is going away.

Before the infant is even a year old, she is making many such social distinctions. She is showing expectations of events of a social nature and she has been involved in a great many social experiences. By the time we encounter the three- or four-year-old child she is by no means a new recruit to learning about social interaction. However, she is just getting started in actually conceptualizing this social world. In early chapters, we have seen that with physical objects and phenomena, the child learns much about the world through her actions in it. Likewise in the social world, the child has done her early learning on the sensorimotor level. She has expectations of how social objects (mother, stranger, etc.) will act, but until she is at the representational level of thought, these are not yet concepts. By the time the child is about eighteen months, she moves out of the sensorimotor period and becomes capable of representational thought (Piaget, 1952).

The preschool child is beginning to construct her conceptual understandings of the social world, of herself and others. To illustrate this difference, let us contrast the one-year-old child's perceptual ability to distinguish male and female faces (Kagan, Kearsley, and Zelago, 1978) with the three-year-old's conceptual ability to think about what males and females do or reflect on how it can be that the person there with a feather on his hat is a man (a discrepancy to resolve). We see many kinds of evidence of this active constructing of knowledge of maleness and femaleness; to pursue this as an example: in the children's acting out of male and female roles in play and their challenging of each other's enactments, in their information-seeking questions, or in their double-takes when a new piece of information appears which doesn't fit an existing "theory" about males and females. Thus the child begins to put together her notions of who's who in the social universe and what makes things happen as they do. But she has a long way to go in acquiring the knowledge and the abilities which form this universe.

The Social-Affective Domain in the Preschool Curriculum

Many have noted the dependence of social understanding on cognitive development, and parents and teachers tend to be aware that there are many things in social interaction, moral judgment, etc., which we cannot yet expect a child to do or to understand because "he is too young." There is evidence to support the relationship between the child's cognitive level and his understanding of social events (e.g., Emmerich , Cocking, and Sigel, in press). This relationship of social understanding and cognitive growth is one reason why the social-affective domain merits close attention in a classroom. It may be useful to examine further why the social-affective domain has important status in the curriculum for the child's development as a thinker.

On the simplest level, of course, anything that sets the child thinking has value for the development of his thought processes. So there is certain value in an area of experience which matters so enormously to the child that its dilemmas, its organization, its puzzling inconsistencies will set him thinking. There are problems to be solved, relationships that need to be understood, cues that need to be interpreted—these are matters of great importance to the child. If there were no other reason for taking very seriously the curriculum in social-affective development, this would suffice. But there is more.

The second point is that it appears that thought processes which are called to use with such ease in one area are not automatically mobilized in another domain. A scientist may be excellent in observing her laboratory animals but be very unobservant with social cues. A doctor may be brilliant in identifying the problem of his patient from the symptoms and yet be very poor at identifying the problem with the way he is using his time or the difficulty with communicating with his mother-in-law. The fact that being a good solver of *impersonal* problems doesn't mean one will be good at *interpersonal* problem-solving has been documented in research investigations as well (e.g., Spivack and Shure, 1974). This commonplace disparity in how "smart" people are in various areas of their lives has many contributing factors, no doubt. But the educator cannot be content to stimulate thinking processes in some domains and leave it to chance that they will be applied automatically in others.

A third point is that the social-affective domain may be particularly good for the development of thought processes in certain respects. There is not a great deal of research on this point, but attempts to work with social-affective understandings have brought some of its special characteristics into focus. Lee C. Lee (1975) mentions two differences in the task of constructing physical "schemes" and that of constructing social "schemes": (1) the greater variableness of external reality of the social world as compared with the objective world and (2) the responsiveness of social objects as compared with physical objects. In her second point, Lee is referring to the fact that when an individual acts on a nonhuman object, the object almost always "reacts," giving the individual feedback, while social partners may give degrees of feedback varying in quality as well as quantity. A toddler puts his finger into his cereal and it "gives"; he does the same with an apple and it doesn't give. The child begins to construct a notion of what objects you can stick your finger into, how the punchable ones look different from the nonpunchable ones. The same toddler, let's say, has found a bug on the floor and takes it to show it to father. Dad says without looking up from his paper, "That's nice, son." Big brother ignores him entirely; sister screams, mother takes it away from him. On a different day his father might have responded with interest, and so on. The child cannot be assured of always getting feedback at all, and the quality and type varies greatly. In this example, it is difficult to construct a coherent notion of what people will do when you take them an object for perusal.

A related characteristic of the social-affective domain is the subtlety and complexity of the inferences it demands, the nuances and fine shadings it involves. It is an area in which there is little black and white and much gray: smiles can have many shades of meaning, people's words have to be interpreted in the context of the situation, and so on. This makes the social-affective domain an interesting one for expanding the child's thought beyond the "literal."

An additional characteristic of the social world, as contrasted with the world of physical objects, is the child's own involvement. Thinking about her unsuccessful attempt to persuade a peer to play, or her mother's reaction to her knocking over a dish, is different from thinking about which objects float or sink. (The difference may only be one of degree for the young child since she has a tendency to be egocentric in her perceptions of the causes of *physical* phenomena as well as social events (Piaget, 1972). It is difficult for the young child to dissociate her own actions from events she is observing. She even thinks the moon is following along with her as she walks!)

When thoughts and feelings themselves are the object of thought, the child has a doubly heavy mental demand to deal with. The phenomena themselves are "invisible" and must be inferred from cues that are sometimes subtle and do not have a simple correspondence with the thought or feelings. In addition, the child has the interference from his own thoughts and feelings—either those he has at the moment or those he remembers from similar situations in the past. He knows that he cries when he's sad or hurt, for example, and he sees someone crying when receiving an Oscar. He says, "What's wrong with the lady, Mama?" In combination, these characteristics make understanding the actions and emotions of others a mentally demanding arena.

We have been discussing up to this point the reasons from a *cognitive standpoint* for placing the social-affective domain squarely within the early childhood curriculum rather than on its fringes, branded as outside the cognitive part of the program (the concern only of those who remind us that we should not forget to consider "the whole child"). There are, of course, also reasons from the standpoint of *interpersonal adjustment* and *emotional development.*

Research evidence has documented the value of working with children's ability to think about interpersonal situations for their social adjustment (e.g., Shure and Spivack, 1978; Spivack and Shure, 1974). We will be seeing more throughout the chapter of these reasons for dealing with the social-affective domain.

Children during the preschool period have fragments of knowledge about social interaction, about friendship, justice, and equity, for example. The early childhood years are a time when such knowledge can be increasingly integrated (Damon, 1977).

In summary, there are a number of reasons for taking the social-affective domain seriously as a curriculum area. In addition to its importance in the life of the child, it is an area that holds significant cognitive challenges for children. These challenges, along with the high interest and motivation children bring to this area, make the developing of social-affective understandings particularly fruitful ground for cognitive growth.

In each of the areas we have dealt with in the previous chapters (art, construction, movement, music, science), a limitation of scope has been necessary; defining the scope of what to include is particularly necessary with the social-affective domain. Volumes have been written on the child's emotional life, on the growth of interpersonal relationships in the family and school, and on behavior problems and methods of guidance. As in the case of the previous chapters, the scope of our consideration of the social-affective domain is defined by our purpose as reflected in the title of our book, *Educating the Young Thinker: Classroom Strategies for Cognitive Growth.* Our emphasis is on the child's development of understanding of the social context, his thinking about interpersonal problems, and on the teacher's role in promoting this growth. Our focus will be on the cognitive foundations of social-affective understandings and on the classroom environment conducive to "educating the young thinker" about issues that are personal or interpersonal (as well as those that are "impersonal").

We will begin by describing in broad strokes such a classroom, particularly the human environment in which such thinking is stimulated and supported. The interaction among children and the interaction of children with adults will be considered here in general terms as part of our sketching of the crucial elements of the environment and taken up in more detail later in the chapter. In describing the decisions teachers make in creating and maintaining the atmosphere of the classroom, we will focus on the relationship of these decisions to (1) the teacher's goals for the children's development, and (2) the characteristics of the preschool child's thought and social development. Two central aspects of the young child's development as a thinker will be explored: (1) role-taking, that is, the taking of the perspective of another individual, and (2) interpersonal problem-solving. In considering the child's development of these abilities, we will look at some strategies teachers can employ to foster the development of these capacities in the young child.

The Classroom Environment: Goals

Up to this point we have not said much explicitly about the classroom environment. However, we would be poor believers in our own constructivist perspective if we did not assume that you have, consciously or unconsciously, constructed your own notion of what kind of classroom atmosphere we would try to create. Would it be a room in which teachers would discourage peer interaction? Would teachers require children to share or to include all classmates in their play? How about discipline—tight reins? Laissez-faire? In most respects you would probably be quite accurate in your predictions. But it will nonetheless be useful, we believe, to summarize the basic characteristics which have been implicity reflected in our descriptions of classroom interactions to this point. Of course, in doing this we will want to be explicit about the reasons for stressing these characteristics as well. The decisions one makes, the atmosphere one's classroom has, reflect the goals one has for the child. Many programs, particularly those within the "interactionist" perspective, have certain basic goals in common, which we share. Patricia Minuchin (1977) has summed up concisely these central goals for the young child's total development:

—the expansion of trusting relationships to adults beyond the family and to peers;
—the increasing development of channels for expressing and managing fear, helplessness, anger, affection, and excitement;
—the establishment of foundations for cooperative interaction in work and play;
—the maintenance of an exploratory stance toward the environment and of a capacity for choice and initiative;
—the enhancement of a subjective sense of mastery and of the power to communicate and to make an impact on the environment (p. 9).

To these widely shared goals for the child's development, we would add three additional goals:

—the development of interpersonal problem-solving skills;
—the growing awareness of how symbol systems can be used for personal and interpersonal communicating;
—the increasing ability to take a reflective perspective toward social and physical reality.

From these eight goals, along with our point of view about how children learn and develop, we can make some *general* statements as to what the environment should be like. The *specific* decisions a teacher will make are determined, of course, by the resources and the constraints of her teaching situation, by the particular children she is working with—their age, their family backgrounds, etc.,—and by her own personality, her strengths and weaknesses. But whatever specific decisions she makes, there are certain basic characteristics of the environment which follow naturally from the goals articulated above.

The Classroom Environment: Influences

The Shape of the Day

There are a number of global features which set the structure of the child's preschool life and thus indirectly, but critically, affect the child's growth as a social being. The *schedule* of the day should allow opportunities for making choices of how to spend one's time: alone, interacting with this classmate or that group, in the block corner, or quietly sharing a book, etc. Such freedom of choice is important in relation to the goals of the child's development in several respects. First, each child's needs for these various kinds of social activity are individual, as is the timing of these needs. With the availability of opportunities and the freedom of movement to choose among them, the child can seek out what he is ready for. Options are also important to the child's sense of efficacy, his sense of having some control over his life. In addition, the child's freedom of time and movement gives him the opportunity to engage in such activities as make- believe play in which he enacts roles and relationships he observes in the world of adults. As we shall see in the next chapter, such play is a powerful vehicle for the growth of social understanding and competence.

The *arrangement* and *contents* of the classroom also establish the context within which the children live. If the teacher values an atmosphere where children have a sense of control and competence, then materials are accessible, safe, and functional for child use. There is a *variety of activities* to allow children opportunities for mastery and expression through a range of tasks that are appropriate to their developmental level.

The classroom is not static from the first day of school; the materials, the arrangement, and, in some cases the rules and procedures are modified according to the needs and desires of the changing human community which they serve. As the children develop, they are able to understand more of what lies behind rules and procedures and behind the decisions that affect the classroom environment. The children's input into decisions of this kind is elicited. It is important that it *only* be elicited where there is real scope for taking children's opinions and preferences into account. (You may recall the voicing of this concern with *genuine* discussion by the teachers who are considering a group problem-solving session in Chapter 1.) Such involvement of children in decision-making, where realistic, is another reflection of the goals stated earlier for their development within the social context.

The Teacher and the Children

The early childhood classroom is a particular kind of community. It is a community in which one (or two) people have been charged with the care and socialization of a number of other people, some eighteen or more years younger. *Neither* feature of this situation should be overlooked: that the classroom is a community and that it is not a community of peers. As with any group, there must be rules and routines, and the children are not yet ready to judge well in all matters. However, as Shapiro and Biber (1972) assert:

> The teacher's exercise of authority is not an arbitrary function invested in her role, but a rational function that is dependent on group goals and relationships. A system of controls is still necessary—as a safeguard against excessive impulse expression and to protect the work, the play, and the life of the group, but it is built on positive motivation rather than submission to power. . . . The teacher enlists new levels of motivation to take into account the children's capacity for control and to help them understand the functional necessity of classroom rules (p. 69).

For programs which see children as having an active, participatory role in their own learning, it would be unnatural to cast them in a passive role in their relationship to the social world. It is natural to see their active efforts to understand as involving the same "indivisible intelligence," as Kamii (1974) has called it.

Teachers who are genuinely interested in what children think will be just as curious regarding the children's construction of their social universe. The teacher's authentic interest is indispensable to the classroom environment. It is communicated when a teacher willingly waits as the children grope for words, as they struggle with formulating and communicating their thoughts. The teacher is not interested in the child giving a right answer or an adult-oriented platitude; she is interested in what the child is really thinking or feeling. This interest brings to the child, as to an individual of any age, a sense of his worth and of the reciprocal enjoyment in exchanging ideas and feelings. This sense of openness is particularly crucial in the highly charged area of interpersonal problems and feelings. When the teacher asks a question, it is important that the child not see it as a hidden command ("Do we allow hitting in the classroom?") or moralizing ("Do you think it's fair for one child to have more cookies than the others?"). For this reason it is important for the teacher to be clear in her own mind what she is up to. If the purpose of her interaction is to remind a child of a rule that he is not following, she should handle it differently than if she is setting out to explore with him possible alternatives to a problem, find out his perception of a situation, etc. For example, when the teacher sees two boys chasing each other, she may simply say, "Remember, boys, walk in the classroom. Running is for outdoors." When she first introduced this rule, she discussed the reasoning behind it with the children, eliciting their ideas about possible outcomes of running in the class and communicating her thinking about it. At some later points, with individual children who haven't seemed to understand initially, some further discussion may be advisable. But this kind of discussion need not be attempted *each* time there is an infraction by children who know the rule and the reasoning behind it perfectly well, but have simply forgotten or chosen to disregard it. Such "discussions" have the effects of confusing the child about *real* discussions.

If the teacher wants children to come to feel that a discussion of an interpersonal situation is a time for thinking and honest communication, the teacher must also realize that she may have to counteract what the children have experienced with parents or other adults. Take, for example, the classic, "How do you think Teddy feels when you. . . ?" In itself, there is nothing wrong with this question, which seemingly tries to engage the child in taking the perspective of the other, a crucial step in social and moral maturity. However, in addition to the fact that the mental demand which the question poses may be excessive for the young child (more on that later in the chapter), there is the fact that this kind of question has often been used in a "loaded" way. Much of the time it is asked, it would be best translated as "You've done wrong. You've made Teddy feel bad." So even when the teacher *does* mean the question in a different way, she should take into account what the child's interpretation of it may be. A teacher who hopes to be able to discuss with children what they actually feel and perceive in interpersonal situations would do well to avoid such questions altogether, at least until she has solidly established with the children the genuine openness of her inquiry. And even then she must be aware that the child may misinterpret her intention.

Later in the chapter, in our discussion of the teacher's role in the development of children's role-taking and problem-solving abilities, we will look at some specific strategies and examples for helping children think through interpersonal situations and their own emotional reactions. These are delicate but critical issues since it is in the context of real-life situations, in the social-affective area as in all areas of the curriculum, that the greatest development takes place.

Children and Their Peers

It has been implicit in our discussion so far that the child's opportunity to be with other children is a significant part of the school experience. This peer contact is often the number one reason for parents' decision to place their child in a preschool group experience. In this priority they are quite right. Nor does the importance of this aspect of school life end with the preschool years, though it has received more universal recognition and attention for the young child. A wide range of programs agree on the value of children's experiences

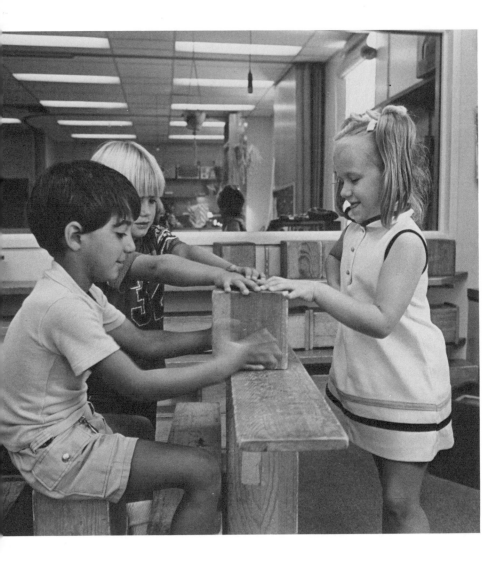

with peers for their growth in dealing with conflict, forming friendships, communicating their ideas or desires, and functioning within a group. Teachers and parents are also usually aware of the value of being exposed to age-appropriate models in whose actions children witness behaviors they can learn from, ranging from engaging in dramatic play to making overtures to another child (not to mention some of the behaviors adults deem less desirable, such as aggression).

Piaget and others who have focused on the child's cognitive development have likewise emphasized the child's experience with peers. The young child, Piaget (1959) has argued, is *egocentric*. She sees the world from her own perspective and has difficulty understanding that others have perspectives which differ from her own. This is not a question of "selfishness"—such a label is not meaningful at this point when the child has not reached the point of understanding that others' perspectives even exist. Take, for example, a revealing feature of children's speech, the use of pronouns without antecedents. In describing an event, the child tends to say things such as "He took it and hid it in that place." Who is "he"? What is "it"? Where is "that place"? Parents and other adults have a tendency to accommodate to such egocentricity. They have the mental capacity, they often have the advantage of having sufficient familiarity with the child's world to be able to surmise what the child is talking about—and they have plenty of practice! Ever since the child was an infant and parents had to determine what the child's outstretched hand was reaching for (if they wanted to put an end to her crying), they have learned to make educated guesses from minimal cues. Peers are not intellectually or emotionally equipped to make such accommodations. When confronted with the demand to "bring me that," they are likely to look blank or say "Huh?" As Piaget (1959) has pointed out, the need to makes oneself understood is a continuing pressure towards the construction of a less egocentric reality.

What is the teacher's role with respect to peer interaction? Most simply, her decisions about schedule and space determine the opportunities children have for spontaneous interaction. If children are ushered from one structured, teacher-directed activity to another, their opportunities to learn from one another will be minimal. There are other things which teachers do to facilitate interaction besides allowing it to take place. For example, you will see illustrations of other teacher roles in facilitating spontaneous interaction in the chapter on make-believe play, which happens to be a particularly rich arena for the development of communicative and interactive abilities. In the case of make-believe play, by providing the setting, the materials, and the input which encourage children's enactment of adult roles and situations, teachers indirectly influence the likelihood of social encounters.

Another implication of valuing peer interaction is that the teacher does not rush in and "make the peace" each time there is a quarrel or a potential one. Decisions about when to intervene are not clear-cut and observation of what is happening is essential. Is one child winning her way once again by bullying or manipulation? The teacher has many factors to consider, but she can be guided by an awareness, on the one hand, of the potential values of arguments and breakdowns in communication between children, and a recognition, on the other hand, that in some cases she can be valuable in providing mediation, a sounding board, an example of useful interpersonal behaviors which the child can add to his repertoire.

We will be focusing on two areas of development which seem to lie at the heart of growth in social understanding and competence: (1) the development of role-taking (the ability to take the perspective of another into account), and (2) the development of problem-solving in interpersonal situations. Let us first look at why so much attention is given to the child's development in role-taking.

Role-Taking

Development of role-taking and communication skills seems to us to be critical from three points of view: (1) from a concern with socialization goals, (2) from a concern with affective development, and (3) from the standpoint of cognitive development and school learning. Just as we have stressed the value of teachers subjecting their curriculum plans to the *why* question, it will be helpful for us to consider explicitly why we would put so much energy into facilitating role-taking.

Role-Taking and Socialization

There are social realities with which we must contend. We live in a world with others where rules, laws, and conventions exist. Problems emerge in the social context for which workable solutions must be found and agreed upon. The child is better equipped to function in his present social world if he understands that he will not always immediately be understood, that others have different information, feelings, and motives from his own. And in adult life he will need far more fully developed abilities in communication and role-taking. As Flavell says:

> Other human beings are our most important stimulus objects, after all, and making good inferences about what is going on inside these objects permits us some measure of understanding, prediction, and control in our daily interactions with them (1968, v.).

Is there any evidence that increasing role-taking skills brings improvement in relations with others? The work that has been done to date tends to support the idea that development in role-taking skills is related to improvement in social relations, for example, less antisocial behavior (Chandler, 1973) and more sharing and helping (Staub, 1971). Role-taking has also been found to be related to children's moral judgment (Damon, 1977; Selman, 1971). It would seem to be a case of "necessary but not sufficient." Although role-taking skills would not invariably lead to improved social interactions, it is hard to see how significant improvement in communication could occur without the individual first gaining the ability to make appropriate social inferences about what the other person is like and what his perspective is.

Role-Taking and Affective Development

It is frustrating when others do not understand us or we do not understand them. Just being aware that such a thing is possible can help reduce frustration in two ways:

(1) When the individual realizes that the other may not understand or agree (or that she herself may not understand correctly if she is the listener),

frustration from miscommunication may not develop in the first place. Failure to understand or be understood is not attributed to meanness or stubbornness; it is recognized as a possibility inherent in the communication process. *You don't get so frustrated when you know people don't always understand each other.*

(2) You may still get somewhat frustrated but your knowledge of the possibility of communication failure helps you deal with your frustration after the fact. *You still get upset but you are able to calm down and not be hostile toward the other person because you understand that differing perspectives and difficulties in understanding are just part of the way things are.* And being calmer and less hostile is more conducive to getting the message clarified, the mutually agreeable solution found. From the point of view of affective development, the use of these constructive actions is likely to increase the individual's feeling of efficacy, of being able to have an influence on situations.

Of course, there are additional ways, besides the reduction of frustration, in which communication and role-taking skills are related to affective development. As the child increases in his ability to think about what others are experiencing, how their characteristics or roles affect their perception of situations, etc., his understanding of his own affective reactions will gain in depth and subtlety.

Role-Taking and Cognitive Development/School Learning

As we will be seeing throughout the next section of the chapter, role-taking and communication skills are very much cognitive activities. Without getting too far ahead of ourselves, let's make one simple point which will be elaborated later: developmentally appropriate situations or activities of a role-taking nature—challenging but just within reach—provide excellent opportunities for the growth of the child's cognitive processes (e.g., decentering, inference, internal representation).

The ability to infer the perspective of the other and to take it into account continues to be a crucial tool in school learning in the later grades (and it is not an ability that is acquired equally by all children as they increase in age). Let's take three examples:

(1) Mr. Johnson's third grade is studying the early settling of their state in the West. Mr. Jones asks the children why they think the people would have wanted to move west. To think about and understand the settlers' motives the children have to infer the perspective—the thoughts, motives, feelings—of people in a very different situation from anything the children themselves have directly experienced.

(2) Ms. Grantham's fourth grade is having a simulated election as part of a discussion of the upcoming presidential election. Supporters of each candidate are given a problem: to plan what their spokesperson should say in addressing the "undecideds." Children must think of what arguments would be persuasive—what would make these people who aren't for either candidate favor the one they do.

(3) The sixth grade in a small Vermont town is discussing the Civil War. Some class members see the South simply as "bad" and as totally to blame for the war. The teacher, Mrs. Lane, asks if the class can think of any reasons why the South acted as it did.

For people of all ages the ability to be aware of the perspectives of others underlies any genuine understanding of social systems and customs, of history and political science, of literature, philosophy, and so on. This ability is also an implicit (and often overlooked) basis for the communication skills which the school tries to foster—effective speaking and writing in various contexts and for various audiences. Much of this, of course, is a bit down the road for the young child. Let's return now to where the four- or five-year-old child is in terms of developing role-taking abilities.

The Development of Role-Taking Abilities

It is easy to be fooled into believing the child's ability to engage in taking the perspective of another person is greater than it is. Beth tiptoes when her father says he has a headache. Tim cries when he sees his friend is hurt. Paul persuades his mother that he can go outside by saying that he won't get dirty. All of these actions would seem to be based on the ability to understand what the other feels or thinks, but are they? Beth may be tiptoeing because she has seen Mother do this when Daddy has a headache. Tim may cry when his friend is hurt because his memory of his own past hurts is triggered, which is merely an association. In the case of Paul's clever persuasion tactics, he may not have an understanding of his mother's motivation, which differs from his own, but may merely be remembering that staying clean has been mentioned in the past as a condition for being allowed to go outside. The child can look socially savvy in many ways and yet as far as his actual understanding goes, he is just beginning to construct his social knowledge.

The actions of Beth, Tim, and Paul do not require real *role-taking*. As we have mentioned, this term is used to refer to the ability to take the position of another person and in so doing to infer what his perspective is. To do this, the child must emerge from *egocentrism*, the inability to mentally take the other's position and thus understand his perspective. Piaget (1926), says that in communicating with others the young child, because he is egocentric, tends to assume that his listener automatically understands him perfectly. Likewise, when the child is the listener, he assumes that his own understanding of the message is complete even when it is not. The young child's egocentrism is probably not this extreme in every situation, but there is abundant evidence of this tendency to fail to recognize that other persons may see, feel, or think differently than he does.

Role-taking is not, of course, an all-or-none phenomenon that clicks into the child's cognitive repertoire overnight. Nor is it the result of his simply adding more and more to his store of knowledge about people. As Shantz (1975) puts it:

Understanding others is not merely a matter of "learning more" about people in some quantitative sense; it is organizing what one knows into systems of meaning or belief. What one learns from his experiences with others depends heavily on the structuring of those experiences by the person (p. 266).

Children's Inferences About Others

In looking at the child's emerging role-taking ability, his system of beliefs about the "other," there are several different kinds of other-knowledge that he may have. In an excellent review of the development of social cognition, Carolyn Shantz (1975) divides the types of social inferences as follows: (1) What is the other seeing? (2) What is the other feeling? (3) What is the other thinking? (4) What is the other intending? and (5) What is the other like? To better understand the preschool child's level with respect to such inferences, or deductions about the other, it will be helpful to look at some of the highlights and generalizations from Shantz's extensive review.

To infer what the other is *seeing* is the least "social" of the various types of inference and certain simple levels of visual perspective-taking are acquired early in the preschool period. A child of four can tell that a person on the other side of a barrier from him can't see what he has before him. He realizes that someone seated opposite him sees a book differently. But there are more difficult visual perspective-taking tasks which are later to develop. For example, a late skill to emerge is the child's ability to reverse right and left in figuring out what a person seated opposite him is seeing. As Flavell and his collaborators (1968) report, the child develops the ability to infer with increasing specificity the visual perspective of the other. First, he simply knows whether the other can or cannot see an object from a visual perspective differing from his own. Next, the child develops the ability to determine *how* objects appear from different locations. Still later come the more refined adjustments like the left-right reversal.

Another type of inference is what the other is *feeling*. Young children, even infants, often startle us in their sensitivity to the feelings of those around them. Some of these deceptive "sensitivities" are the result of direct physical effects. For example, Mother is tensed up about breast-feeding her infant; the infant "gets tense" because there is physical difficulty in getting the milk. But even where there is no physical effect on the child, there are many examples of children picking up on the feelings of those around them. This is sometimes called "emotional contagion" or "empathic distress."[1] As the term suggests,

---

[1]Terms such as *empathy, altruism,* and *sympathy* are used in the literature with widely ranging operational definitions and often with little attempt to state what cognitive processes are involved. We have avoided the terms for this reason and in the belief that they may obscure the cognitive issues. That the kinds of development we are describing are closely linked to concepts such as empathy, altruism, sympathy, and kindness is apparent.

this kind of reaction does not involve a role-taking inference about the feelings of the other. It does not depend on an *awareness* of the other's feelings from understanding his or her perspective. The child is affected by another's emotion as a pet might be; such picking up on feelings can take place without the child distinguishing the self from the other and inferring what the other—a separate, different individual—would feel.

So, the preschool child is *affected* by the emotions of others. What other characteristics or abilities are typical of this age level which have bearing on inferences about the feelings of others? By this age the child typically recognizes that certain situations evoke certain emotions. For example, he has formed a generalization that receiving a present is likely to make one happy and that having something grabbed away is likely to make one angry. The child of this age can also tell what emotions a person is feeling from the facial cues (in the usual correspondences he has encountered, e.g., smiling face means happy, tears mean sadness or anger). As Shantz (1975) points out, in its earliest forms this ability need not be more than matching of feeling with cue from association. Nonetheless, it is well to remember what the child can do in this area as well as what he cannot do. He comes to the preschool knowing some things about feelings; he has experienced various emotions himself and can remember in what situations some of these have typically occurred, he can recognize common emotions in others by their facial expressions (either in real life or in pictures), and he has had numerous experiences in which he cannot have helped but notice others reacting to events differently from himself.

One of the crucial difficulties for the young child in role-taking is becoming simultaneously aware of the point of view of the other and his own point of view. Lee C. Lee (1975) illustrates another way in which the difficulty the child has in *decentering* (Piaget's term for noticing and considering more than one aspect of a situation at once) can lead him to inaccurate inferences about another's feeling. A child seeing a person cry will assume he is sad even when the occasion is a birthday party and everyone else is laughing, singing, and giving him gifts. It is very difficult for the young child to *decenter* from one aspect or cue in the situation; his inferences about the affective responses of others are consequently limited.

A third type of social inference which the child has to make is in regard to what the other is *thinking*. Some investigators have found that in laboratory-type situations until children are about six they are not capable of recognizing that another person may view social actions differently from themselves depending on the information that each has (Selman, 1973; Selman and Byrne, 1974). But other observers have noted that laboratory experiments tend to underestimate what children are capable of under optimal circumstances (e.g., Flavell et al., 1968). There are many examples of preschoolers knowing that others have different (less, more) information than they themselves. For instance, children's many questions to adults—different from those they ask other children—are one example of their belief that adults have knowledge that they themselves lack. There are also instances of the other sort. The child shows surprise when a stranger approaches him knowing his name—if the child assumes that everyone knows what he knows, why the surprise? But this knowledge that others know different things or think different things from the self is often intuitive and sketchy, as we have found in general with the thought of the preschool child. The child does not have a clear concept of how he has arrived at his inferences about what the other knows. He would have an even more difficult time, of course, figuring out what the differences in the other's knowledge would mean specificially in the view of a situation. (For example, that when Mom doesn't know with whom Kevin played today, she won't know whom he means if he says, "He hit me and I don't like him anymore.") As we have seen elsewhere above, where further inferential steps are required, the difficulty of the mental task is increased.

The fourth type of social inference for which Shantz summarizes the developmental findings is inferring the *intention* of the other. The child's ability to infer whether an action was accidental or deliberate has been the subject of much interest, largely because of Piaget's (1965) assertion that younger children do not take intention into account in judging moral behavior. He found children judged a hypothetical child's naughtiness on the basis of damages rather than intentions. Refinements on Piaget's original method have raised some doubt about the extent of this failure to take intention into account. At the least, these studies have found children judging acts in terms of intention at a younger age than Piaget asserts (e.g., Chandler, Greenspan, and Barenboim, 1973). However, it does appear that inference about intent increases over the preschool period (Baldwin and Baldwin, 1970; King, 1971).

Underlying the four types of inference discussed to this point (what the other sees, feels, thinks, intends) is inference about *what the other is like.* This area of inference has also been of considerable interest in its own right. In general, as children develop, they note more "psychological" aspects of others—thoughts, feelings, and perceptions—rather than appearance, possessions, and so forth. On tasks requiring explanations of events, younger children produce fewer causal explanations, especially in terms of psychological factors rather than situational (Flapan, 1968). That is, they tend to provide explanations such as "He's crying because his mother left" rather than "He's crying because he's afraid his mother won't come back." Given the lesser verbal skills of the younger children, such results are best taken with a grain of salt, as the investigators themselves are generally quick to point out.

Another group of studies in the general area of inferences about what the other is like have concerned themselves with the classifications the child is making in his social world. What kinds of distinctions does the child make early in approaching the great conglomerations of others? The answers to this question are not only informative for understanding how the child mentally constructs his social world, but also have bearing on role-taking communication situations. For example, along what lines does the child classify people into age categories? Does he notice age differences between himself and children a year or two older or younger than himself? How does he modify his behavior in attempting to communicate with younger children vs. adults vs peers (Shatz and Gelman, 1973)? What are his notions of kinship (Piaget, 1959)? As Lee C. Lee (1975) points out, identifications of social objects start out global and diffuse, lacking defining properties. As she writes, "Daddy is daddy is daddy!" With time and increased social experience, the child starts to differentiate aspects of the person and context. He puts together more systematized notions of what makes up daddy: he's a man, he's big, he goes to work every day, etc. This is true of the child's concept of himself as well. Development proceeds in the direction of more differentiated and systematic concepts of what others (and the self) are like and how various aspects of others make a difference in communicating with them.

We have looked briefly at what sorts of inferences young children make about the other—about what the other is seeing, feeling, thinking, intending, about what the other is like. It is important for teachers to have a developmental perspective to see how for young children many of the skills we take for granted are very difficult or impossible. This is certainly the case in trying to understand the development of children's role-taking and communication skills, which we will be focusing on in the next section of the chapter.

Components of Role-Taking Ability

One of the most helpful sources of understanding what is involved in role-taking and communication skills is the work of John Flavell and his colleagues (1968). One important step which Flavell and his collaborators took was to try to specify the *subskills* that are involved in role-taking and provide a description of the sequence of development. If a child doesn't just wake up one morning able to Take the Perspective of the Other, what are the first signs of his moving in this direction? What are the first levels of knowledge and skill which underlie the full acquisition of role-taking ability? Flavell suggests that the starting point is simply realizing that the possibility of other perspectives exists. He describes five subskills. They are not a straightforward sequence, each coming in full-blown before the next, but the subskills do refer to different levels of role-taking which Flavell was able to identify by determining what children could do on a variety of tasks with role-taking demands. The subskills are as follows:

1. *Existence*—the child knows that there is such a thing as perspective, that what another person sees, thinks, or feels in a given situation does not necessarily coincide with what he himself sees, thinks, or feels.
2. *Need*—the child recognizes that in the particular situation at hand, an analysis of the other's perspective is called for (and would aid in achieving his goal).

3. *Prediction*—the child knows how to carry out this analysis; he is able to accurately discriminate what factors about the other need to be taken into account in communicating.

4. *Maintenance*—the child is capable of maintaining an awareness of what he has inferred to be the perspective of the other, even though it may actively compete with his own.

5. *Application*—the child knows how to translate what he has inferred about his listener's attributes into an effective message.

   Complete acquisition of these abilities is not attained for a long time after the early childhood years. Nonetheless, for the preschool teacher, an awareness of the differing subskills of role-taking ability will help in understanding where individual children have problems in communication situations and other situations where role-taking is called for. Such an awareness should also help the teacher in creating teaching situations which engage these abilities.

The subskills in turn depend on the attainment of other abilities, as Flavell, Shantz, and most workers in the area have noted. Progress on Flavell's subskills (existence, need, prediction, maintenance, and application) is a function of several processes which are undergoing development during childhood. We think three are particularly apparent:

—increasing ability in *drawing inferences* from available information
—increasing capability of *decentering* from one aspect of a situation
—increasing *representational capacities*[2]

The child's development with respect to these processes, we suggest, underlies the attainment of the various components of role-taking skills outlined by Flavell and his collaborators (1968).

In any given situation, the individual's abilities in making inferences, decentering, and representing are called on to a degree. Let's look at an example of how these mental demands are involved in a specific situation.

Jon is playing in the sandpile with Diane and Phillip. Diane repeatedly tries to grab Phillip's digging tool. He yells for her to stop it and when she doesn't, he angrily throws sand in her face. Diane begins to cry. We will focus on Jon's understanding of what has taken place. What inferential, decentering, and representational demands are involved in his interpreting this situation?

First, let's consider the *inferential* demands. An inference is involved in Jon's realizing how Diane and Phillip are feeling, though it is probably not a very difficult one. Diane is crying and rubbing her eyes; Phillip is yelling and

[2]We are aware that these three developing processes are not independent of each other. Decentering, for example, requires some representational ability if one is to simultaneously consider more than one aspect or perspective. However, we do think they refer to sufficiently different processes or dimensions of mental ability that they are useful in viewing role-taking situations.

red in the face. Jon has seen these cues many times and, together with the situational cues, they give him a rather clear picture of the emotional states of Diane and Phillip. Nor is it as difficult as it is in many interpersonal situations to infer the cause of each child's reaction. Diane is crying because Phillip threw sand in her face and that hurts. Phillip is angry because Diane kept taking his toy. These are familiar cause-effect sequences for Jon and it is likely that understanding the connection is within his inferential ability (this would *not* be true of a younger child). The additional causal inference that Diane kept taking Phillip's toy because she wanted it and it was the only one is also on familiar ground for Jon since he has had the usual range of peer experiences. If he were an only child and had not had much experience with other children or shortages of toys, the inference of what Diane was up to could have been more demanding. As it is, he knows this kind of situation (and he knows grabby Diane!) so the inference is again a relatively easy one.

Next, let's think about the *representational demands* of the situation. The events take place before Jon's eyes so he does not have the representational demands of interpreting the events via a verbal account, a series of pictures, etc. Jon does have to use his past experiences to interpret Diane's and Phillip's actions and reactions. Since the situations Jon has seen in the past are very similar to the current one, the mental job of making the link between past experience to the present situation is not as difficult as it would otherwise be. Jon may anticipate at various points what will happen next, which is also based on representation of past experiences. In addition, using these past experiences as a basis, Jon probably constructs some internal representation of Diane's and Phillip's thoughts and feelings. Very little is known about how crude or schematic the child's notion of the feelings of others in such a situation might be. We do know that the representation of psychological states is generally more difficult than representing concrete objects. An additional demand on Jon's representational competence is holding *two* such representations in mind at once.

What are the *decentering demands* in the current situation? As we have said, decentering involves simultaneously considering more than one aspect of a situation, for example, not just Phillip's sand-throwing but Diane's toy-grabbing, not just how Phillip feels but how Diane feels as well. Such a double focus is difficult for the young child, but it is likely to be *less* difficult if he is not directly involved. It is easier for the child to decenter enough to see both perspectives when one of them is not his own. (Easier for adults too!) We should remember, though, that even with impersonal situations such as considering both the length *and* the density of rows of pennies in judging the equivalence of number, children have difficulty considering multiple aspects of a situation (see Chapter 6 for discussion of decentration). It follows that mentally coordinating the perspectives of two participants in an interpersonal conflict *is* taxing for the child; however, it is not as taxing as it would be if he were one of the participants.

The Teacher and Children's Role-Taking

It may be useful for the teacher to think of how each of these three types of mental demands (decentering, inferring, and representing) are involved to a greater or lesser degree in what a child is having to do in any role-taking or communication situation. These mental demands are always involved in a role-taking situation, but they are not equally demanding across all situations. For example, in the case of inferring, the degree of difficulty or complexity varies markedly from one activity to another. There are numerous factors which might make a difference. Here are three examples:

CASE 1   (How explicit are the "instructions" to engage in role-taking? How many inferential steps are required?)

On a visit to an elderly aunt, Mother says to Jane just before knocking on the door, "Aunt Lucy is old and doesn't hear very well. You should speak loudly so that she can hear what you're saying." Notice the difference between Mother's saying this and her saying "Aunt Lucy is old. You should speak so that she can hear what you're saying." In the second case more of an inference is called for on the part of the child. She must infer that being old would make it harder for Aunt Lucy to hear and that increasing the volume of her speech is the way to offset this difficulty (rather than the speed, the pitch, etc.). If Mother hadn't spoken to Jane on the subject at all, Jane would have had to make the further inference that there is a *need* to adjust (perhaps on the basis of Aunt Lucy's appearance, misunderstanding, etc.). This would be much more difficult.

CASE 2   (How directly or overtly do the cues convey the situation?)

Cassie says to Beth, her face red and upset, "I don't want to be your friend anymore. I don't like you." Beth can infer that Cassie is speaking in anger with more ease than when her older brother says, in a calm voice (after Beth has angered him), "You can't draw very well, can you, Beth?"

CASE 3   (How "overt" and/or concrete is what the child must infer?)

Tom is looking at a book and sees that a boy in the story is wearing a heavy coat, mittens, and a hat. He infers that it is cold. He turns the page to a picture of a man looking at a broken car and scowling. Tom is likely to have more difficulty inferring the person's emotion than he did in inferring the cold in the previous picture. He may say that the person is mean, for example, or that he is old (due to the wrinkled brow). On the whole, where the task demand involves thinking in terms of psychological causality, the child is likelier to have difficulty than when it is physical causality which must be inferred. The exception is in cases where the correspondences between the cues and the psychological states are so straightforward and familiar that even the young child can make correct inferences of the thoughts and feelings; e.g., a smile means the person is happy. As Shantz (1975) has pointed out, such cases might even be called association rather than inference—smile = happy.

These examples illustrate how inferential demands on the child vary with a number of factors. The same range exists in the case of decentering or representing. This awareness should help the teacher to think through the demands of a given situation. With these considerations in mind, she is equipped to learn more about the child's thinking from the situations she sees him grappling with. She is also equipped to (1) think of ways she could profitably give the child assistance in dealing with role-taking situations he encounters and (2) design learning situations which will be appropriate to the child's level, and useful for his growth. With respect to inference, for example, the teacher could proceed by *reducing the level of the inferential demands* on the child in some way. Or she could go on to *highlight for the child the nature of the inference,* specifying it or assisting the child in doing so. Let's look at some examples of how thinking about the cognitive demands on the child guides the teacher's actions, first in a spontaneous situation and then in several planned activities.

Considering the Cognitive Demands in Handling a Classroom Conflict

Mark and David are playing and have a falling out. Mark tells David, as he often has in the past, that he doesn't like him anymore and isn't his friend. David is very upset. The teacher, Jeanne, thinks that it might help David if he recognized that Mark is speaking from temporary anger. She realizes that just telling David this is not likely to be very effective, nor to help him in future encounters. The following interaction between her and David takes place.

After establishing that Mark has told David that he's no longer his friend, Jeanne says, "David, I can see why that would hurt your feelings." Encouraging David to reconstruct past experiences which may have a bearing on the current one, Jeanne continues, "Has Mark ever said to you before that you weren't friends anymore?" David replies, "Yeah, he said it to me when we were at the duck pond." "Earlier this week," Jeanne says. "Yes, I remember that. Did you stop being friends then?" David shakes his head, "No, we got friends again." Then, remembering his current distress, he wails, "He says he doesn't like me and won't be friends now." Jeanne says "Hmm, so Mark said he wasn't ever gonna be your friend again and then he was. I wonder what made that happen." David, still staring disconsolately at Mark, makes no reply.

Jeanne decides to move for the moment to another aspect of the situation which later will link to what she and David have discussed. She says, "Let's think about what happened here and what Mark is thinking." She engages David in observing Mark's facial expression, etc., and in describing what took place. With attention focused on these more specific, objective aspects, David is able to identify Mark's state as anger ("He did get real mad.").

Jeanne's aim is to focus David's attention on inferring what a person is feeling from cues—situational, verbal, facial, etc. Since David is young, upset, and inexperienced in peer quarrels, Jeanne judges this interaction to be sufficient and doesn't try to get him to go further. The cause-effect connection she articulates herself, hoping to leave David something to think about. She says, "Sometimes when people are very mad, they say things they don't mean for very long. I wonder if Mark won't be changing his mind pretty soon. And I'll be seeing you two playing together like always."

Jeanne's interaction with David helps in several ways. The comfort of her presence and her reassuring it's-not-the-end-of-the-world tone lend emotional support to David. The cognitive thrust of Jeanne's conversation with David is in (1) getting him to call to mind an instance in which the social partner has said something which wasn't true or didn't remain in force for long and (2) encouraging him to infer from cues (facial, situational) in the current situation that this is a case where someone is angry. She herself articulates the connection, confining her inquiry to other mental demands on a more limited level. In asking David about an earlier incident when Mark spoke in anger, Jeanne is encouraging the application of past experience to a new situation. The representational demand in this case is not excessive. With her inquiry about cues in Mark's appearance and behavior, Jeanne is trying to provide some experience (and a model) in observing relevant cues as a basis for making an inference. She sticks to the *observable* as a basis for deducing how Mark feels. She is very explicit in asking about how Mark looks and how he acted, not leaving it to David to realize the *need* for inference, which she judges to be too taxing a cognitive demand in this situation for this child.

The teacher does not bring to each new situation a ready formula for interacting with the child. No two situations are the same; in each case the participants, the events, the emotions involved present the teacher with unique decisions. One of the indispensable elements of the teacher's effectiveness is, of course, sensitivity to the emotional needs of the children. We are suggesting that it is also very important for the teacher to be tuned in to the cognitive demands of the situation in hand. This awareness will also be an ingredient in the teacher's educational planning.

Activating Cognitive Demands Through Planned Activities

Let's look at several activities which Jeanne and Denise planned to give the children experiences with decentering and inferring and representing the perspective of another.

Activity 1. What do the mouse and the giraffe see?

Several objects are placed before the group, a chair, a toy car, etc. The teacher engages the children in a discussion such as the following: "Let's think about what a mouse is like. Can you show me with your hands about how big a mouse is. Hmm—like that, eh? Well, let's think about a mouse being under this chair. Let's try to think about what the *mouse* could see. Could he see the legs of the chair? . . . Do you think he could see the part you sit on, the top of the seat? Show me what part of the seat he could see, Jimmy. Now, how about this tiny toy car. How do you think it would look to a mouse or an ant? . . . What is something that would look small to a mouse?" The children suggest ideas. The teacher continues, "Now what's a very large animal? A giraffe, an elephant, a dinosaur—ok, let's think of any of those. What do you think a giraffe would see if he were standing near the chair?" and so on.

Reasoning: The teacher's choice of this activity involved several considerations. They chose a perspective-taking situation in which the cognitive demands are limited in several respects. (1) The inferences involved are of another's *visual perspective,* which is on the whole easier than inferring feelings or motives, particularly when the predictions which are called for are not the more highly subtle type (such as left-right reversals) but the straightforward can-he-see-it-or-not variety. (2) As Flavell's work has indicated, a large part of the difficulty is inferring that someone's perspective is different, that there is *need* for perspective-taking. This is why the teachers have chosen size as the characteristic which is linked to what is seen, and have used creatures of drastically different size. In addition, the teacher draws the children's attention to the difference in size and explicitly wonders what difference if any that will make in what the creature sees. This explicitness reduces the cognitive demand to a more manageable level: the child has to think about what it would be like to be the small mouse, but he is helped to notice that things may look different for the mouse. For the children who are not able to predict this visual perspective themselves, hearing and discussing other children's predictions may create the kind of discrepancy which will lead to reduction of egocentrism.

Activity 2. Communication game: Helping your partner pick the right card
(Children play this game individually with the teacher as their partner.)

The teacher sits on one side of a screen and the child on the other. The child is shown that the teacher has the same cards on her side as he has in front of him. He's told that his job is to pick a card and then tell the teacher everything she'll need to know to pick the same card from her set. The procedure, which is like that employed in much of the research on children's communication skills (e.g., Krauss and Glucksberg, 1969), is designed to maximize the need for effective verbal communication. To increase the value of the game as a learning experience, the feature of feedback from the listener (the teacher) is added.[3]

The game can be played with cards varying along any dimensions the teacher chooses. In this case Jeanne designs sets which vary in features which

[3]The game is a classroom form of the procedure employed in Copple, Coon, and Lipscomb (1977), which was found to be an effective format for giving children experience with various kinds of listener feedback.

she knows the children are familiar with: color, size, position on the card, and geometric shape (circle, square, and triangle). Thus the difficulty is not in knowing how to describe features, but in recognizing and taking into account what the listener needs to know. There are eight cards in each set, as shown in Figure 7-1. As you can see, an adequate description of a card would include some mention of each of three features, for example, size, color, and shape in the first set—"The big black square."

Figure 7-1.
Two sample sets of cards for communication game.

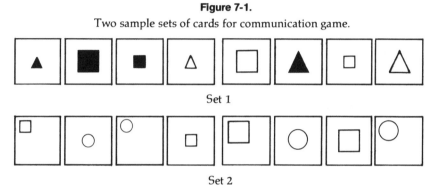

Set 1

Set 2

Children often describe their selected card more minimally—"The black one." The teacher gives the child some form of feedback which indicates the inadequacy of his description—"There are several black ones. I don't know which one to pick." Along with this verbal feedback, the teacher will in some cases show the child the one she has picked (she'll pick the wrong one—having surreptitiously peeked at the child's choice—until the child gives her more information). She asks the child to try again to tell her what she needs to know to pick the right card. There are many variations of feedback which the teacher can give, depending on the level of the child. Showing the child her wrong choice is a very direct form of feedback and has been found to result in an improvement in the specificity of the child's descriptions (Copple, Coon, and Lipscomb, 1977). But this is also the easiest form of feedback for the child to respond to. As the child becomes more adept at supplying additional information after seeing the teacher's wrong choice, the teacher can try more indirect feedback. For example, she might pause as she looks over the choices saying to herself, "Hmm, I wonder which one he means" or "Let's see, I'm not sure I can tell which card he's picked if all I know is that it's a square."
Reasoning: The young child, as we have noted, has difficulty with communication tasks which depend on his recognizing his listener's perspective as different from his own. In this game the child must *decenter* from his own perspective (that of knowing which card he has picked) to that of the teacher (that of needing specific descriptions—"little white triangle"). Since the cards vary in a number of ways, the child must also decenter from a particular feature in order to give an adequate message.

The kind of feedback the teacher gives in this game is simply a more systematic and focused form of the kind of feedback children get from the environment and by which they progress from egocentrism to communicative competence. As we noted in discussing peer interchange, when someone doesn't know what you're talking about because of the way you say it, you are jarred into further attempts to get your message across. A situation which removes possibilities such as pointing requires the child to think of what needs to be said, with listener feedback letting him know when he has not succeeded in giving the listener sufficient information.

Activity 3. Easel story: Michelle tries to join other children in play

The teacher tells the children a story accompanied by simple, hand-drawn pictures. In the story a little girl, Michelle, wants someone to play with. The first group she approaches are building with blocks. Trying to join in, she picks up a block from a stack and begins to make a new stack. The children are angry because the block she moves was the top of *their* tower and they yell at her to go away. Several incidents of this kind occur and Michelle gets progressively more and more upset. The teacher's questions for each situation are about what Michelle wanted and what the other children she approached thought she was doing. Ways that Michelle could have avoided the misleading communication are discussed as they arise, but most of the teacher's questions focus on who is thinking what and why.

Reasoning: This story has a strong role-taking message. Each event is described though Michelle's eyes and also through the eyes of the other children. The cause of the problem is the failure of each party to take the other party's perspective into account; the children in the story do not try to understand the source of each others' actions. For the children in the class *decentering* is involved in trying to move from one perspective to the other in each episode—first, they see what Michelle is trying to do, then they are told how the other children see this, then back to Michelle, and so on. This shifting may be helpful in building up the child's ability to *represent* two perspectives simultaneously, that is, to keep one in mind when confronted with another. Stories about the kind of situations children face, but removed from their own individual situations, can often be helpful. They are more likely to be able to see both perspectives when not involved and in a story such as this the different perspectives are described dramatically and highlighted by teacher questions.

Role-Taking: Summary

Role-taking has been viewed as central in the child's social development from the standpoint of theory (e.g., Flavell et al., 1968; Selman, 1971, 1973; Shantz, 1975) and from the standpoint of the facilitation of social understanding and development (e.g., Copple, Moore, and Warman, 1979; Elardo,

1977). The young child is limited in his ability to infer the perspective of the other and to use this understanding in communication. Underlying progress in this ability is the child's development in decentering, in making inferences, and in representation. The classroom is an environment with excellent potential for developing these abilities. Peer interaction plays a substantial role in confronting the child with others' perspectives. Sometimes these peer encounters require some involvement from the teacher (because, for example, of the endangerment of life and limb, the great distress of one or more parties, or the breaking of classroom rules); on such occasions the teacher's awareness of the cognitive demands of the situation is as important as her sensitivity to the emotional needs of the children. Awareness of the cognitive demands of a situation on the part of the teacher should guide her interactions with children in spontaneous classroom situations and her planning of activities for the social-affective curriculum.

The teacher's strategies for facilitating children's social-affective growth can be further developed by recognizing the importance of the classroom in improving interpersonal problem-solving skills.

Interpersonal Problem-Solving

Learning to Think Through a Problem

Herb and George are reading together in the quiet area. Laurie and Amy, excited by the class activity of marching to music which has just ended, pick up cymbals and tambourine to "play band." George tells them to be quiet. Laurie replies, "No, we're a band. We have to make noise!" George starts to get up and push Laurie, but sees Denise watching him and instead says to her, "They won't go away. I asked them to first." Denise says, "Do you still want them to be quiet?" (The boys nod their heads emphatically.) "And you, Laurie and Amy, are you still wanting to play your instruments?" "Yes!" the girls shout. "Then I guess we have a problem we have to talk over," Denise says and asks the children to sit down with her on the floor for a few minutes to work something out.

Laurie begins describing her grievance immediately; "He wants us to be quiet (pointing at George) but we can't 'cause we're a band." "Do you know why he wants you to be quiet?" Denise asks the girls. Amy responds, "It hurts his ears. He's a baby." "Is that it?" Denise inquires, "Does the noise make your ears hurt, George?" "No! I'm trying to read this book!" "So what? We aren't stopping you," Laurie contends. Denise turns to George and Herb, "Hmm, help us to understand this, boys. Don't you read with your eyes?"

Now Herb speaks up, "Yeah, but the noise is bad when we're trying to read. I can't think!" "Well," Laurie says, "they could cover their ears." "What do you think about that idea, Herb? George?"

Herb refuses this idea because he wouldn't be able to turn pages. Denise encourages the children to think of other solutions to the problem. In one form or another, the following suggestions are made:

1. That the girls do something else besides playing instruments (Herb's suggestion)
2. That the girls play instruments that make less noise (George's suggestion)
3. That the girls play outside in the hall (George's suggestion)
4. That the boys do something besides reading (Laurie's suggestion) or, (following Denise's ascertaining that the boys still want to read) that they move somewhere else
5. That the boys go home (Amy's giggling suggestion)

In some cases objections are made to particular suggestions as they are offered (often rather nonspecific objections such as "No way!" or "You're crazy!" which Denise attempts to get the protestors to clarify). More evaluation of the suggestions will follow, but Denise at this point wants to encourage the children to continue suggesting alternatives. In this effort she makes comments such as, "That's one thing we could do. Can anyone think of another idea?"

When the above suggestions have all been offered, Denise raises some of them for more consideration. In some cases, she directs the children's attention to problems they might not have considered. For example, when the suggestion is made that the girls play outside in the hall, it meets with a favorable reaction; the novelty appeals to the girls. Denise comments, "That would help Herb and George to have more quiet. But let's think a bit more. Is there any other problem with that idea. What would be near to the place where the girls would be." The children remember nearby classrooms and they all laugh about how Mrs. Harris likes to have it real quiet for story time.

Denise realizes that there isn't time for a full evaluation of each suggestion and that the children will lose interest if she tries to get them to evaluate ideas that they find very unappealing. She also chooses which ideas to discuss further by thinking of the alternatives which have particularly interesting implications for interpersonal problem-solving.

Let's follow the children's evaluation of one of the alternatives. When the hallway is ruled out as a place for the band to play and the suggestion is made that the girls move someplace elsewhere within the room, Laurie and Amy do not immediately reject this possibility. This solution seems to have some viability, and at the same time seems to involve a number of problems which will require some challenging cause-effect thinking and role-taking on the part of the children. So Denise finds this alternative a good one for further discussion. Generally the children overlook difficulties with possible places initially, as we would expect of young children with their tendency to center on one aspect of a given situation. For example, the boys spot an area which is far away from their reading area—the area near the water table. Laurie, no more capable of decentering than the boys but having a different vested interest, exclaims, "Yech!" "What's the problem?" Denise asks, "You don't seem to like that idea." "It's all wet," Laurie says. To establish what Laurie is thinking and to encourage her verbalizing the cause-effect relation so the others can see her point, Denise pursues this statement, "Why is being wet a problem?" "We'll slip and we'll get our feet wet." "Oh, I see, so you think that area wouldn't work too well for a marching band. Where else might be better?"

The art area is the next place suggested. Denise is curious to see if the boys will be able to recognize that the children in the art area will have the same sort of problem they themselves have just complained of. She inquires, "Does anyone see any problem with Laurie and Amy moving over there?" No one indicates that they do. Denise says, "Do you think it will be OK with Chris, Todd, and Molly (the children who are working in the art area)?" Making the problem still more specific, but still trying to encourage the children doing the thinking, she adds, "Imagine you're sitting at the art table. Now imagine there's a band playing nearby (she shows through gesture the playing of cymbals)." Laurie says she thinks it would be nice. "I like bands," she says. But George winces. With his recent experience of cymbals crashing near his ears, he is able to represent what it would be like to be drawing under the same conditions. He doesn't verbalize this at a specific level ("Ugh"), but from his facial expression Denise sees a manifestation that George is sensing the perspective of the others (one of the frequent cases in which role-taking demands are involved in evaluating alternatives in interpersonal problem situations).

The children have stuck with this problem-solving session for quite a long time, so after the next suggestion is made and discussed (a reasonably remote corner where only the guinea pig's ears will have band music inflicted upon them), Denise begins to bring the discussion to a close. "That idea seems OK with you, boys? And you, Laurie and Amy? (They nod.) It seems like a good idea. You all did a good job of thinking of a way to solve that problem. Now Herb and George can enjoy their book and Laurie and Amy can enjoy making music."

The children in this situation had a problem. Denise's decision to work with them on it was two-edged: (1) she decided not to solve the problem for them and (2) she decided not leave them alone to solve it without assistance. Both of these options, of course, are valid under some circumstances. The first option: Denise could have provided a solution; for example, she could have asked the girls to move to another area of the room. There will be times when it is advisable for teachers to make a given decision unilaterally, either because time is short—teachers cannot always take the time as Denise did here—or because of the nature of the situation. The situation may require at least a short-run solution from the teacher herself, because of a child's emotional distress, because of the disruptiveness to an ongoing activity, etc. Even in these cases, the teacher usually provides the reasoning which underlines her solution—"You'll need to take the band to the corner where no one is reading or working on something, Amy and Laurie. This is the quiet area and we need to keep it quiet enough for reading." In the situation above, however, Denise concluded that there was time for a discussion and none of the parties was too distressed to be able to work the problem through. In addition, she saw this as a situation with multiple alternatives within the children's capacity to generate and evaluate.

If Denise felt that this was a situation which was conducive to the children's "working through," she could have taken the second option (above): letting the children go at it on their own rather than engaging in an interaction with them. This hands-off course of action also would be an appropriate decision in some circumstances. As we mentioned earlier in describing the value of peer interchange, children gain from being confronted directly with the need to accommodate to the perspective of a peer. Valuable interchanges often take place when children must deal with each other. If the teacher invariably entered such conflicts (even assuming this were feasible) the children would never get the opportunity to practice their problem-solving skills independently. Overdependence on the teacher as a mediator might be an outcome. But on an occasional basis, children can benefit from the teacher's involvement. She may be a sounding board, a buffer for hot tempers; her questions and comments provide a model of problem-solving strategies. She engages the children in each of the problem-solving processes or steps and activates their cause-effect thinking. In on-the-spot problems between children, a balance of involvement and standing back is desirable. Given the fact that the teacher sees the advantage of getting involved in working through problems with children *some* of the time, her decision about engagement in a particular situation is affected by such factors as the children's willingness to accept her assistance and the degree to which the individuals involved tend to work through problems independently as opposed to seeking teacher assistance. Denise concluded that in this case (the standoff between the grand tradition of John Philip Sousa and the well-respected tradition of the library hush), all signals were go. As she decided to attempt to do some problem-solving with the children, what *specifically* was Denise attempting to do?

One way of looking at the teacher's interaction with the children is to look at the various components or steps of problem-solving skill which she encourages in them. In our example, Denise works with the children in (1) identifying the problem, (2) generating alternative solutions, and (3) evaluating the alternatives.

Identifying the problem may seem redundant when the children are at each other's throats over a grievance. They already know they have a problem, right? Right and wrong. Herb knows the girls' noise is making it hard to read—that's his notion of the problem. Laurie knows she wants to play her instruments and George is trying to stop her—that's her idea of the problem. Nearly always, as in this situation, the child's idea of an interpersonal problem is one-sided. Often the child's notion of the problem is very undefined as well, if not incorrect.

Denise's initial questions were aimed at getting the problem identified. She wanted to know about the individual children's construction of the problem and she wanted to get both sides of the issue brought out. In the process of achieving these goals, Denise's behaviors also provide a model of behaviors which are effective in identifying/clarifying a problem between individuals. An example is her asking the boys for clarification of their perspective. She asks the girls if they know why George wants them to be quiet. When confronted with this question, which may not have occurred to her at all, Amy voices her own construction: that the noise "hurts" George's ears. Through Denise's questions, Laurie and Amy see that this isn't quite the way the boys see it; they also learn that you can get a better idea of what someone else thinks the problem is by asking them.

Denise realizes that young children cannot be expected to engage in such discussions *ad infinitum*. After minimal steps to ensure that the problem has been identified, she proceeds to invite the children's thoughts on how the problem can be solved. Not every step of the problem-solving process can be the focus of lengthy discussion in a single session. In this situation Denise opts for less discussion in identifying the problem, which is relatively straightforward here, and more in generating and evaluating alternative solutions.

Generating possible solutions to a problem is a critical part of the problem-solving process which Denise encourages here. As the research of Spivack and Shure (1974) indicates, children vary widely in the quantity and quality of alternative solutions they suggest for a given interpersonal situation. Children who are better adjusted in their classroom behavior suggest a wider range of alternatives. In the example, Denise encourages the children to suggest as many alternatives as they can. One child's idea is often triggered by the suggestion made by another child. Denise wants the children to have experiences with "brainstorming," with the free flow of ideas, in on-the-spot situations as well as in planned activities. She continues to elicit ideas which show children that in solving a problem it is a good idea to go on beyond the first alternative that comes into your head. This strategy prevails across all curriculum areas. The general classroom atmosphere of all-ideas-welcome underlies the teacher's being able here to promote in the children a feeling of freedom to suggest any idea. Children over the course of the year learn that when the teacher says things like "That's one way; can you think of another way we could do it?" she isn't rejecting Idea 1. They learn that this is just the way to go about finding a good solution to a problem.

The teacher also plays a role in encouraging the children's *evaluating of possible solutions*. She encourages them to think of what each solution will be like when implemented. Imagining the outcome of an action calls on the child to mentally construct the event. For example, if you say to the child, "What would happen if I put up my umbrella in this crowd?" the child must mentally represent this situation. It is the same here. Laurie contructs a mental representation of what it would be like to be marching in the area near the water table. George has an internal representation of how it would be if he were working in the art area and someone played an instrument nearby. Mentally representing (in whatever form) the outcome of a given alternative is indispensable to evaluating the solution.

Let's suppose the child does form a representation—what else is involved in evaluation? Sometimes the child will quickly see a problem or an undesirable feature of an envisioned outcome, as Laurie does when she says, "Yech!. ...We'll slip." Sometimes in centering on one aspect of a situation the child will overlook problems. Another way of saying this is that she will not look at the solution in relation to various criteria. This is why Denise sometimes tried to get the children to think further when they saw no problem with a given solution initially. In some cases, she mentioned other criteria that the children were not considering, such as whether anyone else would be affected by a proposed move of the band. Through questions or comments which extend the children's evaluation, the teacher is giving them an encounter with additional criteria to consider; e.g., it anyone else affected? Even more important, she's encouraging the tendency and the ability to think through the desirability of a solution in relation to *all* relevant factors.

Research of Effects of Interpersonal Problem-Solving

Myrna Shure and George Spivack have done extensive work on the relationship of the ability to think through real-life problems and behavioral adjustment. They began by doing background studies to determine the kinds of thinking skills lacking in poorly adjusted individuals. They first worked with adults, adolescents, and preadolescents (Shure and Spivack, 1970; Spivack and Levine, 1963). Then studies were done with four-to-five-year-olds to relate behavioral adjustment in classroom situations to the ability to solve interpersonal problems. *The Preschool Interpersonal Problem-Solving (PIPS) Test* was devised to tap each child's ability to name alternative solutions to real-life problems presented by the interviewer (e.g., how to obtain a toy from another child). Children who were judged as well-adjusted in the classroom were markedly superior to their less-adjusted peers in thinking of more relevant alternative solutions to such problems. In the classroom, these children were able to wait their turn, were less aggressive towards their peers, and were not highly emotional when things did not go their way. They were more likely to be liked by peers and to show more autonomy and initiative in their classroom behavior. It should be noted that, although there is a correlation between "alternative thinking" ability (as measured by the PIPS) and intelligence (as measured by the Stanford-Binet Intelligence Test), classroom behavioral adjustment is predicted much better by the measures of alternative thinking than by intelligence. One of the major contributions of the Spivack and Shure work is the evidence provided that the abilities involved in *interpersonal* problem-solving (even in interview situations, as opposed to on the spot) are not identical to those involved in solving *impersonal* intellectual tasks.

After these studies had confirmed the authors' notion that there was a relationship between behavioral adjustment and interpersonal problem-solving skills, studies were planned to develop such skills in children and assess improvement in behavioral adjustment. At the completion of this program, the children had improved markedly in their classroom behavior through gains made in interpersonal problem-solving skills (Shure and Spivack, 1972, 1973; Shure, Spivack, and Gordon, 1972).

In their training of problem-solving skills the teachers in the Shure and Spivak project worked with children in both on-the-spot situations and in planned activities. Presenting children with a hypothetical problem to solve was a frequent technique, which we have found useful as well. There are both advantages and disadvantages in comparison with on-the-spot discussions. Emotions are cooler, which may diminish the interest in solving the problem but also allows for more thorough and objective thought than in the heat of the moment. Since the teacher can pose the problem situations she chooses, the children will be presented with challenging but developmentally appropriate problems with elements with which the teacher wants to confront the children. For example, Denise may engage small groups of children in an activity in which they are selecting gifts for members of a hypothetical family. The children's role-taking abilities will be called on and Denise will have the opportunity to learn more about their skills (or lack of skills) in this kind of task. There is need in the social-affective curriculum for guided problem-solving opportunities of this kind. In these encounters children have the chance to strengthen and expand their skills in various problem-solving processes, which they can use in the real-life situations they meet. These real problems remain the crucial proving-ground for problem-solving skills.

In looking at the classroom situation with Herb, George, Laurie, and Amy we saw a situation in which the teacher decided to deal with a problem on the spot. The children were at an impasse and were willing to think about a solution. Even in a classroom where such talking through is common, children are not always receptive; nor do teachers always have time for extended dialogues. Another kind of teacher decision about a real classroom problem is to discuss it with the children at a later point as a group (or perhaps in smaller groupings). You may recall that in Chapter 1 the teachers were considering having a group discussion of the block-monopolizing problem. The major benefits to such a decision are (1) that the teachers and the children find out what the class reactions to the problem are, (2) that the problem is dealt with as a general class problem removed from particular individuals, and (3) that the children have an experience with group problem-solving. Let's look at such a discussion in action. The session we will examine was based on a problem situation much like that discussed in Chapter 1.[4] The boys were always in the block corner and did not allow the girls to play there. One day a few girls complained to the teachers, who had been aware that there was a problem

[4]The script is an edited version of a discussion held between Eloise Warman and her class at the Child Care Research Center, Educational Testing Service, Princeton, New Jersey, in February 1978.

brewing. The teachers decided to have a group discussion of the problem that day. We find them just settling down to discuss.

Teacher:	Here's the problem. Girls are telling me that they don't get a chance to play with blocks because the boys are always playing with them and won't let them join.
Sam:	Good!
Teacher:	How about this? Suppose the girls would play with the blocks and no boys allowed?
Boys:	(a roar of protest)
Teacher:	Tim and Randy are making a sound that really sounds like they don't like that idea.
Marie:	I've got an idea. Everybody plays with everything.
Teacher:	Well, Marie, that's the rule we have now, but why do we have a problem?
	(no response)
Teacher:	Kids, isn't that the way the school is run now—that anyone can play with anything they want?
Linda:	I've got an idea. If the girls want to play with the blocks, they can just take them.
Teacher:	(repeating Linda's suggestion so all can hear): If the girls want to play with blocks, they can just take them from the boys' building.
Sam:	I'll play army on them.
Linda:	Then we would do it back to you.
Sally:	(makes a quiet suggestion inaudible to the group)
Teacher:	Sally said we should make the boys go home early so the girls can play with the blocks when the boys aren't here. Is that what you said, Sally?
Boys:	Roar! (their protest noise)
Teacher:	Do you think we should let the girls go out for recess at a different time, so the boys can build, and when the boys are at recess the girls can build?
Boys:	Roar!
Girls:	Yes!
Stephen:	I got an idea, I got an idea, Eloise.
Teacher:	What, Stephen?
Stephen:	The boys can use the big blocks and the girls can use those little blocks.
Sharon:	I don't want to do that (shaking her head with conviction).
Teacher:	Look at Sharon. She's doesn't seem to like that idea at all! Stephen says the boys can play with the big blocks and the girls can play with the little blocks.
Tim:	No way!
Sharon:	Girls play with big blocks and boys play with little blocks.
Teacher:	Hmm.
Randy:	No, I'm not gonna play with any small blocks. I'm just gonna play with big fat blocks.
Teacher:	Why just big fat blocks?

Randy:	'Cause I like them. You can go under 'em.
Stephen:	I can make a big block out of the little blocks. . .for the girls to play with.
Teacher:	Is that a good idea? (Seeing Sharon shaking her head) No, Sharon doesn't like that either. How about this: The first free play for boys in the big blocks and the second free play for girls in the big blocks.
Sharon:	No, first girls and then boys.
Teacher:	First girls and then boys.
Boys:	No! Roar!
	I hate that!
Teacher:	Would that give the girls a chance to play? They're saying they don't get a chance to play with the blocks now. (pause—no reply)
Stephen:	Yes! They can! I got an idea. I got an idea.
Teacher:	Stephen has another idea.
Stephen:	How about the boys share the little blocks and the girls share the big blocks and the little blocks?
Randy:	We wouldn't have enough then.
Teacher:	Stephen, that sounds like a reasonable idea, but that's how it is supposed to be now and boys seem to use the blocks all the time and the girls are complaining that they don't get a chance.
Bill:	Eloise, I'll let Molly play with me in the blocks.
Teacher:	You'll let Molly play with you?
Sharon:	That's not fair, he just wants *little* girls.
Teacher:	Why isn't it fair, Sharon?
Sharon:	Because the *other* girls don't get to play.
Peter:	I got one idea.
Teacher:	Peter's got an idea. Let's hear it.
Peter:	The girls can play with the big blocks only on two days.
Teacher:	Hey, listen, we come to school four days a week. If the girls play with blocks on two days (holding up two fingers), that gives the boys two other days (showing two other fingers) to play with blocks. Does that sound fair?
Children:	Yeah! No! No way!

The discussion continues. This is undeniably an ambitious undertaking but one which is rich in benefits. The willingness to engage children in such discussions is based on several premises.

First, the teachers think that the children benefit from working through a problem as a group. This can help in several ways. In hearing each others' ideas, they think of new ones. And they are forcefully confronted with opposing viewpoints. We see both of these advantages operating in the discussion about the block corner.

Let's take as an example Stephen's idea of making big blocks out of little blocks for the girls to play with. This suggestion is made when the girls reject the idea of being confined to play with little blocks only. Stephen's idea involves some good thinking and some important realizations. He has apparently taken into account the girls' rejection of small-blocks-only. Grasping that they want "large block capacity" and that the boys do not want to yield the large blocks, Stephen thinks of a way to use the little-valued small blocks to supply the need. His idea has little appeal for the girls, but it is impressive problem-solving all the same. There is a solution of a physical problem in Stephen's thinking of putting small blocks together to form large blocks. On an interpersonal level he is responding to the desires of two parties with an alternative which takes both sides into account—a genuine, albeit undesirable, compromise. It is the teacher's belief that Stephen is more likely to do this kind of thinking in a situation where (1) he hears other ideas which he modifies and (2) he is confronted with two parties wanting two imcompatible outcomes and the need to satisfy both.

Another reason for the teachers' decision to have these group problem-solving sessions is to increase their own awareness of what the children think. The children's views and suggestions are input to teacher decision-making about the class problem. This is based on the belief that what children think about some problem in the classroom is important to what's decided.

The teachers also see benefit in the children experiencing what a community making a decision is really like. You and your friends think you have a great solution and those people over there don't like it a bit. Sometimes the way something is said makes all the difference to whether it's accepted or rejected. And so on. The rough-and-tumble atmosphere of *real* group decision-making, the teachers believe, should be allowed to be a part of the child's experience from the start.

Summary: Problem Solving

Among the most valuable skills which a human being can have are problem-solving skills, particularly with respect to interpersonal situations. An example of a classroom problem shows the value of teacher involvement in encouraging the children to *identify the problem, generate possible solutions,* and *evaluate solutions.* Research by Spivack and Shure confirms the relationship between interpersonal problem-solving skills and behavioral adjustment. Like Spivack and Shure, we have found value both in hypothetical problem-solving activities and in real-life situations. Another method for working with problem-solving skills is through group discussion, which has its own particular advantages and limitations.

Summary

The child comes to the classroom with a history of living in a social context, but he or she has a long way to go in acquiring the knowledge and abilities which form this universe. The social-affective domain has important status in the curriculum for the child's development as a thinker. In addition to its importance in the life of the child, it is an area that holds significant cognitive challenges for children. The chapter focuses on the cognitive foundations of social-affective understandings and on the classroom environment conducive to educating the young thinker.

We describe such a classroom environment in terms of basing decisions on goals for the child and on the characteristics of the preschool child's thought and social development. Two areas are discussed as central to social understanding and competence: the development of role-taking abilities and the development of problem-solving in interpersonal situations. The applicability of these areas to teachers' curriculum planning and classroom strategies is illustrated through examples.

Suggested Resources

Bingham, A. *Improving Children's Facility in Problem Solving* (New York: Teachers College, 1958).

Elardo, P. T. "Project AWARE: A School Program to Facilitate Social Development of Children." In *Social Development in Childhood: Day-Care Programs and Research*, edited by R. A. Webb (Baltimore, Md.: John Hopkins University Press, 1977).

Elardo, P. T., and Cooper, M. *Project AWARE: A Handbook for Teachers* (Menlo Park, Calif.: Addison-Wesley, 1977).

Emmerich, W. "Structure and Development of Personal-Social Behaviors in Preschool Settings," In *Head Start Longitudinal Study* (Princeton, N.J.: Educational Testing Service, 1971).

Flavell, J. H., Botkin, P. T., Fry, C. L., Wright, J. W., and Jarvis, P. E. *The Development of Role taking and Communication skills in Children* (New York: John Wiley, and Sons, 1968).

Frost, J. L., and Kissinger, J. B. "Enhancing Affective Development: Motivating and Managing Behavior," In *The Young Child and the Educative Process* (New York: Holt, Rinehart and Winston, 1976).

Gesten, E., de Apodaca, R. F., Rains, M., Weissberg, R., and Cowen, E. "Promoting Peer-Related Social Competence in School," In M. W. Kent and J. E. Rolf, eds. *The Primary Prevention of Psychopathology*, Vol. 3: *Promoting Social Competence and Coping in Children*, edited by M. W. Kent and J. E. Rolf (Hanover, N. H.: University Press of New England, 1979).

Minuchin, P. "Affective and Social Learning in the Early School Environment," In *Early Childhood Education*, edited by B. Spodek and H. J. Walberg (Berkeley, Calif.: McCutchan, 1977).

Shantz, C. U. "The Development of Social Cognition," In *Review of Child Development Research*, Vol. 5, edited by E. M. Hetherington, (Chicago: University of Chicago 1975).

Shure, M. B., and Spivack, G. *Problem-Solving Techniques in Child-Rearing* (San Francisco: Jossey-Bass, 1978).

Spivack, G., and Shure, M. B. *Social Adjustment of Young Children* (San Francisco: Jossey-Bass, 1974).

Wolfgang, C. H. *Helping Aggressive and Passive Preschoolers Through Play* (Columbus, Ohio: Charles E. Merrill, 1977).

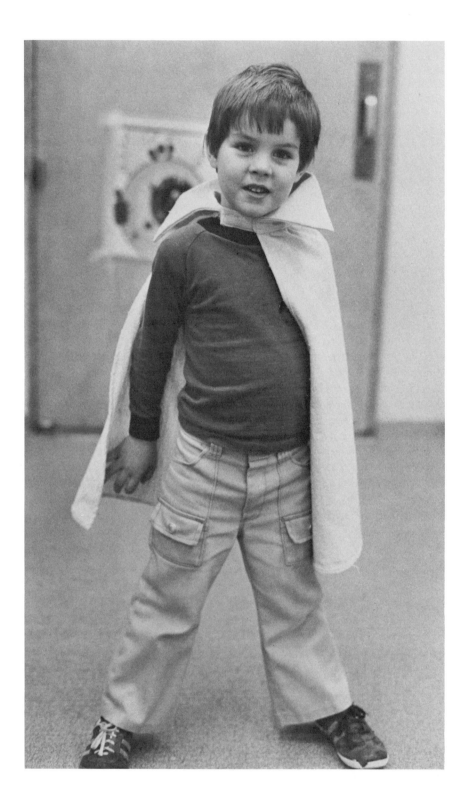

Imaginative Play

One of the most fascinating of the young child's activities is make-believe or imaginative play. We find ourselves charmed by the sight of children playing at being daddies, mommies, police officers, pirates, and doctors. This play of young children is not merely charming; it is very significant for their cognitive and social development.

The earliest forms of play with a representational or imaginative element begin to appear at about one and a half to two years of age. In fact, observations of such play by Piaget (1951), El'Konin (1971), and others have been a major source of evidence that the child is becoming capable of symbolic or representational thought at about this age. For example, when Piaget's daughter was one year, six months old, she was observed pretending to eat and drink without having anything in her hand (Piaget, 1951). Parents do not have to deliberately nurture or reward this kind of play. Without direct parental training, or even conscious adult attention, symbolic play blossoms throughout the preschool years. The particular kind of symbolic or imaginative play in which the child takes on a role is known as *dramatic play*. It reaches a peak at around the age of four or five. Later, make-believe play and imagination take somewhat different forms. In the group games of middle childhood, for example, we find children employing elements of make-believe. Daydreaming, which is prominent in adolescence and continues in adult life, involves a mental make-believe attitude of sorts. We cannot be precise in stating what changes there may be with age in the function of imaginative or make-believe activity. But no one would dispute that imaginative activity continues throughout life to serve both affective and cognitive functions. For example, there is some evidence that the predisposition to take on a make-believe and or playful mental attitude is linked with the divergent thinking processes required for creative production (e.g., Helson, 1965; Schaefer, 1969).

In this chapter we will be examining the prominent and perhaps unique role of make-believe play in the life of the preschool child, focusing on implications for the early childhood teacher. Our initial discussion is organized around two major points. The first is a consideration of the functions of make-believe play. Such play emerges for the most part spontaneously and looms large in the play of the young child. This being the case, it is important to examine what function make-believe play serves in the development of the child. In considering its function we will look at *what makes the child want to do it* and at *what adaptive or developmental function it serves*.

Next, we will look at the other side of the coin: Although most children engage in make-believe play of some kind, some children do not develop beyond the most rudimentary forms (Smilansky, 1968). It is important to consider the *set of conditions* which foster the development of dramatic play and other forms of make-believe activity. Research has shown, for example, that children from economically deprived families often do not engage in dramatic play at the same level as their middle-class peers. We will be examining the environmental inputs which are conducive to "high quality" dramatic play. Specifically, we will consider the teacher's roles with respect to dramatic play in the classroom.

The Origins and Functions of Dramatic Play

As a starting point, let's consider the interesting fact that dramatic play emerges in young children of many (though not all) families and cultures. The question arises: What makes children engage in such behavior? If so many children engage in it with so little direct parental or educational emphasis on encouraging it, the children must find it appealing—why?

A related question comes on the heels of the first: What good does make-believe play do the child? What are the short-run and long-run benefits to the child from engaging in dramatic play and other forms of imaginative activity? Let's first look at why the child *wants* to engage in such play.

Why Does the Child Seek to Engage in Dramatic Play?

Opie and Opie have studied the play and lore of children all over the world (1959, 1969). They find the element of make-believe to be quite pervasive in children's play, in organized games as well as in dramatic play. They describe the appeal as follows:

> As long as the action of the game is of the child's own making he is ready, even anxious, to sample the perils of which this world has such plentiful supply. In the security of the game he makes acquaintance with insecurity, he is able to rationalize absurdities, reconcile himself to not getting his own way, assimilate reality (Piaget), act heroically without being in danger. (1969, p. 300).

Opie and Opie suggest various aspects of the appeal that the make-believe framework has for children. Children enjoy being in command. We see them trying out roles and situations which in reality they cannot experience—being a parent, a teacher, a policeman; making a purchase, cooking, driving a car. The children seem to be grappling with what they only partially know, trying to get a firmer grip on aspects of their encounters with the world which especially interest, puzzle, or frighten them. By working with these elements in play, the child is able to assimilate them to his own conceptual framework.

Let's look at a four-year-old, Brad, who is told that his dog must go to the "animal doctor." Brad gets to go no further than the veterinarian's waiting room. His mother tells him that this doctor "takes care of animals and makes them feel better, like Dr. Jones takes care of you." Brad is very interested in this new place and personage, as well as a little nervous for his dog, Hannibal. Later at home he plays "animal doctor." He must make do with his own limited knowledge of what this role might involve. He *assimilates* the animal doctor into his construction of what doctors do and since Brad's most memorable skirmish with a doctor was when he had his tonsils removed, in his play he removes the dog's tonsils. He also includes a nurse who gives the dogs lollipops for being "big boys." (Certain evidence can also be seen that Brad is *accomodating* his current doctor concept to the new information he has encountered and to what he knows about the difference between dogs and people. He builds the examining table short to fit dogs and he tells the patient to "bark if it hurts.")

Why is Brad engaging in this play about the veterinarian? One reason is the child's attraction to adult roles, to the mysterious and impressive competence which they display. Brad cannot *be* the animal doctor, so he pretends that he is. As Smilansky (1968) and others have convincingly argued, it is not that the child wants to "escape reality." He would like as realistically as possible to experience being the animal doctor and do the things the doctor does, but since it is not in his power to do so, he bridges the gap with fantasy.

There is another aspect to Brad's play which might be pointed out by the psychologist or psychiatrist focusing on the child's emotional life—that the child has chosen to enact this situation because it was fear-producing. Dramatic play provides an excellent vehicle for working out emotional distress. When encounters with life throw us off balance emotionally (rather than being unsettling only to our intellect), we have an additional need to work this through in some way. But both kinds of unsettling, intellectual and emotional, lead to attempts to assimilate through play.

Play is a safe and satisfying way to work things through in several respects. It is *physically* safe—the bull is not really charging, the diving board is only one foot to the ground, etc. In an *emotional* sense, play is safe because the child deals with only as much of the raw reality as he can handle. Just by being in the play context there is removal from the original source of anger, fear, guilt, etc. And, as play therapists can testify, there is sometimes further removal through the transformation in play of the true identity of the anxiety-producing persons or events. An angry father may appear as a villainous giant or a bear; this masking is also believed to lie behind the appeal of many children's stories. Observations of children's play after upsetting events in their lives, such as a family death, confirm that a trauma is often dealt with through a play vehicle (Brown and Curry, 1971; McDonald, 1964).

In play the child is in control. Not only can he create situations which are as realistic or as fantastic as his emotional needs require (father as father or father as bear), he can also play out outcomes which suit his purposes, and battle perils with no danger. The child can limit and transform his doses of reality. It is not just in these two ways, physically and emotionally, that control is important to the satisfactions of dramatic play. There are other respects in which the child's control is significant in the appeal of dramatic play.

The child's active role in determining and controlling the course of dramatic play is key to its appeal in two other ways: (1) such play involves a strong *feeling of efficacy*, the joy of making things happen (Groos's "joy of being a cause"), and (2) the ability of the child in play to maintain the satisfying balance between being bored by too much familiarity or overwhelmed by too much novelty, a balance Piaget and others (e.g., Berlyne, 1960) have called *moderate novelty*. We have encountered these notions before, but let's look at them now in more detail with special reference to dramatic play.

In Chapter 4, Art and Construction, we noted that one of the reasons for children's typically ready and intense involvement with these activities is the feeling of efficacy produced by the creating of immediate, visible results. In dramatic play, the feeling of efficacy or competence may often have an element of *identification* with competent adult models who are able to make things happen. In addition, by enacting adult actions and roles through play the child is able to *operate within a reduced world*, a world where the child himself can make things happen and enact the adult forms of competence successfully. For example, instead of having to be a passive witness, the child himself can make dinner, cutting pieces of clay, putting them in a pot on the toy stove, and then serving them on a plate. Sutton-Smith (1971b) raises the interesting point that adults contribute to children's opportunity to have a scaled-down world where they can operate effectively. We provide indestructible dishes for them to wash, plastic lawnmowers for them to push, wooden trucks for them to drive around. We need think about children's toys for only a moment to be struck by the extent to which they are based on the objects used in adult roles. This is by no means unique to Western culture or to the present century. The widespread extent of the phenomenon would seem to almost certainly reflect, among other things, an adult awareness of children's absorption with adult roles and their enjoyment of enacting these roles at a level which they can handle.

In all of the child's activity—in her exploration of physical phenomena, her interpersonal ventures, her art, construction, music and dance—the name of the game is Making Things Happen. The special kind of Making Things Happen which takes place in the child's dramatic play is making things happen which she *cannot* ordinarily make happen in the real world—disciplining or comforting a baby, stopping traffic, putting out a fire. Heady stuff, and important for a child growing up in a world where there are many, many things she cannot yet do.

Another aspect of the individual's motivation for competence is the tendency to explore, to seek novelty, to avoid monotony or boredom (e.g., Berlyne, 1960). In Chapter 6 we discussed children's natural tendency to explore in the context of their spontaneous investigation of physical phenomena. Even though we human beings seek novelty and change, we do not enjoy situations or material which are totally beyond our present level of knowledge. We can be overwhelmed or frightened. In other cases we simply find no interest in these totally unfamiliar situations because we have nothing to relate them to, no way to understand them. Like the rest of us, the child needs a certain amount of novelty and he needs the chance to assimilate new material. Speaking of the joy of imaginative play, Singer (1973) states:

> One can begin to consider the possibility that the imaginative play of children represents an effort to *organize the available experience and at the same time utilize motor and cognitive capacities to their fullest* [italics ours]. The consequence of this position is that to the extent that the child interacts with novel material, which is within his capacity for mastery, he will continue to show interest, alertness, and positive emotional reaction (p. 23).

In spontaneous dramatic and imaginative activity the child sets his own level of play. He incorporates new material from the environment, but he fits it into old schemes. The individual child finds for himself—as only he can—the blend of novelty and familiarity which is at once satisfying and stimulating.

So far we have been considering why the child wants to engage in dramatic play. Let's turn now to asking what function such play serves in development.

What Good Does It Do the Child to Engage in Dramatic Play?

One way to respond to this question is to ask whether children who have engaged in such play are different from those who have not. This is not certain ground, as Sutton-Smith (1971a) has pointed out. Discovering that there are certain cognitive capabilities that we find in children who engage in dramatic play does not tell us whether the dramatic play has influenced this cognitive development. It could be just a "symptom" of the cognitive abilities. As Sutton-Smith (1971a) has neatly put it, the question remains "Does the player learn anything by playing?" (p. 256).

In considering this question we will look principally at what theory and observation tell us about what is activated and elaborated in the child through his dramatic play, without an extended account of the research on which these ideas are based. Let's begin by listing the benefits which have been alleged to come to the child through dramatic play. For the moment we will not be examining the potential role of the adult and the environment in affecting the extent to which dramatic play will bear these fruits.

These are the major ways in which dramatic play has been said to promote the development, well-being, or learning of the child:

1. By increasing the *capacity and/or tendency to use internal representation*
2. By providing a vehicle for *active assimilation of new material* and thus for *more elaborated mental structures*
3. By strengthening the *"as-if mental attitude,"* the ability to deal with nonpresent or hypothetical situations
4. By increasing *social competence* because adult roles are tried out and practiced and because of the rich occasions for interaction among the players.

Now let's look in more detail at each of these ways in which dramatic imaginative play is thought to play important developmental functions.

Use of Internal Representation

To deal thoroughly with this question would be a formidable task beyond the scope of this book. We will have to be content with making a few simple points. The first point is an obvious one. Suppose we see a child, Mary, pretending to be a storekeeper (ringing up sales, placing her goods on shelves, etc.). We must assume that in doing this she must be calling on her internal representations of the way stores look and operate. In choosing the toy typewriter to be the cash register she must use internal representations of what cash registers look like and what she has seen people do with them. In placing the cash register counter at the end of two aisles, Mary has had to mentally reconstruct the spatial arrangement of the store. She also has had to reconstruct the sequence of events that she and her parents have followed in their shopping expeditions. Mary gives her customers shopping bags as soon as they come into the store area. They put items in the bags and bring them to the counter; she rings up the sales and gives them change from the register (though they don't give her money). Mary has reconstructed, though with less than perfect accuracy, the sequence of shopping for groceries. She has some steps of the actual sequence correct and others not.

The process of remembering, as we have stressed, is not an automatic replay, particularly when what is being remembered has many parts and one has to think of how they were related to each other. Calling on internal representations and actively reconstructing nonpresent actions, places, and objects are a major part of dramatic play. It seems reasonable to assume, though perhaps difficult to document, the importance of this representational process for later development. To the extent that dramatic play and other types of imaginative play are among the forms that this "reprocessing" of experience takes, such play has an important role in the refinement, eleboration, and organization of thought. This is closely related to the next point.

Elaboration of Mental Structures Through Active Assimilation of New Material

The young child is continually deluged with new sights and sounds, new information and experience. Without the opportunity to actively assimilate this material, to "mull it over" in some way, new input will have little impact on the mental constructions of the child. As adults, we are more capable of doing this kind of mulling over entirely in our minds. The child is growing in this ability, but the capacity to engage in covert "working through" is still quite limited in early childhood. With dramatic play as a strategy of assimilation, the child has a useful tool for processing and incorporating new facts and ideas; more elaborate constructions of the social world, etc., can be expected to result.

Ability to Adopt Hypothetical Mental Attitude

In imaginative play the child takes a mental stance in which objects, events, and persons are treated as other than what they are. As a number of writers have commented (e.g., Sigel, 1970; Smilansky, 1968; Sutton-Smith, 1971b), such a mental stance is also involved in dealing with hypothetical situations of the kind that are frequent in school learning (e.g., "If John had twelve cents. . . "), indeed in problem-solving in or out of school. The ability to take the mental attitude of accepting a contrary-to-fact premise, e.g., "Suppose we lived in the Middle Ages" or "What if the water supply was suddenly cut off in our town. . . ?" has been hypothesized to be enhanced by play which is based on imagining contrary-to-fact circumstances.

Social Understanding and Social Competence

Of the various kinds of play which children engage in, manipulative table activities, art activities, etc., dramatic play involves the most peer interaction (Charlesworth and Hartup, 1967) and requires considerable give-and take. In an extensive study of peer interaction, Lee C. Lee (1975) repeatedly finds the interactions in role-playing episodes to be among the richest peer interchanges in terms of cognitive and communicative demands. An example from one of her protocols (1975) illustrates this point. Jeff and Morgan are talking:

> "I'll be cooking and you telephone, okay?" suggest Morgan. "I'll be the daddy," he adds, "okay?" "No, no, mommies cook," protests Jeff, walking over to the counter beside Morgan. "Oh," says Morgan, then reconsidering, "I'll cook; I'll be the mommy." "Uh?" asks Jeff. "I'll be the mommy," repeats Morgan. "And I'll be the daddy," says Jeff, walking toward the cabinet, " 'cause I'm the. . . .Good." "You'll be ironing," says Morgan. "Yes Daddy'll be ironing," confirms Jeff. "Mommies iron, mommies iron. Not boys. . .daddies," remembers Morgan. "Oh," says Jeff, "an' you can cook," as he turns back to the ironing board in spite of what Morgan has just told him. "No, no, mommies, daddies don't iron," says Morgan, walking over to the ironing board and holding the iron flat against the ironing board to prevent Jeff from ironing. "But," says Jeff, "when mommies are gone, daddies iron." "Oh," says Morgan, releasing his hold on the iron and returning to the counter (p. 220).

As Lee points out, in role-playing there are many opportunities for testing social strategies and learning skills of communication. Children must often come to shared decisions, as Jeff and Morgan did about who would be the mommy and who the daddy and what each role will involve. In this decision-making process Jeff is faced with a problem. Morgan has already co-opted the juicier role of mommy, which includes the opportunity to cook. And now he claims daddies don't iron! Jeff must convince Morgan that it is appropriate for him to be ironing or, given the boys' limited knowledge of the activities of daddies, he'll be left with nothing fun to do. Jeff uses his wits to retain the right to iron (a joy he may not struggle for later) by saying the daddies can iron when mommies are gone. Morgan is so stunned by this *coup de grâce* that he overlooks the fact that he, the mommy, is not gone.

Notice that Jeff must win this battle within the confines of the dramatic play situation, within its premises. He doesn't say, "Get out of my way—I'll iron if I want," or "Don't be bossy, Morgan." Challenges of role-appropriateness such as Morgan's are generally taken seriously and there is either some modification of behavior or some justification within the terms of the dramatic play roles. Such situations are particularly rich in promoting social development in two ways. First, there are many meaty occasions for persuading and negotiating due to the *complex and interdependent nature of the play*. Second, the *content of the discussions between children are social in nature*, as in deciding what constitutes role-appropriate behavior. Being confronted with alternative views of how things should be in the social situations is a spur to the child's construction of his own social understanding.

Dramatic play is a channel through which children try out various social roles and explore interpersonal relationships. Children construct notions of what behaviors accompany certain social roles and practice enacting them. Pretending to be the mother is part of the child's growing awareness of what it is like to be a mother. The child assimilates behaviors, and perhaps feelings, which are involved in mothering. When a child playing a mother scolds or reprimands recalcitrant children, for example, he or she is assimilating past experiences and constructing a concept of the mother role. When peers react to these role behaviors, the child's experience of what it is like to be Mother is further extended. Dramatic play provides a critical means for assimilating a variety of social roles and exploring the nature of social relationships and thus makes an important contribution to the growth of children's social understanding and competence.

In summary, there is much that children can gain from their involvement in imaginative play. The tendency to engage in imaginative play is a skill which is founded on capacities characteristic of the human organism (such as the ability to represent, the tendency to assimilate, etc.) and characteristic particularly of the ages around two to six years. The skill develops from the *interaction* of these capacities with an environment which provides stimulation and encouragement for such development.

A Fertile Environment for the Emergence of Make-Believe Play

The next question is what such an environment is like. There is evidence that not just any environment will do. Differences have repeatedly been found in the quantity and quality of make-believe play among children of varying social class and family background (Freyberg, 1973; Pines, 1969; Sigel and McBane, 1967; Smilansky, 1968). It is important not to leave it at that. We need to attempt to specify what it is about these home environments that make some children engage in abundant fantasy and dramatic play while others engage in little or none. Based on home observations and parental interviews (Freyberg, 1973; Pines, 1969; Smilansky, 1968), we know something about what features of the home environment are important in fostering dramatic play. There is considerable overlap in the home influences which various investigators have found. The list that Smilansky provides is fairly representative. She suggests that the following influences have an *indirect influence* on the quality of dramatic play:

1. Providing for normal emotional relationships, essential for healthy identification.
2. Providing for conceptual, informational and verbal means essential for the understanding of human behavior and social relationships.
3. Developing the power of abstraction and imagination, the ability to rise above the concretely present toward verbally described hypothetical existences.
4. Encouragement of positive social relationships of the child both with parents and peers based on tolerance and self-discipline (1971, p. 44).

   With respect to 1 and 4 we do not have a great deal to add. The full picture of how the child's emotional and social history relates to his involvement in dramatic play is not much more than hypothesis at this point. There does seem to be evidence for the importance to dramatic play of the child's emotional bond with a parent or other adult as a precondition (Singer, 1973). The relationship of the child to peers may not be as crucial for make-believe or dramatic play *per se;* play with other children is more significant in the development of what is known as *sociodramatic play.* Sociodramatic play is defined as dramatic play in which the theme is elaborated in cooperation with at least one other role-player (Smilansky, 1968). As we have seen, there are benefits to the child, both social and cognitive, which are only actualized through this interactive type of role-play as opposed to solitary dramatic play.
   What is meant by 2, "providing for conceptual, informational and verbal means for the understanding of human behavior and social relationships"? Let's recall Brad and his role-playing of the veterinarian. If it were not for Brad's having certain concepts, information, and verbal skills, he would not have had the basis for this role enactment. His conceptual and informational base concerning what doctors do is the necessary starting point from which he formulates a notion of what an animal doctor might do, Without sufficient abilities to comprehend language Brad would have understood very little of the doctor's role in previous visits to his own doctor. He also needs his verbal skills

to relate these previous experiences to this new situation through understanding mother's statement that this man "takes care of animals and makes them feel better like Dr. Jones takes care of you."

What Smilansky is talking about in 3 is intimately related to what we have called *distancing*, the ability to deal with nonpresent objects and events through mental representation. In Chapters 2–7 we have described the kinds of interactions which we believe contribute to the development of this ability. Such interactions can take place, of course, not only in the classroom but in the home. Research indicates that parental "distancing" behaviors are important in the child's development of the ability to deal with that which is not concretely present (e.g., McGillicuddy-DeLisi, Sigel, Johnson, 1979).

The degree to which the child's environment has included the "indirect influences" (Smilansky's 1–4) affects, of course, the extent to which other *direct influences* have an impact on the child's dramatic play. These direct influences as listed by Smilansky include:

1. Providing for conditions that encourage sociodramatic play; friends to play with, toys, place, time and so on.
2. Teaching the child directly to imitate different behavior patterns in a playful manner and reinforcing this.
3. Teaching the child to use make-believe in action and verbal expression (1971, p. 44).

In order to be useful to the teacher in classroom decision-making, Smilansky's descriptions of the influences on dramatic play need more specification. It is particularly important to specify what one means by "teaching the child to use make-believe in action and verbal expression," a phrase which would not be interpreted the same by all early childhood educators. To describe our own perspective on the role of the teacher in facilitating dramatic play, we will begin with examples of classroom episodes where Jeanne and Denise are faced with making decisions about whether and how to involve themselves in the children's play.

The Teacher and Children's Dramatic Play

Episode 1. Jeanne had placed some props near to the block corner to stimulate dramatic play, and perhaps block construction, around a store theme: a toy cash register (with plastic discs in the cash drawer), some plain cans, cardboard boxes, jars of various sizes, and several large paper bags. Kevin and Sandy are in the area. Kevin is handling the objects in a way that appears to be purely physical exploration (fitting boxes inside each other, making towers, etc.). Sandy is poking the keys of the cash register in the appropriate way but with no evidence of taking on the role of storekeeper. Jeanne approaches the cash register and addresses Sandy, "I'd like these things, please." Sandy bangs the keys for a few moments. Jeanne then hands her a piece of paper, saying, "Here's a ten-dollar bill. Can you give me change?"

Episode 2. Denise is watching Amy, Molly, and Sam in the housekeeping area. Molly has taken the mother role and drafted Sam for the father and Amy for the daughter. Dressed in an orange vest and purple high heels, Molly says to Amy, "Your father and I are going out to a movie. While we're gone, you should make dinner for the baby." Denise watches Amy curiously since she has never seen Amy use make-believe objects or take on a role in dramatic play. As she expects, Amy is at a loss. She looks to the area where the snack has been served, as if that would be the only place she could think of to find dinner. Denise says, "Your mother and dad gave you a job of making dinner for your baby sister. Have you ever done that before?" (Amy shakes her head.) "Well, I think your mother keeps her things for baby's dinner in that cabinet." She points to a set of shelves where miscellaneous items are stored, allowing Amy to make the choice. Amy takes a cup and on another shelf finds a spoon. (If she had not made a choice, Denise would have offered to help her look. Going through the items, she would have held up several items saying something like, "How about one of these? Which one do you think you'd need for baby's dinner?")

Episode 3. Jeff, Randy, and Michelle are playing policemen, which consists of arresting "bad guys" and hauling them off to jail. They come to arrest the teacher, Jeanne, and she asks Randy, "What have I done, Officer?" Randy replies, putting the handcuffs on her, "You drove too fast." Jeanne asks a few questions (on the way to jail, of course) and finds that Randy's concept of imprisonment is that policemen put people in jail if they do anything wrong and leave them there until they want to let them out. She realizes also that she has never seen the children enacting any of the roles of police officers other than arresting people and taking them to jail. She decides that it might be a good idea at another time to give them a broader base of information, including acquaintance with other roles police officers perform or with what happens *after* someone is arrested. Jeanne decides to discuss the pros and cons of various possibilities with Denise: a field trip to the police station or to court, a visit from a police officer, a film, a book, a group discussion. Then they can follow up by making some additions or changes in the props or the physical arrangement which might stimulate continuation of the children's playing out their interest in law officers.

Episode 4. A fourth example of the teacher confronted by a decision about the children's dramatic play, which you may wish to reread, appears on pages 45–48 in Chapter 3. The teacher goes along for the ride in the children's "airplane-boat."

The set of four episodes have one thing in common. In each case, the teacher did decide that there was a valid role for her to perform. The cases where such a decision is appropriate are probably in the minority. Teachers see much ongoing dramatic play in the course of the day, and in most situations their best course is simply to watch. (Dramatic play is, by the way, one of the most delightful and informative observation opportunities for teachers. They can learn about the children's emotional concerns, patterns of social inter-action, language, and problem-solving skills, in addition to the imagination, creativity, and representational abilities their play manifests.) The three episodes here and the additional one in Chapter 3 are all cases in which the teacher did decide to take some action. To make sound decisions on when and how to enter the children's play, the teacher needs a set of guiding principles, based on knowledge of the characteristics of dramatic play. Entry into children's play of any kind requires great care, but this is particularly so in the case of dramatic play. There it is not just a question of possibly interrupting the child's activity, but of jarring his involvement with what he is imagining. Great thoughtfulness is required on the part of the teacher and the rule "when in doubt, don't" may be a good one. With this warning in mind, let's examine what principles these two teachers consider in deciding when and how to get involved.

Nurturing Dramatic Play: When to Act

1. When it does not involve disengaging the child from what he or she is involved in. This is always a good rule of thumb for the teacher when she is considering interacting with a child. If the child is intensely involved in something, the teacher should *at the most* join him, perhaps engaging in parallel play, such as taking a lump of clay near the child who is playing with clay, as she unobtrusively observes. One thing she will try to do is get a sense of what the child is involved in. She may discover, for example, that the child is deeply absorbed in exploring the materials, as Kevin was with the boxes in Episode 1. Such a time would not be a good one for trying to extend the child's level of participation in dramatic play. It wouldn't work and it would interrupt the child's own valid pursuit. You may recall another example of this concern in Chapter 3 when Jeanne was watching Jeff and Tricia constructing a doghouse. When she observed that their real interest was in the construction of the house—not with pretending to be dogs—she realized that any interaction she might have with them should be about the construction task.

This concern would tell Jeanne not to try to shift Kevin's interest (Episode 1). But Sandy, on the other hand, is imitating what she has seen cashiers do with the register. Jeanne decides that Sandy is perhaps at a receptive point for going further with the storekeeper/cashier role. From what Jeanne can tell, it may be a good moment to help Sandy move forward to more use of make-believe, to acquaint her with new possibilities of dramatic play.

Another example of a potentially good time for the teacher to stimulate the children's play appears in Chapter 3 when the children's boat-plane episode had run out of steam. One of the difficulties young children have with dramatic play is sustaining an extended sequence of events. The gaps in their knowledge of adult roles, as well as their limited social skills, are often the cause. When dramatic play is about to break down for these reasons, an open-ended boost from the teacher is well timed.

Another aspect of the teacher's concern with not going against the grain of the children's interest is noting the specific focus of the ongoing dramatic play. Episode 3 illustrates this consideration. The teacher saw that the children's police play was limited to arresting people and throwing them in jail. Her first thought was the children seemed unaware of all the ways police officers help people—directing traffic, coming to their aid in emergencies, etc. But a few questions and some reflection convinced her that they did know a little about these various roles (as much as they did about arrest!); these roles simply were not where their interest lay at the moment. So Jeanne directs her attempt to provide additional information not toward sidetracking their interest but toward extending it in a natural direction—what happens after an arrest, what the police officer's next job is. This is another application of the principle that when children are highly engaged in one kind of enterprise it is not the time to shift them to another.

2. When the child appears to find the next step overwhelming. As Smilansky (1971) has written, the teacher need not "leave the child alone to face the immense task of solving all the problems he encounters in his efforts at self-expression alone and unaided" (p. 46). A child can find these problems too overwhelming to deal with for a number of reasons: physical, emotional, social, and cognitive. Let's look at Amy in Episode 2. When a child is somewhat shy, younger than the others in the group, or from a different cultural group, she may lack skills of approaching the others and carving out a role for herself, as well as a sufficient understanding of the specific content of their play. Thus, in a circular fashion these factors will limit the child's exposure to the experiences with peers which would provide the models and opportunities for interaction necessary for further growth. Amy seems to have had this kind of history and, as a result of this and her limited exposure to parent modeling of pretend play, she has had little exposure to a make-believe or nonliteral attitude to objects and actions—too little such experience to enable her to deal with Molly's demand. She wants to play but she doesn't know how to begin. Peers can be valuable models of pretending, but in their own egocentric involvement they are no help when the child doesn't know where to start. The impetus to play may come from peers, as in this example, but the assistance in solving the problem must come from the teacher.

To this point the "When-to-Act" principles we have listed have been (1) to avoid disengaging a child from something he is interested in and (2) to watch for occasions when the child gives evidence of needing assistance to enter play or to meet the demands of the dramatic play situation. There is a third consideration in judging when teacher action may be useful: when play seems to be proceeding at a restricted level. In order to describe clearly what we mean by this we will at some points be describing how teachers might act as well as when. Systematic discussion of the "hows" of facilitating children's dramatic play will be the next section.

3. When play seems to be proceeding at a restricted level. What is meant by "restricted level"? Dramatic play can be limited or restricted in two ways:

a. In terms of the limited nature of the children's knowledge of the role(s), the setting, etc. Children usually do not know a great deal about what is really involved in adult roles, particularly those outside the scope of the home. (This greater acquaintance with the home setting, incidentally, is partially responsible for the popularity of home themes and roles with children, along with their great emotional involvement in these situations, of course.) It may be noted that the complexity and sophistication of the interactions and the level of the imagination are usually highest when the child is on familiar ground. But often children have little knowledge of the role to work with—they have seen only a few behaviors performed by the model (policeman, quarterback, astronaut) and have even less understanding of what lies behind these behaviors. Episode 3 is an example of this: the children are familiar only with the aspect of the policeman's role which involves taking people to jail. They have vague or incorrect notions of offenses and their relation to imprisonment and no concept of the legal system, its limitations on what the policeman does, and where he fits into this system. The restricted nature of the children's play is partially a function of their stereotyped, superficial knowledge. Yet the children seem to be interested in something about imprisonment for wrongdoing. The teacher sees the need for supplementing their knowledge. Talking with the children in the course of their play and at other opportunities, she discovers that other functions of policemen such as traffic control are not of current concern to the children. So adding some information about the court seems a natural direction. She reads a story involving a court case and then talks it over with them, reenacting the trial in the book. The next day a large box is placed in one area of the room and the teachers make several benches out of blocks. At the beginning of free play, the children's attention is drawn to this "in case you want to play trial." Now, at a simple level, the teacher sees the beginnings of a richer kind of play: one child tries to convince the Judge that the speeder has done wrong, the speeder claims he wasn't going very fast, the policeman claims he saw it happen, etc. The children do not have an advanced understanding, of course, of equity or the legal system. They borrow many phrases from the story they heard and reenacted the day before, but they make changes as well. A wealth of potential is opened up. The children have a lot to learn and there are limitations on what they will be developmentally capable of understanding. But the cognitive demands and possibilities are at a higher level than those involved in handcuffing people over and over. Now the situation involves active verbal confrontation with the point of view of the other, having to make arguments to persuade someone, and having someone complain of a particular punishment being "too much." The teachers provided some exposure to the simplified steps of a trial; the children selected from this what was of interest to them and what they could understand. It is not just to give the children new information that the teacher acts. Her greater concern is with giving them a basis for role-enactment and interaction on a level that will be more productive for their cognitive and social development.

b. In terms of the level (representational, interactive) of make-believe play. Dramatic or make-believe play is not an all-or-none activity of uniform level.There are changes in the level of dramatic play in complexity and in representational difficulty. The investigations of dramatic play by Smilansky (1968) began by observing children and identifying characteristics of "good" dramatic play. From these investigations Smilansky lists six elements:

1. *Imitative role play.* The child undertakes a make-believe role and expresses it in imitative action and/or verbalizations.
2. *Make-believe with regard to objects.* Movements or verbal declarations are substituted for real objects.
3. *Make-believe in regard to actions and situations.* Verbal descriptions are substituted for actions and situations.
4. *Persistence.* The child persists in a play episode for at least 10 minutes.
5. *Interaction.* There are at least two players interacting in the framework of the play episode.
6. *Verbal communication.* There is some verbal interaction related to the play episode (Smilansky, 1971, p. 41).

Let's expand on what each of these characteristics of children's dramatic play involves.

In element 1, what is meant by saying that the child undertakes a make-believe role? Smilansky is making a distinction of some importance. If a child is sweeping with a broom or drinking from a tiny cup, it may seem that he is taking on a role or engaging in make-believe but this is not necessarily the case. He may be merely imitating adult action. After all, much of children's learning to function in the world is accomplished through *imitation*, or *observational learning* (e.g., Bandura and Walters, 1963). The child listens to what people say and watches what they do. When he imitates these actions, he is not necessarily imagining himself in the adult role. Before children have reached the point in their representational development where they assume roles in play, they nonetheless drink from miniature cups, ride around on toy trucks, steering and honking the horn, etc. They use realistic objects in the way these are used by adults. Often the child is not pretending anything. From the point of the view of the child's cognitive development, a giant step forward is involved in *taking on a role* and *representing an object with an abstract, undefined object* (e.g., a block) or *with verbalization* (e.g., "pretend I have a gun").

Another indication of the child's developing ability to employ mental representation in pretending is his increasing ability to *imagine situations or actions.* The children who use only concrete, realistic objects and give no evidence of taking on roles are unlikely to be able to substitute verbal description for part of an action sequence ("Pretend I drove to work and came back") or set a scene through language ("Let's say this is all water"). A child more advanced in dramatic play will often skip over or abbreviate parts of the action he knows or cares little about, indicating verbally that he is doing so. For example, Jason will say to Molly, "Pretend we flew a long way and now we're getting ready to land." A child whose dramatic play is just getting started is unable to make such leaps of imagination.

Sigel and McBane (1967) found a similar tendency in the doll play of many children of lower-income families. When enacting stories, these children stuck close to the realistic events of their everyday lives. They tended to go through each step of an action sequence, while middle-class children frequently substituted verbal descriptions for parts of the story line, e.g., "He went to the store and now he's home with the groceries."

In summary, as children progess in dramatic play, they show an increased ability to substitute verbalization and, it is assumed, internal representation, for concrete objects and actions.

Children also increase in their ability to *sustain lengthy dramatic play episodes* and to *cooperate with others in developing the make-believe events.* Verbal abilities are crucial in this more complex, interactive make-believe play. With increasing linguistic skills the child becomes able to let another child know what he is pretending. Such communication is necessary for the activity to proceed. For this reason, verbalization is typically more frequent in dramatic play than in other activities; it may also be on a higher level.

The *degree* to which the six elements cited by Smilansky are observed in children's play discriminates restricted, minimal make-believe play from that which is rich and elaborated. The awareness of these differences provides a set of criteria for the teacher's decision-making about when it may be useful to facilitate children's dramatic play. It should be clear that the frequency (and perhaps the manner) of teacher action is a function of the children in a given class. The teacher asks herself to what extent each individual child's play shows an awareness of the full possibilities of dramatic play.

Now suppose the teacher does feel some action is called for. What can she do?

Nurturing Dramatic Play: What to Do

The various categories of teacher action which we will be describing with respect to dramatic play will sound familiar to you from other curriculum areas discussed up to this point. First, we will see again the importance of *providing the opportunity* for children's spontaneous involvement in the activity, in this case for their initiation of dramatic play. Second, we will see that the teacher can make a difference by giving children *experiences which increase their knowledge of and interest in various roles and settings*—through trips, class visitors, discussions, stories, films, etc. Third, the teacher affects children's dramatic play through her *selection of materials*, that is, the objects which can be used as props in imaginative play. Finally, there is influence of the teacher on make-believe play through *interaction* with children, which can take various forms. For example, the teacher may actually take a role in a dramatic play episode or she may address the children in their respective roles without taking on a play identity herself. The use of dramatics in planned activities is a special teacher strategy which we will discuss and illustrate in the final portion of the chapter.

We have seen examples of all these teacher roles, singly and in combination, in the dramatic play episodes earlier in the chapter. Teacher decisions in these four areas often are interlocking, but for the purposes of discussion we will consider them one at a time.

1. Providing opportunities for sustained dramatic play. This one sounds simple enough and indeed it is, but it is sometimes not given suffiient consideration in teacher decision-making. The opportunity for free play is crucial here, of course, as it is in all child-initiated play. For dramatic play to develop optimally, it is important to allow for relatively large blocs of free-play time. Three fifteen-minute periods of free play do not serve the same goal as one forty-five minute period. It may take a while for children to get started and if the time is too short the play may get cut off "just when it's getting good." The development of the ability to sustain and elaborate dramatic play situations should be supported by not breaking up a play episode with lots of interruptions, including well-meant teacher intrusions. We have listed some of the considerations of *when* it is appropriate to enter a dramatic play situation, and when we discuss *interaction* we will have some suggestions regarding *how* this can be done in the least intrusive way. But the overall quantity of the occasions of teacher involvement should not be large.

Peers can also be disruptive to dramatic play, particularly when the children involved are just beginning to develop the ability to immerse themselves in a make-believe situation. Teachers should consider this problem when arranging the classroom. They also need to protect the children's freedom from interruption by reminding other children when they are disturbing their classmates.

The common element in these decisions regarding scheduling, teacher involvement in play, room arrangement, and other measures to reduce peer interruption is the teacher's attitude of respect for spontaneous dramatic play. If she understands the great value of children having the opportunity to develop role-playing situations to the fullest state of elaboration and sustained interaction of which they are capable, she will make decisions which will reduce the interruption of this process.

2. Providing experiences which "prime the pump" for dramatic play. As we have seen, children draw the raw material for their make-believe play from the adult world they see around them, the world they see around them, the world they are trying to understand and enter as fully as possible. Any of the child's experiences with what adults do, how they dress and talk, and with how they relate to others—experiences from home, school, community, or through the media—are grist for the mill.

Parents and teachers alike play a role in determining the range of the

child's exposure, as well as the degree to which the child notices and understands what he is exposed to. Does the child know anything about what people in various jobs do? Does she see and understand what various adults' tasks involve, such as mailing a package, shopping for groceries, entertaining a friend? Sometimes children's encounters with aspects of the adult world are so superficial or incomprehensible that they have no impact. As Smilansky has noted, they "look but they do not see" (1971, p. 45). Experience alone, such as a field trip to the fire station, does not activate dramatic play unless children have already developed a tendency to engage in such play. This is not surprising. If a child does not engage in role-play about the situations and roles he knows well, such as those he sees daily in the home, why should we suppose that a single trip to the fire station will suffice to activate such play? Even for the child who does engage in dramatic play, one exposure to a new setting and new roles may not have an impact. Experiences which broaden the child's acquaintance with adult roles and activities by themselves may not have a direct impact on dramatic play, but this does not mean they are irrelevant. The relevance depends on a number of factors the teacher must consider.

One factor which makes a difference in the impact of new material is the degree to which it is meaningful to the child and the level on which it is meaningful. Sometimes a child imitates the actions of an adult model without understanding a great deal of what is involved. For example, a two-year-old who has watched the World Series with his father squats down and slaps his fist into his other hand, imitating the catcher. This does not require an understanding of the role of catcher or the game of baseball. Likewise, in our example of children's understanding of the role of the police officer, various levels of understanding are possible. The child could imitate the banging of the judge's gavel and say, "Court 'jurned' " without having the slightest notion of what is involved in a trial. But meaningful role-play of what is happening in a court of law is another matter, requiring real understanding on the part of the child. This understanding will, of course, not be complete; for example, we would hardly expect the child to have the notion of the social contract underlying the legal system. But she may understand, for example, that what happens in court is that people talk about whether the person was bad enough to go to jail or not. Such understanding cannot be assumed to occur automatically by a visit to court or a film on the subject. It is for this reason that the teacher must think in terms of experiences which are developmentally appropriate and which will add significant elements to the children's knowledge, and she must think of how she can facilitate their understanding.

By observing the children and by talking with them, the teacher can get an idea of their knowledge of the role or activity in question. Let's go back to Episode 3. Jeanne watched the children play, noting some of the misconceptions and gaps in their enactment of the policeman role and the repetitiveness of their play. When the children arrested her, she had further opportunity to tap their knowledge by asking questions such as, "What have I done wrong?" . . . "What will happen to me next?" etc. Since she does not want to take over the children's play by asking too many questions, Jeanne may want to hold off until later. She can ask the children as a group or in small groups when she sees an opportunity, e.g., "Has anyone heard of court? . . . They have a judge, Sam? What do you suppose a judge does?" With the information she gleans from watching children's play and talking with them about their ideas, the teacher forms a picture of the gaps in the children's knowledge of the role or activity. Now she is ready to think through ways in which to extend the children's understanding of the role. She will take the children's cognitive development into account in this decision. Their developmental level influences the teachers' decisions about both the content and the methods to use in acquainting children with the new role or setting. Direct demonstration or witnessing of the roles, for example, is likelier to be more successful than verbal discussion alone.

In the process of exposing the children to the additional material, the teacher will again need to watch and listen to see what children are grasping. Following Episode 3, Jeanne chose to have the children do a role-play of a courtroom scene at group time for two reasons: one, to provide a warm-up to stimulate children's enactment of these roles in free play and two, to allow her to find out what the children's perceptions of the various roles are. She can thus get an idea of where further explanation or discussion may be useful. This is part of what happened:

Jeanne:	(as the judge): Lawyer Molly, what did this man do wrong?
Molly:	He was going too fast in his car. He ran into a house.
Jeanne:	Is that right, Officer Jeff?
Jeff:	He wrecked the car. We policemen arrested him.
Ken:	(who is supposed to be the defense lawyer): He's bad. Put him in jail.
Jeanne:	(to the accused): Scott, some of these people think you should go to jail. They say you were driving too fast. Were you driving too fast?
Scott:	I was driving just a little fast. Not real fast.

Note that when Ken shows a lack of understanding of his role, or an inability to stay within that role, Jeanne does not try to hold him to the role as *she* understands it. In the course of the film and discussion of courtroom goings-on, Jeanne has explained in simple terms about the two lawyers. But she realizes that grasping this idea and staying within a given perspective in the face of the opposing view is very difficult. Ken's actions show her this is true. She wonders if the notion of arguing one's case "before a judge" might be easier in a situation where the child has his *own* point of view to put forth. This might be something to try out. A real understanding of courtroom procedures and what underlies them would obviously be beyond these children, yet they have managed to understand that after arrest comes a time when the person who is arrested gets to say what happened, etc.

As this example demonstrates, decisions about providing experiences to increase children's familiarity with other roles and settings are not a simple matter of reading a story or going on a field trip. Notice that Jeanne engages in several important processes. Before planning any activities, Jeanne has done the following:

1. She notices the limited nature of the children's police-play, coupled with their great interest in it.

2. She "gathers data" about what the children know and do not know about the police officer role, as well as what aspects they are interested in.
3. She gives thoughtful consideration to the level of the children's cognitive development, both in choosing *what* to acquaint them with and *how* to go about it.

[Jeanne launches the action decided upon in 3.]

4. She listens and observes carefully during and after the activity to see what the children understand and to discover what they may incorporate into their play.

Clarification, discussion, and enrichment of the understanding of a given role or setting is an ongoing process. The teacher builds on the successive experiences and conversations she and the children have. As the children develop, the teacher gives them continuing opportunities to construct a broader and more accurate understanding of the adult world.

3.Providing props for dramatic play. As we have seen, the use of objects as props in role-playing passes through several stages, becoming increasingly representational (Smilansky, 1968). Just because a child reaches the point in his representational level where he can employ an abstract object in a symbolic way does not mean that from this time on it is ideal to have only such objects around. Realistic objects can still play a role in stimulating the child's initiating or elaborating a theme. For example, suppose the class has been having their annual check-ups and the teacher thinks it is a good time to encourage role-play of the doctor's office. A few realistic props such as perhaps a stethoscope and a doctor's bag placed in the dramatic play area, along with some more undefined play materials (asorted scrap materials, blocks, etc.), increase the chances of the children coming to the area and exploring the theme. The presence of the stethoscope and the doctor's bag actually makes it *moor* likely that children will make representational use of other objects to further their play. They will now be motivated to play the doctor's office situation and, in the absence of some props they need, will create these from the assorted things the teacher has provided.

Mary Ann Pulaski (1973) investigated children's play with objects which are realistic and structured (e.g., toy garages) and with those which are abstract and open-ended (e.g., wooden blocks). She was interested in the appeal of these two types of objects to children and in whether preference is related to the child's predisposition to fantasy. Her results are relevant for us. She reports that children who were *above average in their predisposition to fantasy* showed greater involvement and enjoyment when playing with the *less structured materials*, while children below the average on fantasy appeared to prefer the structured, realistic toys. With the minimally structured toys, there was a greater diversity of themes in the children's play and somewhat greater richness of fantasy play. In comparison, the use of the more structured play objects was confined to what they were designed to do—less was "left to the imagination."

We have discussed various considerations which shape the teacher's decision-making about what kinds of objects to have in the classroom and the playground. To summarize:

1. There is a preference for more concrete replicas among children who are less advanced in dramatic play (children who are younger or who have had a limited background with imaginative play). For children who are at this point in development, the realistic toys are more conducive to imitative play than more abstract or undefined objects like blocks, sticks, pieces of material , etc. However, if the teacher were to provide *only* realistic objects, these children would have little opportunity to develop the ability to use less representational objects.
2. Among children who are more advanced in dramatic play some availability of less-defined play objects is desirable. These objects are more versatile in what they can be, which allows for open-ended possibilities in the child's play. Equally important, the child is able to wean himself from the literal, reality-bound to the more representational use of objects. When a realistic replica is not available, the representational demand on the child is greater.
3. For children who can handle the representational demand of the "abstract" play object, such as a block for an iron, realistic props serve the purpose of providing a stimulus to engage in dramatic play in the first place and to engage in playing along particular themes. That is, if a fireman's hat is available, children are more likely to seize on the idea of role-playing about firemen.

Points 1, 2, and 3 considered together should suggest some implications for the teacher. First, *not all play objects made available should be at the same level of realism/structure.* In addition to the diversity of children within the class in terms of representational level and predisposition towards fantasy, there is the fact that for any given child some toys of each kind can be beneficial. (For the child advanced in make-believe with respect to objects, highly defined, realistic objects can be a stimulus to try a new theme or role; for the child less advanced in make-believe with respect to objects, abstract objects should be available for the child's forward development.)

Second, *the representational level of the play objects would not be expected to be the same throughout the year, since the children are changing.* A gradual transition towards less realistic materials is possible as children gain in the ability and the desire to use objects flexibly.

Other considerations with respect to objects, other than their mere presence, are the spatial arrangement (since utilization of objects is influenced by their placement), the timing of their appearance in the room, and the teacher's actions in involving children with them.

4. Interacting with the children. We have emphasized that it is important for the teacher not to intrude excessively on children's imaginative play. But there are occasions when some teacher involvement is timely and useful. In dis-

cussing the fact that some children engage in little make-believe/dramatic play, we noted that studies of their homes indicated that they had little experience with playful and make-believe interactions (such as a parent pretending to be a bear, feeding a doll, or asking what would happen if we had no grocery store to go to). In other words children in such families were rarely exposed to models of a fantasy or make-believe behavior or attitude. Such interactions apparently play a role in getting the child started in imaginative play (Freyberg, 1973; Sigel and McBane, 1967; Singer, 1973).

Teachers can find abundant opportunities throughout the preschool day for initiating interactions of this kind.

Watch for opportunities on the playground.

Jimmy is at the top of the jungle gym. Denise says to him, "You're way up high, seeing what a bird can see. How do things look from up there, Mr. Bird?" Jimmy replies, "I'm a cardinal." "Oh, Mr. Cardinal, how do things look?". . .

Watch for opportunities in the block corner:

> It's clean-up time and Randy, who has been building with small wooden blocks, does not seem at all eager to clean them up. Jeanne fills a truck with blocks and pulls it up to where Randy is standing near the block shelves. "Here's a load of wood for you to put away. You'll have to work fast 'cause I'll be back soon with the next load. Where do you want me to dump these?"

Take the opportunity of setting a make-believe frame at group times from time to time:

> Take the children on the familiar "Bear Hunt". As you pursue the bear, add novel situations to the familiar obstacles on the hunt (the river, the tall grass, etc.). For example, add a patch of quicksand or a passage which has a very low ceiling. "*How* are we going to get through? Does anyone have any ideas?" you ask. Put yourself into the suspenseful search and the frightened flight, staying within the make-believe context and drawing the child with you.

Sometimes, as in the cases we've just looked at, the teacher is the sole initiator of the make-believe set. Teacher interactions to facilitate dramatic play also take place when children are already involved in some form of imitative activity or in dramatic play itself. There are two major sorts of teacher entry or interaction (with, of course, infinite variations):

1. The teacher *takes on (or is given) a role* in the children's play.
2. In interacting with the children, the teacher *maintains their play roles but does not assume a play identity herself.*

In either case, the teacher may have a variety of motives for choosing to interact with the children. One is to find out more about their thinking, an aim which can sometimes be achieved most effectively when the teacher is more than a passive observer. (An example was Jeanne's interaction with her "captors" in the handcuffing episode).

Another motive for involvement in children's dramatic play is to help them sustain the play episode. As we discussed earlier in the chapter, the social and communicative demands of sustaining an interactive make-believe play episode are great, often too great for the young child. The teacher can serve as a link between the children, for example, responding to a child's ventures into representational use of an object when his play partner ignores him or finding a way for an onlooking child to enter the play. The teacher can also keep the play rolling by contributing an occasional idea as we saw Jeanne do in Chapter 3 when she asked the children what the strange noise was. An open-ended remark of this kind is a good way to provide a boost to children's pretending without taking over the *direction* of their play.

Yet another motive for the teacher's involvement in children's dramatic play is to extend its richness or level of make-believe by introducing an element typically missing from the play of a child or group of children. One example of this is the way the teacher acted in Episode 1 with Sandy. Another example is with Dan, who according to the teachers' observations does not use make-believe with respect to objects. He engages in imitative action only when realistic objects or replicas are available. He and some other children are playing with a stethoscope, listening to each others' hearts. The teacher submits herself to the stethoscope and the scales. Then she holds a small cylindrical block out to Dan and says, "Doctor, I've been taking these pills you gave me, but I'm out. Can you give me some more?" Within the context of the play, she has found a way to suggest the possibility of pretending one object to be another.

In this case, the teacher had a good opportunity to enter the children's play as a patient and in this role encourage Dan's make-believe use of objects. Whenever possible, teachers for their entry should avoid taking on leading roles or restructuring the situation. Sometimes a natural way to become a participant in the play isn't readily available, or there may be other reasons (such as limited time) that the teacher doesn't want to take on a role in the children's play. The teacher may choose instead to address the children without taking on a role. She may ask, "Where is your boat going?" Without becoming a participant in the episode, she nonetheless maintains the *children's roles* in all cases.

A Special Teacher Strategy: Providing Experiences with Dramatization

To this point we have been focusing on the value of spontaneous dramatic play and the classroom strategies for fostering it. We now turn to a related but rather different activity in which the enactment of roles is within the context of a planned drama. This is usually called *dramatization* or *dramatics* (as opposed to *dramatic play*). Here the role of the teacher is somewhat different and typically more active (in questioning, etc.). In fact, although experiences with dramatization do have aspects in common with "free style" dramatic play, these experiences seem to differ significantly in what they involve for the child.

Mary Ann, who is playing mother in the block area, and Jane, who is portraying the mother in a dramatization, are both taking on roles. Both may be immersed in the roles, but Mary Ann is likely to be more so. She is taking on the role of the mother in her own imagination; the locus of her attention is identifying with Mother and imitating actions for her own satisfaction. Jane, in contrast, is to some extent faced with the "audience factor." In her role-enactment the focus is partly on external representation. The nature of the activity of dramatization involves a concern with *how others will know*, for example, that it is mealtime, that one is the mother, or that the characters are going to a fancy party. For the young child, with her difficulty in taking the perspective of another, an awareness of the audience's problems is not always present. In fact, the opportunities provided for activating the children's thought about this problem are part of the reason why dramatization is an effective classroom activity.

We will see more of the implications of the "audience factor" as we look at a specific activity. The ways that a teacher can use dramatization as a tool in facilitating children's development are numerous: for building verbal skills, for providing acceptable ways to express emotions, for fostering cooperative abilities, to name a few. We will focus on two aspects of the teacher's use of dramatization: for increasing children's abilities in planning and problem-solving and for exploring representational problems and concepts, including the communication of messages to others. Let's look at the use of dramatization as a tool in achieving these objectives by turning to some excerpts of the class planning to enact *Hansel and Gretel.*

Activity. Planning and presenting *Hansel and Gretel*

The activity will take place throughout the week. The children will first plan and then rehearse and enact a simple (and less violent) version of *Hansel and Gretel.* In the planning stages the children (sometimes as a group, some-times in small subgroups) will select music, gestures and movements, props, verbalizations, etc. to convey the story to some visitors who will constitute an "audience." (The teachers find that if possible an "outside audience" for whom the dramatization is planned is useful—another class, some adults from the school office, some mothers who are driving the day's carpools. An audience provides a real reason for considering questions of how to represent action, character, and mood: For example, "How are we going to show the audience which one of you is the mother and which is Gretel?. . . How are they going to know the children are scared?" etc.)

Several segments from the week's activity will demonstrate some of the issues the teachers and the children explore.

Monday. Jeanne is talking with the group as a whole about some of the things which will be needed for the play. Second only to the witch's candy house in the children's interest is the bird that eats the bread crumbs. They are eager to portray the bird in their drama.

"How shall we show the bird?" Jeanne asks. "We can make it out of paper," Herb suggests. "It has to fly!" Dan asserts.

"How are you going to show that it's flying?" Jeanne inquires. "I could fly it around with my hand," Laurie offers. "A string," says Jeff, and Keisha adds, "Hang it from the ceiling."

Jeanne says, "Those are ways we could have a bird in the air. Now how about when we have the part where the bird eats the crumbs? Will Laurie's idea work for that part?" Laurie and the others in chorus assert that it will and Laurie demonstrates with her hand how the bird could come in for a landing. "OK," says Jeanne, "How about the other idea—hanging the bird from the ceiling with a string. Will that work for the part where the bird eats the crumbs off the ground?" "It could be a long string," Molly suggests. "So the bird reaches all the way to the ground, Molly?" (Molly nods.) "What about when the bird is flying?" Keisha says that the string can be pulled to make the bird go up and down.

This will make an interesting problem for Keisha and several interested children to work on later (an example of a "science" problem in the dramatization activity). For now the emphasis is on how objects and events can be represented. Jeanne has tried to get the children to identify and solve a problem which is both representational and physical.

Suppose a child had suggested instead that the bird just hang in the air and the people "pretend that it's already eaten." This would have been equally valid and would have been followed up in a different way. Jeanne might proceed to see if the child is able to take the audience's perspective into account—"How will the audience know that the bird has already eaten and isn't just flying over?" " 'Cause Hansel and Gretel are sad," one child offers. Another says, laughingly, "They'll know 'cause the bird will be fat!"

As can be seen in this interaction, dramatization offers a range of interesting problems of communication, representation, and make-believe, as well as physical problems; the potential for exploring "how-will-we-show" types of questions makes dramatization an excellent tool in the early childhood curriculum.

Tuesday. At various times during the week children in groups of three or four work with a teacher in making decisions about the production. The group with Denise on Tuesday (Peg, Jason, Randy, and Laurie) is planning the scene where Hansel and Gretel are lost and cold.

Denise says, "Can you think of some ways we could let the audience know Hansel and Gretel are cold?" "We could tell them," Peg suggests. "Who would do the telling?" Denise inquires. "You could," several children suggest. Others suggest that Hansel and Gretel themselves say they're cold. "That's one way we could do it, then. Hansel and Gretel could talk about being cold," Denise acknowledges. "How else could we let the audience know that the children are cold?"

Becky suggests putting snow on the ground and Jason adds that you could use scraps of white paper. "Oh, if there were snow, people would know it was cold. Good thinking. Let's keep thinking of different ways. You said we could tell the audience that Hansel and Gretel are cold. You said we could use snow. Are there any other ways you can think of that we could let them know it's cold?" The children are stumped.

"OK," Denise says, "imagine it's very cold and windy. You don't even have on a sweater." Several children shiver and two boys move closer together. "Look at Jason and Randy," Denise says. "What are they doing?" The children reply that the boys are sitting close together. "But what does that have to do with the cold?" Denise asks. "You sit together to keep warm," Randy replies. Denise says, "Hmm, I've seen people sit close because they like each other too.

How would the audience know Hansel and Gretel were sitting close because they were cold?" No response is offered, though the children seem to be thinking.

After waiting a bit, Denise goes on: "Laurie, did you see anyone else do something that let you know they were cold? Let's imagine again how it feels in the cold wind." Laurie shivers herself and says, "This." "Shivering," Peg offers. "They could shiver."

Denise proceeds to have the group choose among the alternatives suggested to this point and then moves on to further problems.

If you'll think back to the movement chapter, you'll see many of the strategies discussed there applied in the above example. In fact, dramatization furnishes excellent opportunities for using the strategies we have talked about for activating the children's thinking about representation through each of the modes, as well as for provoking children's taking the perspective of the other in evaluating how messages can be communicated.

Summary

Our concern in this chapter has been children's play which has a symbolic or make-believe element. Of particular interest for the early childhood educator is dramatic play, the type of imaginative play in which the child takes a role. A look at the place of dramatic play in early childhood curricula must begin with an examination of why children engage in such play and what developmental functions it serves.

Much of the attraction of make-believe play lies in the opportunity it provides for the child to be in control, to make things happen. The child sees many things around him which he would like to be able to do and cannot. Through dramatic play he can be in charge and can perform actions which are not possible to him in reality—driving a car, mowing the lawn, etc.

Dramatic play provides a vehicle through which the child can assimilate the new material with which he is continually deluged. In play the child can deal with as much of this material at a time as he wishes; he can establish the pleasurable balance between the too-familiar, which is boring, and the too-novel, which is overwhelming.

There are several kinds of potential benefits to children from their engagement in dramatic play. Make-believe play is believed to promote the child's development in these ways: (1) increasing the child's *capacity and tendency to use internal representation*, (2) providing a vehicle for *active assimilation of new material and thus for more elaborated structures*, (3) strengthening the child's *ability to deal with nonpresent or hypothetical situations*, and (4) increasing *social competence*.

There is evidence that children's development in make-believe play does not flourish equally in all environments. Various conditions seem necessary for the emergence and full development of "High quality" dramatic play. There are undoubtedly certain emotional and social conditions which underlie the emergence of dramatic play, such as having a close relationship with an adult. We have emphasized the cognitive prerequisites, particularly the ability to imagine nonpresent objects and events. This ability begins to develop in the family, but the teacher can make a difference in fostering it and in "making up for lost time" if parental interactions conducive to such development have been lacking.

There are several kinds of action teachers can take to facilitate dramatic play. First, however, they confront the question of when to act to nurture such play. The teacher should not attempt to pull the child away from an activity he is involved in. An opportune moment for teacher assistance may come when the child is watching others play but does not know how to proceed. Or the teacher may decide to take action to extend the level of children's ongoing dramatic play. She may decide to act when children's limited knowledge of roles and settings is constraining the complexity and level of their play. In other cases, the impetus for the teacher to act is from the children's play appearing limited in (1) their tendency or ability to engage in make-believe, (2) their ability to sustain dramatic play episodes for extended periods of time, or (3) their interactive skills in the dramatic play context.

The ways that teachers can nurture fuller and more elaborated forms of dramatic play were discussed. They can act through four major avenues: (1) by *providing opportunities for sustained dramatic play,* (2) by *giving children experiences* which increase their knowledge of and interest in various roles and settings, (3) by *selection of materials* which can be used as props in make-believe play, and (4) through *interaction with the children,* as in providing a model and introducing new elements into children's role-play.

One form of teacher interaction which has an impact on children's make-believe play is the strategy of class dramatizations. Dramatization furnishes opportunities for exploring representation through diverse modes: movement, music, pictures, three-dimensional representation (props), langauge, etc. Thinking about how to convey messages to others—the "audience"—involvesperspective-taking. This aspect is far more prominent in dramatization than in spontaneous dramatic play and teacher encouragement thinking about such problems is accordingly more active in teacher-initated dramatics experiences. Thus, spontaneous dramatic play and teacher-initiated dramatizations are different in some respects, but both kinds of activity are excellent routes for developing children's representational competence.

Suggested Resources

Chaillé, C. "The Child's Conceptions of Play, Pretending, and Toys: Sequences and Structural Parallels." *Human Development,* 21 (1978): 201–210.

Curry, N. "Dramatic Play as a Curricular Tool." In *Play as a Learning Medium,* edited by D. Sponseller (Washington, D.C.: National Association for the Education of Young Children, 1974).

Freyberg, J. T. "Increasing the Imaginative Play of Urban Disadvantaged Kindergarten Children Through Systematic Training." In *The Child's World of Make-Believe: Experimental Studies of Imaginative Play* edited by J. Singer (New York: Academic Press, 1973).

Goodridge, J. *Drama in the Primary School* (London: Heinemann Educational Books, 1969).

Lowndes, B. *Movement and drama in the Primary School* (London: B. T. Batsford, 1970).

Singer, J. "Theories of Play and Origins of Imagination," "Some Theoretical Implications," and "Some Practical Implications of Make-Believe Play." In *The Child's World of Make-Believe: Experimental Studies of Imaginative Play* (New York: Academic Press, 1973).

Smilansky, S. *The Effects of Sociodramatic Play on Disadvantaged Preschool Children* (New York: John Wiley and Sons, 1968).

_____, "Can Adults Facilitate Play in Children?: Theoretical and Practical Considerations." In *Play: The Child Strives toward Self-Realization* (Washington, D.C.: National Association for the Education of Young Children, 1971).

Taylor, L. E. *An Introduction to Dramatics for Children* (Minneapolis: Burgess, 1965).

9

Educating the
Young Thinker:
Strategies and
Objectives

Throughout the last eight chapters we have discussed the principles which are central to our perspectives, illustrating them with extensive samples of classroom dialogues. You have probably noticed that the dialogues always seem to be segments from activities after the school year is well underway. The children have learned what to expect in the classroom and have come to be at ease with their teachers. The teachers are already familiar with the children and have come to know their abilities and interests. Activities, including materials and teacher strategies, seem to have been carefully planned and artfully executed. You may be asking yourself, "How do I get started? What happens when I don't know the children? How does the whole program get started?" In this chapter we want to give you some suggestions for beginning to apply the ideas you've been reading about. We will be looking at some general guidelines that tie together and make explicit some of the ideas in the preceding chapters. Our aim is to help you help yourself improve in your ability to make wise decisions in the classroom.

Let's suppose that on the basis of what you've read and thought about as you went through this book, you have decided to change your teaching approach as of next Monday morning. Now what?

First of all, and only temporarily, forget your role as a teacher and forget about theory. Think about children you've known. Even if you haven't taught before you may have had babysitting experiences, perhaps you played with younger brothers and sisters, and certainly you have had your own childhood experiences to call upon. What activities did you enjoy doing with children (or as a child)? Pick an activity that you have enjoyed, that you think you will feel comfortable participating in, and that you think will sustain the children's interest. Or, pick an activity because you are intrigued by the materials used, because you want to find out how children react to it, or because you think it will elicit behaviors you want to observe. If ideas don't come to mind, try using sand table, water play, or play dough activities—some of the traditional preschool activities. These are intrinsically appealing to young children and lend themselves to easy conversation. The idea is to get an activity with which *you* feel comfortable. This is important because as you try a new approach to teaching, you're going to be doing some demanding intellectual work with interaction strategies and intent listening. Consequently, it is easier to begin with an activity that is comfortable for you.

Starting in this way does not mean that the choice of activities, materials, schedules, and classroom arrangements is up to personal whim. Far from it! Traditions, however, in early childhood education are generally reliable in providing basic notions of materials and activities children enjoy and from which they learn. Traditional wisdom in early education can provide a framework within which you can make modifications of particular teaching strategies, choice of materials, and so forth. You can then concentrate your energies observing the children in your classroom and improving the fine points of your teaching style.

Don't be overwhelmed by the elaborate planning illustrated in previous chapters. As you get to know the interests and abilities of the children in your class, you will find yourself getting many ideas for activities that are particularly appropriate for those children. As you make decisions about the order in which to present the activities (or themes, or units), you'll find yourself doing some long-range planning. But there is no need to have detailed plans ready for an activity that will not begin until some months hence. Detailed planning is generally best done in one- or two-week segments. Often activities are added, eliminated, or modified as the week, or even the particular day, progresses; teachers incorporate new information and pick up signals from watching the children's evolving interests and changing moods, and from noting the difficulties the children encounter in related activities.

If you have an activity in mind that you feel comfortable with, you are ready to come back to considerations of your role as a teacher. How can you make use of the examples and principles we've been discussing through the previous eight chapters? An approach to being a teacher—a philosophy, a style, a set of strategies—cannot be formulated or changed overnight. You will find yourself internalizing the ideas and methods described in this book only gradually and translating them into your own personal style. What should come first is a changed perspective on how the child learns. From this perspective follows a particular notion of where and how the teacher should be involved in the child's learning and development (and where and how she should *not*). We have attempted throughout the book to describe this concept of teacher role and to suggest some of the ways it affects decision-making in the classroom across the various curriculum areas. It will be useful at this point to review the ways in which our perspective on how children learn translates into principles for teacher behavior. Because the teacher's interactions with the children are central, let's begin by looking at the *guidelines for verbal interactions.*

Guidelines for Educating the Young Thinker

Guidelines for Verbal Interactions

1. *Initiate interactions, but do it gently and time them carefully.*

There are times when the teacher makes an active attempt to provoke the child's thought. Try to make your contributions relevant to what the child is already doing, even when your questions are intended to open up a new direction. The timing of initiating interactions is also important. For example, when a child has just made a new discovery, such as how to sink a plate by loading it with pennies, it is not the time to ask him why that works or to ask whether it would work the same way with pieces of styrofoam. The child is absorbed in trying his new discovery again and again. After he has replicated the sinking several times he will be more receptive to a teacher question or comment.

2. *Ask questions rather than giving statements.*

Since this is one of the central strategies of our approach, there are examples on nearly every page. Some of the most important different types and uses of inquiry are outlined in the strategy chart at the end of this chapter. One important thing to remember is to make sure your questions are real questions, not statements in question form. For example, avoid being like the receptionist who asks, "Can you hold, please?" and then puts you on hold before you get a chance to reply.

3. *Answer questions when you're asked, but avoid pedantic replies or doing the child's thinking for him.*

In general: If you are asked about your *own* opinions or interests ("Do you like chocolate pudding?" or "Do you think it will melt?"), answer the question directly and in as thoughtful a way as the situation seems to warrant. You should also generally answer directly a child's question of "social knowledge," that is, a request for information which cannot be acquired through reasoning or exploration but must be transmitted to the child, such as a social rule, the name of a person or place, etc. When the question is one that can be answered by manipulation of materials or by further guided thinking about the problem, respond to the question with another question or suggestion to encourage the child to find his or her own answer.

4. *Ask questions simply.*

As you talk with children and observe them, you'll discover what vocabulary they do and do not understand and where they have trouble because of the complexity of the linguistic structure. Unless you're trying to find out about children's understanding of language *per se*, try to use words and sentence structures that the children already understand. This allows them to devote their mental energies to answering the question rather than trying to figure out what you're trying to say. For example, there is nothing to be gained by asking "What is the reason for the melting of the ice?" rather than "Why is the ice melting?" (See Chapter 6 for more discussion.)

5. *Allow children time to answer questions.*

Wait patiently and expectantly for their answers. Five seconds may seem like forever, especially when you're nervous about how things are going. But children need that time to process your request. Rephrasing a question before this amount of time has elapsed can interfere with children's understanding and formulation of their own answers. If they haven't processed the initial questions, they may view the rephrasing as a totally new question. Make sure that you ask only *one question at a time*. For example, don't ask, "What makes you think the ice is melting? Why is it melting, Johnny?" Each of these is a separate question; in a string of questions, one or both get lost in the shuffle and the machine-gun pace can come across as a barrage.

6. *Ask questions for which you really want to know the child's answer.*

For example, you may want to know about the child's interests or previous experiences in some area or about his or her understanding of a particular

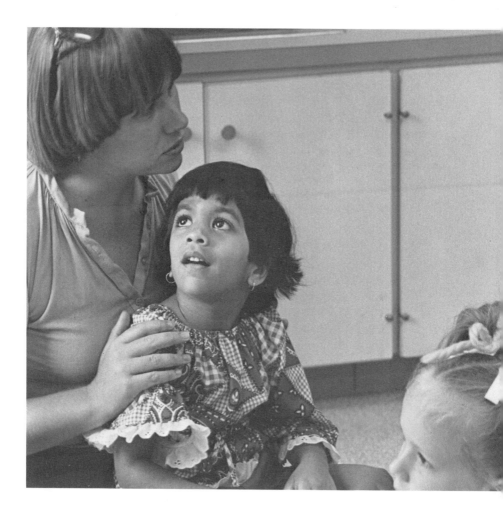

concept. Whatever your interest, the guideline is an important one. One reason is that if you really want to know the answer to a question, you're likely to work hard to pursue it. A second reason is that there is no need to bother children with questions when no one is interested in the answers. Children can often sense when teachers aren't really interested in their responses. It can be counterproductive to ask pointless questions. Why should they bother to give thoughtful responses when no one cares?

7. *Follow up on initial questions in ways that help the child provide adequate answers.*

Don't let your questions drop. If you have a question you really want the answer to, find a way to elicit the information. This often takes considerable ingenuity. Facility in finding the right ways takes lots of experience, thought, and practice. To get you started, here are some of the techniques we've found helpful in getting good answers:

a). *Vary the use of open-ended questions and those which ask for specific information.*
If your first question was very open-ended (such as "What do you like to

do?"), and has elicited only an "I don't know" or a shrug of the shoulders, try more specific questions such as "What do you like to play with in your *room?*" or "Do you like to make things with clay?—what kinds of things?" Sometimes the most open-ended version of a question falls flat because it isn't sufficiently suggestive (either to interest the child or to give him a starting point in his thinking). But open-ended questions are valuable, when they do elicit a response, in the fact that they allow the child to contribute whatever he or she thinks is relevant (rather than to meet a narrow request for information).

b). *It may sometimes be helpful to ask questions that are tangential to the main question you are pursuing.*

Tangential questions are most likely to be helpful when you think the question will do any of the following:

—maintain interest and motivation
—favorably affect the emotional tone of the interaction (e.g., reduce any stress, generally put you both at ease)
—stimulate easy-going conversation and the flow of ideas and/or
—help the child recollect or think through information relevant to answering the original question.

For example, it is often helpful to ask questions about related experiences a child may have had and/or about relevant information the child may possess. This can stimulate the generation of ideas and help the child bring what he or she knows to bear on the problem at hand.

c). Remember to *bring the discussion back to the initial focus after pursuing tangential lines of inquiry.*

For example, children often respond to a question such as "How many cats are there in this puzzle?" with an egocentric statement like "I have a cat at home." You can acknowledge the comment and make use of it in getting back to your original inquiry with a question such as "Do you have as many cats as there are in this puzzle?" Compare this to a question which pursues the tangent in ways that take you even further off focus—"What color is your cat?" "Is your cat the same color as this one?" The first question is unrelated to the puzzle you're discussing as well as to the more specific topic of *how many* cats there are. The second relates the tangential comment to the material at hand (the puzzle) but not to the original question. If the material is being used primarily as a way to find out about the child's understanding of number, then the question related to the material but not to the original question does not serve to bring the discussion back on focus.

d). *Occasionally contribute some suggestions for the children's reactions.*

Outrageous suggestions often add to the child's enjoyment of the exchange and stimulate ideas about appropriate answers. The twinkle in your eye makes it fun; the kind of error you choose to exaggerate guides the child's thoughts about what to consider in providing a reasonable answer. For example, if children are naming things which can fly, you might suggest a bear. When they protest, say "Why not?" The children will enjoy the incongruity and will be provoked to think what characterizes flying things, how a bear *could* fly, etc.

e). *Be honest about your lack of understanding, whether it be of the child's meaning or of the subject matter itself.*

Show puzzlement and ask for clarification. Particularly with young children, you won't get clarification unless you ask for it. In addition, your requests for more explanation show the child that you are genuinely interested in getting information and are not just making mindless conversation in question form.

Guidelines for Considering Effects of Context

The first seven guidelines we have presented are helpful rules of thumb for finding out about the children you work with. At the same time they are valuable guidelines for helping children become better thinkers. The next three guidelines also serve both purposes. These guidelines are more directly related to the context in which strategies are used. As you read through the next three guidelines you'll see the dual role each suggestion plays: (1) it suggests ways to enchance the kind and amount of information which you get about the children, and (2) it points to considerations that help the children's learning and problem-solving through those same interactions. In thinking about the activity you chose at the beginning of this chapter, consider the guidelines below. (It may also be helpful as you read the list to look back over samples of teacher-child dialogues in the previous chapters and to add to each guideline your own list of examples.) Here are the next three guidelines:

8.   *Adjust the classroom setting so as to provide good opportunities both for the children to learn and for you to learn about them.*

As you recall from Chapter 1, you can vary

a). Type and quantity of materials

b). Arrangement of space and materials

c). Rules and schedules for the use of space and materials

d). Teacher presence and role in facilitating change through interactions with individuals and/or through group dynamics.

Variations in these features will call into play different problem-solving capacities of children, will provide them with new challenges, and will help you to learn more about what kinds of interests and abilities the children have. Let's look at a few examples of these areas of decision-making with respect to the classroom setting, some of which appear in earlier chapters.

An example of decision-making about *type of materials* which is significant from our perspective involves the representational specificity of the materials which are available for dramatic play. Factors which should be weighed in selecting the objects are described in Chapter 8 (pp. 196–198).

In deciding about *quantity of materials*, you, the teacher, should think about what you have in mind in providing a particular type of material, let's say the wooden blocks. Your objectives furnish the basis for a preliminary judgment about the quantity of blocks (there should be enough to allow for the children to build fairly elaborate constructions, etc.); your objectives also guide your observations of whether your initial decision about quantity is working out as you hoped. You may want to add more blocks if the number provided seems too constraining or take away some if the block area is too cluttered for the children to work in.

In Chapter 7 we mentioned the importance of accessibility in *arrangement of materials*. When materials are accessible to children, an environment is established where the children can develop independence and a sense of competence. This is particularly important before you have extensive knowledge of the children. The less you know about their interests and abilities, the less equipped you are to select *for* them and the more you need to watch what they select and what they do with their choices. So making accessible a variety of materials with a broad range of potentials will (1) allow the children to find experiences from which they can learn and (2) allow you to find out more about the children's interests and abilities.

The placement of various kinds of materials in relation to each other, such as the proximity of blocks and dramatic play props, is another type of arrangement decision which is important both for the children's activity and for your learning about them as well. An example of teachers making such a decision about the proximity of various kinds of materials to each other is seen in Chapter 1.

Let's look at a few examples of how decisions about the *schedule* affect what you learn about the children as well as what they learn in the classroom environment. Although some flexibility of schedule is crucial to a child-centered classroom, there is much to be said for maintaining a fairly regular schedule. Children begin to formulate some idea of what is coming next in the day, to anticipate both the sequence and the duration of the various periods of activities such as free play, clean-up, circle time. The teacher can get insight into the children's understanding of the temporal sequence and the causal relationships of the day's activities by asking them questions such as "Why don't we clean-up at the very beginning of the day?" "What are some of the things we do before going outside?" Such questions serve the additional purpose, of course, of provoking children's reflection on sequences and relationships of activities they may not have thought about. In other words, the schedule itself can become the object of reflection and discussion; this is done best in the context of some regularity and the building up of expectations on the part of the children. An additional benefit of such conversations is that in children's increased understanding of schedules and other routines, these become less arbitrary and thus less frustrating.

Let's look at the *rule about use of space* and how, in addition to its other functions (such as preventing mayhem), it can influence the children's learning and provide an opportunity for you to add to your understanding of their thinking and their characteristics. Suppose you have set up a learning center for the free-play period which will only accommodate four children. At circle time you discuss with the children that when the four cushions in the area are occupied, they will need to find something else to do and try again later. The need for such a limit will be discussed. You will, of course, need to have interactions with individuals during free play when failures to remember, understand, or comply occur. You will see differences among the children in their behavior with respect to this rule and the notion of the "cushions occupied" reminder. You could handle the limited space problem by just asking children to find a place to play each time the area is in danger of getting too crowded. But by giving them the responsibility of staying within the limit you have put part of the cognitive demand on the child. A demand for pausing and making a judgment is also involved. Not every child will be able to do this from the beginning of the year, but seeing who does and who doesn't, as well as how each progresses over time with the use of such limitations, will be informative to you and show you what individuals may need to work on. At the same time, the children are provided with a cognitive challenge *and* a vote of confidence in their maturity.

Many of the ways in which your interactions with the children allow you simultaneously to promote the children's thinking and increase your knowledge of them were outlined under the first seven guidelines (Guidelines for Verbal Interaction). Now let's look at an example of how you can achieve this two-fold purpose through *actions you take with respect to context*—the decisions you make and opportunities you take advantage of with respect to materials, situations, and other contextual factors rather than your verbal interactions *per se*. Suppose there is a child in your class who never speaks up in circle time or approaches you during free play. When you address comments or questions to her, her replies are minimal and not very illuminating for your understanding of her development level. Is it shyness and inhibition? Does she understand what you and the other children are saying during group time? What is the level of her understanding? One of the actions which you can take to increase your knowledge of the child is to observe her behavior in a variety of contexts, both those she joins in naturally and others which you create, for example, small groups of various sizes, with various other peers, with and without teacher presence. Providing contexts in which the child may show a wider range of behaviors (especially those which you haven't had a chance to see much of) will be good both for the child's ease and growth and for your increased knowledge of her as an individual.

9.   *Use verbal and nonverbal methods to suggest new ways to examine and use materials.*

You might try out the materials yourself, handling them in a tentative way, sometimes accompanying your explorations with comments such as "I wonder if we could find a way to. . ." or "I wonder what would happen if I. . ."

A strategy such as this has several advantages. First, as you work with the materials you get a sense of their sensory attraction as well as the interesting problems that they provoke.

Second, the close involvement can help you see what questions are likely to occur spontaneously and what questions grab children's interest when suggested by someone else. For example, in playing alongside some children with color gels, you find this: the children you're with focus primarily on the variety of objects that change color when viewed through a gel. They do not spontaneously use the gels in combination. You find that when a child sees you combine a yellow and a blue gel and look through them, an interest is provoked which lasts and spreads to the others. However, the children do not get interested, at least on this occasion, in which particular combinations yield which colors. This is the kind of thing which you will discover as you explore the materials alongside the children, observing them and trying out things for yourself. You will begin to get a feel for questions which have a natural interest as opposed to those which are contrived. You will see the value and appeal of asking (at the water table) about how to make the water go up the sides of the container without losing any water; in contrast, you will see that a question about where the water goes when it spills is more contrived and less likely to intrigue the young child. In your parallel play with children exploring materials, you will see the value in asking questions which will help them gather facts about the materials, facts they can use in reasoning about the phenomena they are investigating.

Finally, your active involvement can serve to transmit an interest in the activity. Your enthusiasm and interest will be livelier when you are involved with exploring the materials yourself, and the genuineness of this enthusiasm will be perceived by the children.

This kind of strategy must be practiced with considerable care. The dangers of misuse are just about as great as the advantages gained through proper use. The value of the strategy is completely lost if the teacher takes over the activity. Remember, you want to *generate* enthusiasm in the children, not *supply* them with it; you want children to see the interesting questions and begin to investigate them, not watch you learn.

10. *Adapt both the kinds and numbers of questions to the context.*

Some important contextual variables to consider are:

a). *Familiarity with materials*

On the whole, when a child is involved with exploring new materials, questions relating to the *features* of the material itself are more likely to be effective than, let's say, questions about the uses of the material. The latter are more appropriate after the child has had the time and in some cases the help in exploring the materials. For example, if the child is playing with plastic interlocking blocks for the first time, the teacher might say, "You mean you can hold your stack upside down and these won't fall off! How does that work?" It would be less profitable during the early states of exploration to ask the child if he can think of a way to make a house without windows. Observation of each child's activity will provide the teacher with the best indication of how familiar the child is with the materials and how absorbed he or she is with exploring them. But there is no rush; the time the child spends manipulating materials and learning about their properties is in no sense time wasted.

b). *Personal/emotional aspects*

Is the child showing off for a friend? Is she angry, frustrated, tired, giggly about something unrelated to the activity at hand? Sometimes these are temporary states and can be rechanneled by your helping the child deal with his or her problem or changing his or her mood; sometimes you will want to wait for a better time. Recall the example in Chapter 7 (when two boys' reading was disturbed by the music-making of two girls). The teacher's decision to involve the children in a problem-solving session was based on her assessment that the children were calm enough to be able to deal with the issue cognitively.

The emotional dimension is always a factor for the teacher to consider. There is great pleasure for children in solving problems, working with materials and with friends. But there are other emotional considerations. Shyness in a group decreases the focus on the intellectual aspects of the activity. A question which is fun for one child is threatening to another who is very afraid of being wrong, and so forth. A successful teacher never treats a child as a disembodied mind. Children's desires, emotions, and moods in the classroom are inextricably linked with their intellectual functioning. Teachers must gear their verbal strategies accordingly.

c). *Time*

In all of the wonderful intentions a teacher has for having long and thoughtful conversations with children, there is still reality to consider! Part of the time she is wiping noses, tying shoes, keeping an eye on a group of children who are playing with a new material, and watching Sally, who has been picking fights all morning.

You may be in the sandbox working with Tim on an interesting construction problem when nearby Jeff and Laurie start wrangling over a toy. You don't want to interrupt what you and Tim are doing. Your best move may be to draw Jeff and Laurie into involvement with you and Tim—and *part* of the time, it works! But often you will have to leave an intriguing conversation with one child to save another child from injury at the hands of his playmate in the block corner. When the crisis is over, look to see if the first child is still involved with the same materials you were discussing. You may want to go back and find out what he's up to now. Even if his interest has shifted, your return to acknowledge that you haven't forgotten him will be appreciated.

Even when no crisis arises, spending twenty minutes at a time within an individual child or group is usually not the best use of your time. Move around the room from time to time. Sometimes a good way of exiting from one group is to leave them with a question or problem to work on, returning later to see what they've come up with. They may move on to other things, but that's OK too. Working together (or individually) without a teacher present is something you want to encourage. Coming back to problems later is a way of showing your interest and can also be a good opportunity for mental reconstruction, for example, "You've fixed these boards in a different way, I think. How is it different from the way we had it before?"

d). *Social aspects (group size, composition, etc.)*

We have seen at various points in the book circumstances where the size of a group was a determinant in the type of questions a teacher chose to ask, and vice versa—often the questions you want to explore help determine which format to use for an activity (large group, divided group, informal learning center, small "selected" group in private area, individual interaction).

As an example, a large group is not well-suited to pursuing a line of thought at length and following up on a child's individual responses. On the other hand, when the generating of many ideas is the focus, a large group setting may be ideal.

Sometimes the developmental level of the children needs to be fairly homogeneous—problems which are too easy and boring for some children may be too difficult for others to even perceive. At other times, the teacher can put to advantage the learning from each other and the challenging of each others' perspectives offered by a heterogeneous group. Clearly there are implications of this group composition on verbal strategies. For example, when working with a group where the children are at different levels, the teacher will try to choose questions which can be responded to thoughtfully on a variety of levels.

e). *Noncognitive demands of the task itself*

The teacher needs to consider the nonintellectual demands an activity may place on the child, such as the physical skill and coordination required (for example, cutting with scissors may tax Peg's concentration to the limit and make her far less able to deal with cognitive demands than she usually is); or there may be emotional demands inherent in an activity. For example, children may be visiting an unfamiliar setting; some may not be comfortable enough to do their best thinking at such times. An awareness of this possibility should guide the teacher in both the frequency and the level of her verbal interaction, particularly her asking of questions.

Now think through the activity we suggested you select to try out with some children. Read through the guidelines again thinking through how each one applies in the activity you are planning:

1. Initiate interactions, but do it gently and time them carefully.
2. Ask questions rather than giving statements.
3. Answer questions but avoid doing the child's thinking for him.
4. Ask questions simply.
5. Allow children time to answer questions.
6. Ask questions for which you really want to know the child's answer.
7. Follow up on initial questions.

8. Adjust the classroom setting so as to provide good opportunities for the children to learn and for you to learn about them.
9. Use verbal and nonverbal methods to suggest new ways to examine and use materials.
10. Adapt both the *kinds* and *numbers* of questions to the context.

Thinking through each guideline in turn in relation to your activity, make notes on points you will want to keep in mind as you try it out. If you have the opportunity, it may be helpful to try out your activity once at this point. There will be more refinements to consider later, but these will be easier to incorporate if you have had an initial experience with the activity. You will be more comfortable and what you learn from the children's reactions in the first experience will help you plan the second.

Applying the Guidelines: The Importance of Focus

In previous chapters we have noted some of the variations in the use of these guidelines in accordance with differing environmental contexts, children's developmental levels, and considerations of specific interests, personality traits, and social situations. In spite of the differences, however, all interactions shared an important feature: all were characterized by having a focus. As teachers arranged the physical environment, provided social settings, and engaged in verbal interactions, they did so with specific purposes in mind. Furthermore, the purpose was rather finely specified. Why? What are the advantages to be gained?

Because the answers to these questions are particularly easy to see for verbal interactions, and because the skillful use of such interactions plays a vital but all too frequently overlooked role in the child's construction of knowledge, we will concentrate here on a discussion of verbal interactions, leaving the implications for other kinds of teacher behavior for you to work out.

You have probably noticed a predominance of questions in the teacher verbalizations of the dialogues in the preceding chapters and an emphasis on questioning in the preceding guidelines. This is no accident. Expertise in the use of inquiry is one of a teacher's most valuable assets. It is difficult to acquire, and its proper exercise demands considerable sensitivity and perceptiveness. But its benefits make it well worth the effort. The most valuable dialogues are those with a sustained focus. Skillful inquiry strategies will contribute to such sustained focus. They are useful because when they are applied wisely they

1). can help teachers find out *what* and *how* children think
2). can motivate children to become intellectually active (as they take delight in the fact that some important adult is interested in their thoughts)
3). can enhance cognitive development through the introduction of discrepancies, the activation of problem-solving processes, and the focus of persistent attention on interesting and fruitful issues.

4). can help children become aware of their own thought processes as they clarify for themselves what they do and do not know

5). can provide the direction and guidance needed for children to think through challenging issues

6). can encourage thorough examinations of a problem or interest by providing time, emotional support, and intellectual help (so that children experience the joys of finding a solution, devising an explanation, etc.).

Skillful inquiry strategies have clear benefits. Certainly they are well worth acquiring. We'll be describing and summarizing some specific strategies and some ways of developing skill in inquiry later in this chapter, but first a few words are in order concerning the general nature of focused inquiry and the application of it to various contexts.

To better understand the importance of focused inquiry, let's consider the experience of a young interviewer, Mr. Kent, who has been granted thirty minutes of time with a popular screen personality. He wants to know about three major areas of the actress's life: (1) her future career plans, (2) her views on the women's movement, and (3) her love life. Mr. Kent talks with the actress for thirty minutes and finds her very cordial. When he listens to his tape, however, he is amazed to find that he has learned very little about the actress's thoughts in any of the three areas he'd planned to write about. He has two good quotes about her love life but not much else. He groans when he hears himself change to different topics or pursue tangents just when he should have followed up on some interesting comment or intriguing contradiction.

As suggested in guideline 7, skillful inquiry requires follow-up. An initial question must be followed with other related questions: (1) to allow the interviewer (or teacher) to gain a coherent and in-depth understanding of what the interviewee thinks about the issue or problem at hand and (2) to stimulate in the interviewee (or child) sustained thought about a problem or a set of interrelated questions.

Your interviewees, particularly when they are young children, will not have thought through in advance what they think and want to communicate about the question you have asked. In a successful interview (or learning encounter), you and your interviewee will figure this out together. In working toward shared meanings each of you will come to understand some of the other's initial ideas, and together you will generate new thoughts on the matter at hand. This feature is what makes the inquiry process so valuable for enhancing development. In finding out about *what* and *how* children think, teachers are also provoking and sharing in the children's construction of new understandings. Let's look at a segment from a focused inquiry which appeared in Chapter 5:

Stopping the film after the sound of the helicopter, Denise asks, "What was that one?" Some children shout immediately, "A plane!" and others, "A helicopter!"

Feeling that for some of them "plane" may encompass helicopter, Denise tries to clarify what they are thinking. "Some of you said a helicopter and some a plane. Mark, did you mean any special kind of plane or a regular jet plane, or what?" Mark replies, "A jet." Several other children changing or clarifying their original statement to "plane" say, "A helicopter! A chopper."

Denise notes, "Some of you thought you were hearing a jet and some a helicopter. Would they sound the same, do you think? Maybe they make the same noise? Would you like to hear this one again? Get your ears ready to listen—here it comes."

Mark and some other children now exclaim, "It *is* a helicopter," while a chorus of mostly younger children are still saying "a plane," "a jet," or changing to imitate the others.

Denise asks one of the helicopter indentifiers, "Laurie, what makes you think we're hearing a helicopter?" Mark breaks in, "I hear the 'pellor." Denise sees a nod from Laurie and says, "Laurie, you heard the propellor?""(Another nod.) To try to see if Laurie is really understanding, she asks, "What part of the helicopter is the propellor?" and Laurie makes a circular motion with her hand.

The focus of this activity is not on distinctive features of different planes and vehicles nor on the cause-effect relationship behind the sounds, i.e., *why* the propellor makes a certain sound, so Denise does not stop to pursue Laurie's concepts of these aspects. Instead, she proceeds, "But before when some of you said it was a jet and some said a helicopter, *nobody* said it was a rowboat. How come? There was a rowboat in the film. How did you know that wasn't what we were hearing?"

Modification of Focus

Having a sustained focus in your interactions with children does *not* mean that a predetermined focus is inflexibly adhered to regardless of how the child responds. A skilled interviewer may find one line of questioning unproductive or find intriguing aspects he hadn't anticipated which appear to merit further exploration. The same may happen with teachers and children. Sometimes what comes up can be dealt with as an interesting side road and merely explored briefly before returning to the original focus. At other times the child's responses tell the teacher that the focus of the inquiry as a whole should be modified. There are a number of legitimate ways in which focus may be modified.

One possibility is that you may *narrow the focus* from the one you had in mind. This is usually done in order to expand in greater depth on some part of the original focus. For example, you may have defined your focus beforehand as discussing with the children their ideas about the changes that occur in growing up, which you expected to include changes in how people look, what they can do, and what their lives are like. The physical changes, which you had anticipated to be of less appeal, turn out to be of great concern and interest. The children's contradictory notions furnish a great deal of interchange; you become fascinated by their understandings. It is a valid decision to choose to narrow the focus and spend the entire group time talking with the children about the physical changes in growing up and aging.

Another type of narrowing of focus occurs when you have planned to include several components of the problem-solving process in an activity (e.g., generating and evaluating ideas) but find as the activity proceeds that it would be best to focus on one or the other. Perhaps you find that the children get very involved in coming up with alternatives. You may legitimately decide to continue to encourage the children's generating of ideas rather than moving them on to scrutinizing a few of the alternatives in detail. Or it may happen that the first idea or two suggested are intriguing to the children and have many interesting aspects to evaluate; you may decide to pare down your intention of having the children generate a variety of alternatives before evaluating a few in detail and concentrate only on the latter.

The focus of an activity can legitimately be narrowed either in content or process. The focus can also be *shifted* with respect to either content or process and for reasons of the same kind described above. There are two types of situations which most commonly necessitate narrowing or modifying the focus of your inquiry.

(1) *If the children are more interested in an aspect of the problem which wasn't originally planned as the focus* (but which has rich potential). For example, in Chapter 3 Denise had planned to work with the children in discussing various problems in arranging the playground, employing a diagram as a tool in evaluation. She had brought pieces of paper to use in working with the diagram, planning to ask a few questions about representing the pieces of equipment with these flat pieces before presenting some problems of equipment arrangement. However, the children got interested in issues of representing things on the diagram. Their opinions and reasoning, their disagreements and solutions were just what Denise might have labored long to provoke another day—too good to pass up in the interest of remaining with her planned focus! Denise doesn't abandon the use of focused inquiry, however. Her questioning and her presentation of problems are just as strongly focused when she decides to shift; it is simply that she makes a change in what she focuses on.

(2) *If you misjudged the difficulty of some part of the activity and now find some aspect is harder (or easier) than you anticipated.* It is hard to judge how difficult a certain question or series of questions will be for individual children. In thinking about an activity you may have planned a sequence of questions or problems (roughly, of course—the skilled use of inquiry would never include going through a set of predetermined questions by rote); now you find that the children find even the first few questions very difficult. Instead of proceeding to your original focus, you may need to redefine it more modestly, concentrating on "A" and not worrying about getting to "B" and "C."

On the other hand, you may find that children respond to your questions *too* easily. They find the answers obvious; there is no disagreement among the children—this too is a waste of time. Suppose your focus was to have the children make predictions about which end of the balance beam will go down as you place various combinations of items in the pans. You might have thought that in this activity, the first of a series, the children would find sufficient challenge in predicting that the balance will tip if more wooden cubes are placed on one side than the other, that color doesn't matter, and that equal numbers make it balance. But the children find all of this absurdly obvious. They're ready for more difficult problems such as the discrepancy of three balsa cubes being outweighed by two of the regular wooden cubes. Careful thought beforehand will prepare you for some of these shifts; realizing that children may be able to go farther than you think, you bring some materials and thoughts of possible extensions just in case. But this doesn't always happen. Be flexible, ready to take cues from the children, and unconcerned about having everything mapped out ahead of time. It is a healthy learning experience for the children to see, for example, that sometimes one has to obtain additional materials to explore new problems as they arise; they can help you think of what's needed and how to get it.

Developing Skills in Focused Inquiry

Practicing Through Small Group Activities

After you have tried to apply the guidelines in a general way, you are ready to do some hard, detailed work on your own strategies. One of the best ways to do this is in a small group setting, with a teacher-directed activity. There are several advantages to beginning this way.

First, this is the situation in which you can do the maximum amount of thinking through in advance and have the minimum amount of management problems to contend with. You can practice your strategies and concentrate on the children's responses in a somewhat controlled situation. Just as you wouldn't take your first driving lesson in a sleet storm, there is no need to take on additional problems when you're trying to learn new teaching skills.

Second, it is easier to stay with a focus if you know ahead of time what the focus is and have thought through ways of pursuing it. Although in any interaction you have with a child there should be a sustained focus to your inquiry, there is a continuum in the degree to which this focus is derived from your planning and initiated by you, the teacher. In free-play situations the cue for the focus is taken from the child and is more likely to shift in the currents of free-play activity. In the small group situation which is initiated by the teacher the focus is decided upon in advance and although it is subject to modifications of the kinds discussed in the previous section, you still have a considerably easier job concentrating on trying new strategies than when you have to do *all* your thinking on your feet.

A third advantage to using the small group setting as a preliminary situation for developing your teaching strategies is that you can more easily tape-record the activity and use this aid in evaluating your experience. This is an advantage which should not be underestimated. It is amazing how helpful a tape recording or outside observer can be in helping you notice aspects of the activity which you don't even pick up when involved in the activity. (Videotaping, of course, is even more eye-opening and helpful, but is not as easily available to most teachers.)

Now, think of your activity again. You may or may not have done it as a small group the first time you tried it out. If it is adaptable to this format, stick with the same activity; if it is not, come up with another activity which you feel comfortable with and would like to try with a few children. Consider the following practical points for your next attempt at focused inquiry.

Some Pointers for Your Initial Attempts

WHEN?　　During free play at a time when no special festivities are going on (such as the presence of a visiting pet, the making of popcorn); at the beginning of the day when a few children have arrived early and your teaching partner is on hand to greet the others.

WHERE?　　Out of the mainstream; in an area that is cozy, quiet, uncluttered—no tempting materials to be held or explored.

WHO?　　The children you know best, feel most comfortable with; the most cooperative children and in a group which can be expected to work well together. (You need reasonably "easy" children while you're focusing all your efforts on developing your own strategies.)

WHAT?　　An activity you like and have reason to think the children will like; avoid run and chase games, ball games, activities that require lots of materials or materials that are hard to handle. (You need to concentrate your energies on thinking, not on managing materials.)

WHY?　　Think about the goals for this activity:

(a) *What will you work on in yourself?*

Choose a strategy (or several) that you want to concentrate on. For example, you may decide you need to work on following up on questions. Keep this in mind both in planning and in carrying out the activity; don't expect to get better at everything at once.

(b) *What is the objective for the children?*

There are various levels of specificity with which you might respond to this question and some are too general to be helpful in planning (e.g., to learn, become more creative). In the strategy chart at the end of this chapter you will see objectives at a broad level, such as "Elaborate and/or refine a specific representation or idea." In the Appendix you will see some sample lesson plans. The "Reasoning" section will give you an idea of how specifically the objectives are defined for a particular activity. Both levels of objective need to be considered in planning an activity, for example, "elaborate a specific idea" and "mentally reconstruct the sequence of events in the operation of pressing cider."

HOW?   (a) *Preparing yourself for the activity.*
Based on your objectives for the activity, think about the strategies you will use, including the questions you will ask; consider what the children's possible responses might be and how you will respond if they do not understand, give irrelevant answers, etc. This preparation will make you feel more secure and help you keep from panicking if everything doesn't go as you envisioned.
(b) *Getting the children to the activity.*
You have prepared an activity which you think children will enjoy. Approach them with this in mind—never be apologetic in inviting children to join you for an activity!
(c) *Setting the stage.*
Make it clear when you start the activity and when it is over. Tell the children what the activity is—not "I'm going to read you a book" but "I'm going to read a book, we're going to think about it, and talk over some parts of it."
(d) *Make the activity brief and to the point; end on a high note.* For example, don't read a second story even if the children request it; instead, first end the group and then read the story to those who requested it in a new place in the room. As your skills increase, there will be times you may decide to keep going with an activity longer than anticipated, but always you should try to end on a high note—not by the children losing interest.

Now you're ready to try out your activity. When you have finished, try to find time to sit down and think about what happened. If you have made a tape recording, listen to it, making notes of points you want to think about. Look back over the guidelines and ask yourself how well you followed each. Think about how you would do the activity differently if you were doing it again. You may decide to actually do it again. With this experience behind you, you will be better prepared to read the following section more thoughtfully.

The Whys and Hows: Thinking about Objectives and Strategies

We began this book by looking at teachers in a decision-making situation. There is not a page of the subsequent chapters which does not deal with teachers' decisions. We have presented our own perspective on many of these decisions. At an even more basic level, our message has been *to be sure to ask yourself why* in each choice you make in the classroom. In concluding the book we would like to summarize the central teaching objectives and strategies of our perspective. Here again the important point to think about is the relationship between the whys and the hows.

We have listed ten goals which we believe are the crux of educating the young thinker:

1. To become increasingly aware of objects and events, and one's reactions to them.

2. To understand and use a variety of methods for finding out about objects and events.
3. To elaborate and/or refine a specific representation or idea.
4. To search one's internal representations for those meeting specific criteria.
5. To become acquainted with elements of representational systems.
6. To understand representational use of systems.
7. To understand and use a variety of representational systems.
8. To seek out, perceive, or identify problems.
9. To generate solutions and alternatives.
10. To evaluate through reasoning.

The list is not exhaustive. You will note that we do not include goals for children's physical development, emotional development, etc. We are concentrating on *cognitive goals*, although we have attempted to make it clear that cognitive processes are involved in all aspects of the children's development—their social competence, their understanding of themselves and others, their awareness of the elements of body movement.

Each goal as stated is rather general; each could be divided into subgoals. The ten goals can be viewed as "organizers" under which more specific teacher objectives can be grouped. These ten categories of teacher objectives cover, we believe, much of what teachers across many programs see as important. They may not be worded the same way by all teachers and programs, but there is much that is shared. But more important than the particular objectives is a way of thinking about activities which is reflected in these outlines of the goals and strategies.

If you will look at the first page of the objectives strategies (p. 231), you will see that it is divided into Decision Point 1, which includes *What Goals for the Interaction* and *Why These Goals*, and Decision Point 2, which includes *What Strategies to Use in Accomplishing These Goals* and three types of *Consideration Involved in This Choice of Strategies* (Cognitive Demands, Motivational Considerations, and Diagnostic Considerations). Both of these decision points are extremely important and they should always occur in this order: first you think about your *goals* for the interaction and then you think about the *strategies* to use in accomplishing them. The strategies should be chosen with three sets of considerations in mind. Strategies should be judged as to whether they place on the child those cognitive demands which are the purpose of the interaction.

Strategies should also be evaluated with respect to their effectiveness motivationally. Will they engage the child? Will he or she find the activity interesting? Do the questions activate *intrinsic motivation* in the children (rather than requiring external reinforcement, such as praise)?

A third criterion for choosing strategies is that they help the teacher find out about the children's knowledge, interests, and thought. Good strategies are those which are effective in all three respects: they place appropriate cognitive demands on the child, they activate the child's interest, and they allow the teacher to learn what she needs to learn about the children.

The strategies listed in the outlines which follow are only examples. We have found each of them consistently effective on all three counts. The choice of which to use in a particular situation and the devising of others will be easier and easier for you as you begin to internalize the kind of reasoning these outlines reflect.

Objectives→Strategies

1. Awareness of Environment:

BECOME INCREASINGLY AWARE OF OBJECTS AND EVENTS AND ONE'S REACTIONS TO THEM

Decision Point 1
What Goals for the Interaction

Enlarge children's acquaintance with objects, sensations, physical attributes, responses of others.
Increase children's awareness of their own reactions to aspects of objects, events, and interactions.

Why These Goals

Expand children's experiences and provide ideas to think about, to wonder about, to use in creating and solving problems.
Broaden children's knowledge as a base for subsequent effective problem-solving.
Encourage analytic thinking; help children to develop the tendency to notice details instead of just getting global impressions.
Increase children's sensitivity to objects and events in the world for the pleasure this provides.

Decision Point 2
What Strategies to Use in Accomplishing These Goals

(a) Elicit children's ideas and impressions through direct or indirect open-ended questions, e.g.,

Tell me about this.
What do you know about this?

What kinds of things can we say about this?
This can be done with the object or event available only through one sense, e.g., through touching (in a bag,) through hearing (on tape or behind a screen).

(b) Ask about specific attributes such as color, shape, texture, size, flexibility, etc., e.g.,

Tell me about its color.
What else feels like this?
Does it smell like anything you've smelled before?
Does this taste like the first one? How is it different?

(c) Highlight features of objects by performing (or asking about) a transformation, e.g.,

How would I make mine feel like yours? (About the surface of a piece of clay)
What would you have to do to make that go through here?
(With a cylindrical piece and a round hole)

Considerations Involved in This Choice of Strategies
  Cognitive Demands:

Being asked to notice and describe how an object or event feels, looks, etc., requires the child to *relate the object to others he or she has experienced in the past, noting similarities and/or differences* in attributes and in his or her own reactions. (a and b)
The strategy of eliminating information through some sensory channels *reduces the difficulty of the "filtering out" task and* thus increases awareness of previously unnoticed features (as we notice sound more in the dark). (a)

Motivational Considerations:

Strategies which are effective from a motivational standpoint here are often those which include a specific reason for very careful observing or a problem to be solved—to find out what a mystery object is, to describe an experience to someone who hasn't had it, etc.

Diagnostic Considerations:

The open-ended questions allow the teacher to learn what features are noticed by the children; the extent and nature of the children's knowledge and interests are tapped. The more specific questions provide information on children's utilization of past experience in relation to new objects, events, reactions.

2. Awareness of Environment:

UNDERSTAND AND USE A VARIETY OF METHODS FOR FINDING OUT ABOUT OBJECTS AND EVENTS

Decision Point 1
  What Goals for the Interaction

Increase children's acquaintance with various methods of learning about objects and phenomena.
Help children to become aware of methods at an explicit and differentiated level, rather than to explore only globally and unreflectively.

Why These Goals

Increase the methods children are familiar with for learning about the world and thus improve the specificity and effectiveness of their investigations and problem-solving.
Develop in children the tendency and ability to evaluate a given method for finding out about something so as to make them more efficient and thorough investigators.

Decision Point 2
  What Strategies to Use in Accomplishing These Goals

(a)   Ask the children how they arrived at a conclusion or discovered a property, e.g.,
How could you tell the pudding was very hot?
(b)   Ask
What else can we do to find out about it? (With a concealed or unfamiliar object, for example)
Suppose we want to find out how hard it is. What could we do to find out? What else could we do?
You think it might be something to eat? But suppose we couldn't take a bite yet—how else could we find out?
(c)   Place restraints on methods which can be used, e.g.,
Suppose you couldn't use your hands. How could you find out about what's in here?
(d)   Give a suggestion the children will reject and ask them to explain why it wouldn't help, e.g.,
Do you think if we hid it that would help?

Considerations Involved in This Choice of Strategies
  Cognitive Demands:

Strategies such as (a) and (d) require children to *reflect on the means through which particular kinds of things about a stimulus can be learned.* They are asked not just about their conclusions, but about their methods.

In (b) and (c) the teacher's questions require the children to go beyond the first few ideas that come to mind. When some of the obvious ways to investigate something are eliminated, the children must *search their minds and experience for other possibilities.*

They must *consider the appropriateness of a given method to the particular kind of information desired.*

Motivational Considerations:

As with Objective 1, the children are more engaged when the problem to be investigated is an interesting one. Strategies which enhance the children's notion of themselves as competent seekers of answers ("detectives," "scientists") are good motivators. Children enjoy pointing out that a teacher suggestion (as in d) won't work and often redouble their efforts to suggest useful methods in its place.

Diagnostic Considerations:

The teacher can learn which kinds of methods are harder to think of, for the group and for individual children. She can discover what sorts of inferences the children make in reaching their conclusion (e.g., "I know the pudding's hot because it got dark").

3. Representational Competence:
(Internal Representation)

ELABORATE AND/OR REFINE A SPECIFIC
REPRESENTATION OR IDEA

Decision Point 1
  What Goals for the Interaction

Get children to attend to their own thought, and to clarify for themselves memories, images, or ideas.
Help children learn how to sharpen their ideas.
Help children see the importance of having clear ideas.

Why These Goals

Encourage children's tendency to actively reconstruct what they've experienced, thus adding to the richness, as well as the accuracy of their mental representations.
Increase children's tendency and/or ability to clarify an internal repre-

sentation before representing it externally or putting it to use in solving a problem.

Decision Point 2
What Strategies to Use in Accomplishing These Goals

(a)   In telling a story, describing an object, character, or situation verbally and, providing no picture, encourage the children to form a mental representation of it. In some cases, your questions or comments can further encourage the elaboration and refinement of these representations, e.g.,

> Think about what the body of the monster is like. What is your monster's skin like?
> Now this huge monster is going to sit down in the princess's little chair. Picture in your mind what that will be like.

b)   Elicit children's descriptions (of objects, places, events) verbally or through other modes such as drawing or gesture. Ask about specific details of appearance, sequence, or spatial arrangement, e.g.,

> What did your grandmother do after you gave her the present?
> Was the cookie jar on a low shelf or a high shelf when it fell?

(c)   Draw the children's attention to a reason for thinking about (and showing) how a thing looked in clear and elaborate form. For example, after a field trip to the airport make a tape describing what was seen to another class. Ask

> Jane said the helicopter had a fast propeller. How will they know we're not talking about the jet? Think—did they look different?

(d)   When the children are engaging in problem-solving encourage their mental reconstruction of similar experiences; comment on the occasions when clarifying an internal representation pays off, e.g.,

> Todd said he remembered that butter needs to be melted before you stir it in and that worked.

Considerations Involved in This Choice of Strategies
Cognitive Demands:

Questions about specific details and relationships are intended to *involve children in active reconstruction of internal representations.* Increasingly they will *call on reasoning along with "simple" memory,* in putting together the picture or the account of how things were or predicting how they will be (for example, "I must have been wearing my gloves when I walked downtownbecause it was very cold").

Attempts to draw or imitate through movement how something looks also require mental attention to the specifics of what is to be represented; this can be enhanced by encouraging the child to articulate mentaily his or her idea of how something looked or moved.

Motivational Considerations:

When the child is motivated to express or convey something (the way something looked, what happened, etc.), the time is opportune for asking questions which call for refining or elaborating the mental representation of it. Children will also be engaged when there is a problem at hand, the solution of which depends on mentally reconstructing a relevant piece of information or past situation.

Diagnostic Considerations:

In (a) the teacher learns what the children's individual concepts and images are when the appearance, etc., are left to their imagination rather than being provided. The children's abilities to refine or to elaborate their mental representations will often not be accurately reflected in only one mode of expression, such as verbal. Some children might have highly elaborated images of how the clowns looked, but not be able to describe these verbally, while in movement or in pictures they show aspects of their detailed recollections.

4. Representational Competence:
(Internal Representation)

SEARCH ONE'S INTERNAL REPRESENTATIONS FOR THOSE MEETING SPECIFIC CRITERIA

Decision Point 1
  What Goals for the Interaction

Increase children's facility in reflecting on their own thoughts.
Increase children's awareness of similarities and differences.

Why These Goals

Provide experience in internal scanning
Increase flexibility of thought: the tendency to consider a wide range of options and ability to "break set."

Increase attention to specific features of the stimulus or category of stimuli. Increase classificatory skill (with single and multiple criteria for classification).

Decision Point 2
What Strategies to Use in Accomplishing These Goals

(a)   Ask for ideas which meet specific criteria, e.g.,

Think of things that are green.
Think of things that are green and good to eat.
Can anyone think of anything that is green and good to eat that isn't a vegetable?
Have you ever eaten anything else that was green? (To help in breaking out of set, if necessary)

(b)   Show children an object (or let them listen to a sound) and ask them to think of as many things as they can that look (sound) like it. Do this with a variety of sensory qualities and a variety of objects. More demanding questions require children to think of things having combinations of qualities (e.g., things that sound like this and feel hard).

(c)   Use "What Could This Be?" games with pantomime (as in Chapter 5, p.86), music (Chapter 5, p.98), and drawing (in which part of an object is drawn and children suggest all the things it could be).

Considerations Involved in This Choice of Strategies
Cognitive Demands:

The children must *search their minds for an idea which meets one or more criterion and must ignore irrelevant characteristics.*

In being challenged to come up with more than one or two ideas, the children must *"conduct a thorough search," not resting with the few that come most effortlessly to mind.*

Restrictions (such as green *and* good to eat) serve this purpose of *widening the range of mental search,* as when children have named only things such as trees and grass; at the same time, they place a demand for *holding in mind and applying more than one criterion.*

Understanding that many items can fit a set of criteria or a partial description requires the child to get *beyond a convergent type of thought.*

Motivational Considerations:

The game-like nature of these strategies is exciting to children; they enjoy the challenge of coming up with an idea that fits the criteria. The atmosphere, however, is not competitive or right-answer oriented. The teacher should take care to ask questions to which there are numerous answers and convey to the children that the fun is in the thinking itself.

Diagnostic Considerations:

Strategies such as these allow the teacher to find out about the children's knowledge and concepts. For example, if she asks them to think of the people in their families and finds they don't include grandparents, aunts, etc., she learns what their construction of "family" is. Difficulties in dealing with multiple criteria (e.g., four-legged and on a farm) will often be revealed. The teacher will also see children's individual style differences, such as the tendency to give a lot of ideas including some that don't fit the criteria vs. a few ideas that fit on all counts.

5. Representational Competence: (External Representation)

BECOME ACQUAINTED WITH ELEMENTS OF REPRESENTATIONAL SYSTEMS

Decision Point 1
  What Goals for the Interaction

Help children to discriminate elements of the system. Get children to understand how elements of the system can be combined (e.g., tempo and rhythm in music, color and form in pictures).

Why These Goals

Enhance children's enjoyment of creations in the given midium. Increase children's ability to engage in problem-solving in the medium, that is, to achieve a desired effect. Expand familiarity with elements which will help children to use systems representationally.

Decision Point 2
  What Strategies to Use in Accomplishing These Goals

(a)   Manipulate the elements (e.g., vary the rhythm, darken the color; combine high and loud in contrast to low and loud, etc.) in presenting examples of the mode to children.

Involve them in manipulation of the elements by the materials you provide, by mutual imitation and variation. For instance, the child is playing with a certain beat; you play this beat along with him and then introduce a modification.

(b)   Make selections (in the songs you teach, the pieces you have on tape, the pictures you display, etc.) which have salient characteristics, such as

pronounced changes in rhythm, direction, hue, etc., or can be juxtaposed with selections that contrast with them clearly.
Have children classify, e.g.,

Which ones seem to go together to you?
(Or seriate) You think some of these are faster than others?
Well, let's see which of these songs is the very slowest, the next slowest, and the fastest.

(c)   Give children a problem and get them to generate possibilities, e.g., in a movement problem, possible pathways from this place to that; draw attention to the different solutions children have found: curved, straight, zigzag.

Considerations Involved in This Choice of Strategies
Cognitive Demands:

Children must *discriminate a given element, usually noticing it in the midst of other elements.* For example, if it is a question of the child noticing a rhythm difference between Piece A and Piece B, the two have many other differences as well as rhythm.
Decentering from one aspect of a musical selection, painting, etc., is also difficult for the child; this is *particularly challenging when more than one element is varied independently,* as when one movement is slow and smooth, one fast and jerky.

Motivational Considerations:

Young children prefer exploring and actively manipulating the modes (music, movement, etc.). Pleasant sensory experiences are a better context for becoming familiar with the elements of a given system than are selections or examples which are illustrative but unlovely. Solving problems is a motivating way to learn, here as elsewhere.

Diagnostic Considerations:

When the teacher provides problems to the class, she sets up an opportunity for observing how the various children respond in the given mode and with the particular media: their awareness of the elements and their ability to manipulate them to achieve desired effects. By having the children respond in the given mode rather than always verbally, the teacher gets a fuller picture of the children's familiarity with the elements of the system.

6. Representational Competence:
(External Representation)

UNDERSTAND REPRESENTATIONAL USE OF SYSTEMS

Decision Point 1
  What Goals for the Interaction

> Acquaint children with basic labels and symbols for objects, properties, feelings, etc. and/or where they apply.
> Increase children's understanding of how a given representational system is used, what the potentials and limitations are for conveying messages.
> Increase children's awareness of the link between the symbol and that which it represents (where this connection is other than arbitrary).

Why These Goals

Enable children to share *standard* symbols for communication (1) for the activity at hand and (2) for life in this society.
Develop children's thinking skills within various representational systems.
Give children a more reflective view of the communicative use of representational systems so they can use them efficiently.

Decision Point 2
  What Strategies to Use in Accomplishing These Goals

(a) Ask children what things (events, feelings, etc.) are called, helping them draw on past experience where appropriate, e.g.,

> Have you ever seen anything like this before?

Provide label or symbol if child doesn't know it.
Ask children about the application of labels or symbols to new objects and in new contexts, e.g.,

> What do you call this? Oh, this is a _____ _____ too?

(b) Present children with representational problems, e.g.,

> Show us what character you are by the way you move.

Ask questions or make comments which focus on need to communicate, e.g.,

> How are they going to know you're an *old* man?

Ask children how they know what a representation is, e.g.,
    How do you know Jon is being a monkey?
    How can you tell the man in the picture is angry?

Considerations Involved in This Choice of Strategies
    Cognitive Demands:

As a child learns a given symbol or label he *constructs an understanding of the objects or situations to which it applies;* as he is confronted with cases which are discrepant with his constructions, he must *resolve this discrepancy by modifying his notion of what is meant by the label or symbol.* Through this continuing process the child increasingly learns the meaning of a symbol or label as it is standard in society.

When the child is dealing with a representation which he is to interpret, he must compare *features of it to his mental representations of objects and events.* The strategies described (especially c) require the child to *reflect on what cues he used* in making his judgment.

When the child is producing a representation himself, he must call *to mind the internal representation(s)* he has of the object, movement, etc., and think of how he could convey it to others. In doing this, he must (1) *analyze the features of the referent and select the features which are distinctive* so as to communicate effectively to a person who doesn't know what the thing is (e.g., the trunk of the elephant is more distinctive than his tail and thus more *communicative)* and (2) *invent the means for representing these relevant features* through available resources, e.g., the parts of his own body and the ways of moving it (in the case of mime), the forms he can produce in drawing, etc.

Motivational Considerations:

When children are asked for their ideas of what something means or what it applies to, the message is that they are not merely recipients of teacher knowledge but people who have lived in the world and learned something about it. This creates a better motivational atmosphere and increases the desire to bring past experience to bear. Strategies with representation problems capitalize on the pleasure in responding to challenges to "find a way."

Diagnostic Considerations:

The teacher finds out about the child's conception of what a given word or symbol means rather than assuming (a) that the child's notion is complete and accurate, or (b) that the child has no previous knowledge which is relevant to gaining an understanding of the new label or symbol.

The teacher gains information about how children use a representational system: What elements they choose to use and how they manipulate them. Likewise, in asking children about *how* they know what a representation refers to, the teacher gains insight into what elements of the system children note and understand.

7. Representational Competence:
(External Representation)

UNDERSTAND AND USE A VARIETY OF REPRESENTATIONAL SYSTEMS

Decision Point 1
  What Goals for the Interaction

Get the children to use a variety of ways to express feelings, concepts, descriptions of physical attributes.
Get children to express a message from one mode in another mode.

Why these Goals

Enable children to understand communication in different modes (and using different media) and to use different ways to communicate depending on the demands of the situation and the nature of the material to be conveyed.
Increase children's ability to transform a message from one mode to another and to understand what is "conserved" and what is added or lost.

Decision Point 2
  What Strategies to Use in Accomplishing These Goals

(a)   Ask about alternative ways of expressing something, e.g.,

  Show me how soft it is. . .*Tell* me how soft it is, etc.
  If we want to let the others know there's a storm (in a play, for example), what are some ways we could do it? Can you think of any other ways?

Place restrictions to encourage children to think of ways of representing the same thing in other modes or media. In the above, for example,

  Suppose the lights were out. Is there any way they could know it was a storm?

(b)   Ask questions or make comments which focus on
(1)   the fact that the *meaning* is conveyed through alternate means of representation ("conservation of meaning"), e.g.,

Jane made a drawing of an animal and Ted made an animal out of clay. (Have children indicate what the animal is)
How can you tell both of them are rabbits when one is on a flat page, one is green, etc.?
Peg told us which animal she was by talking about how he looks. She said he has a trunk and is very big. But Timmy didn't talk at all. How did you know *he* was an elephant?

(2)   the capacity one mode/medium has for conveying *different kinds of information* from that which can be conveyed by another, e.g.,

Ted's rabbit has a little round tail. Does Jane's rabbit have a tail?. . .Why *can't* we tell what Jane's rabbit's tail is like?
Peg let us know her elephant was a green one. What color was the Timmy-elephant?. . .You couldn't tell—why not?

Considerations Involved in This Choice of Strategies
  Cognitive Demands:

Rather than a child's using only the one mode which seems easiest or most natural for expressing a given meaning, by the strategies in (a) he is provoked to *think about how to convey the message through other modes* which may be more difficult.
Strategies such as those in (b-1) require children to *recognize that diverse expressions stand for the same thing*, which is a kind of "conservation of meaning."
Questions regarding what information is lost or added when a message in one mode is translated into another require the child to *reflect on the nature of the modes themselves*. To do so involves an *awareness of the vehicle as well as the meaning* (as in metalinguistic awareness).

Motivational Demands:

The challenge of having to find a way to communicate a message when certain ways are precluded is motivating to children. Strategies in (b) and (c) point to a discrepancy, activating the children's thought to figure out a resolution.

Diagnostic Considerations:

Using both open-ended request ("What's a way you can show X?") and more constraining ones ("Can you show X without moving?") allows the teachers to find out children's preferred modes of representation and their abilities to switch from one medium of expression to another.

Questions on how meaning is conveyed in a given mode provide information as to what individual children understand *about* each of the systems (instead of just what they understand *through* the system).

8. Problem-Solving:

SEEK OUT, PERCEIVE, OR IDENTIFY PROBLEMS

Decision Point 1
  What Goals for the Interaction

Help children to notice discrepancies.
Get children to look at situations not yielding desired outcomes in terms of where the specific problem lies (rather than globally, as a failure).

Why These Goals

Increase children's tendency to notice worthwhile problems to work through.
Increase children's ability to see where an inconsistency or conflict lies.

Decision Point 2
  What Strategies to Use in Accomplishing These Goals

(a)   Model relevant behaviors, e.g.,

Now let me see. . . I guess I need to find out how big a space we'll need before I build.
Hmm, something's not working here. I wonder what the problem is.

(b)   Provide incongruous situations, novel and/or surprising items; what is novel, surprising, or incongruous depends on the developmental level and particular experiences of the child.
(c)   Focus child's attention on the aspect(s) where the problem or discrepancy lies, e.g.,

What looks different about those spools that could be making them roll differently? Do you see anything that might be causing the problem?

Considerations Involved in This Choice of Strategies
  Cognitive Demands:

The first strategy requires the child to *imitate and to generalize to new situations the teacher's problem-solving process—trying to identify the specific problem.*

To perceive the discrepancy in an incongruous situation the child *must have an expectation or mental construction which is violated.*

Motivational Considerations:

When the teacher herself shows puzzlement or curiosity, the children often become intrigued. The tendency to wonder about relationships, to seek out and notice problems is thus enhanced. Surprising events motivate children to reduce their confusion by discrepancy resolution.

Diagnostic Considerations:

When the teacher provides all problems to the children herself, she never learns what problems/discrepancies the children see on their own. From noting what is incongruous for children, the teacher can infer what theories and ideas they have had.

9. Problem-Solving:

GENERATE SOLUTIONS AND ALTERNATIVES

Decision Point 1
  What Goals for the Interaction

Get children to think of various possible solutions to a problem, preferably distinctly different alternatives.
Encourage children to look at the reasons for the applicability of these solutions.

Why These Goals

Increase children's flexibility and openness in generating multiple alternatives so that (1) the individual does not get stuck in one method of attack and thus fail to find the best alternative and (2) additional alternatives are available when one fails.
Enchance children's awareness of reasoning employed, which makes the methods more available in later situations.

Decision Point 2
  What Strategies to Use in Accomplishing These Goals

(a)   Groups are often conducive to idea-generation since the flow of ideas is likely to trigger new thoughts from the individual. A brainstorming atmosphere is established.

(b)   List children's ideas on a large pad or blackboard. Make it clear that at this point *many* ideas are wanted.

(c)   Ask

Suppose we want the other group to know what animal we've picked. What are some ways we could let them know?

If children give several answers of a similar kind ("draw it with crayons," "paint it," "draw it with a pencil"), state a restriction or suggestion which will open up a new set of possibilities, e.g.,

What if we didn't have any paper?
What if we just had to use our bodies?

Considerations Involved in This Choice of Strategies
  Cognitive Demands:

Children must draw on past experience to come up with possible solutions. In some cases the children will provide ideas that have worked in other similar situations in the past. In these cases they have to *assess relevant aspects that make the former solution appropriate to the new problem.*

In other cases children will construct alternatives which are "new"—they *combine features of past solutions in new ways or adapt known solutions to the penalities of the new problem.*

Hearing other children's ideas confronts the child with other ways of looking at the problem or solving it.

Motivational Considerations:

Giving children problems which are meaningful, important, and challenging is the first consideration. Asking them for their ideas and acknowledging these enhances the children's sense of competence and gives them the opportunity to see how enjoyable it is to generate ideas. When this is done in a group, here are motivational benefits in the stimulation of others' ideas, in the group feeling that accompanies collective idea-generation, and in the reduction of the feeling of being on the spot.

Diagnostic Considerations:

The teacher learns about the level of the children's spontaneous ideas in response to problems/questions she poses. She learns about the range of the children's information and experience, but more important about how they use these in dealing with problems. Misconceptions and shortcomings in causal reasoning manifest themselves. Over a period of time the teacher learns about the flexibility, the originality, and the flow of the individual children's idea-generation.

10.   Problem-Solving:

EVALUATE THROUGH REASONING

Decision Point 1
  What Goals for the Interaction

Get children to subject an alternative to thoughtful consideration. Increase children's familiarity with criteria by which ideas or potential solutions should be evaluated.

Why These Goals

Enable children to assess better a range of ideas to select the best one for their purposes.
Foster the habit and the ability of examining an idea for ways it can be improved.

Decision Point 2
  What Strategies to Use in Accomplishing These Goals

(a)   Ask questions that encourage evaluation, e.g.,

Would that work?
How would that help?
Would it stop the water?
Would it do anything else?

(b   Suggest other criteria the children haven't used in their spontaneous evaluations, e.g.,

Could we do that with just the things in this box?
So, that would be a cage the guinea pig wouldn't get out of.
Do you think it would be a good place for him to live?. . .
What are some of the things he likes to do?

(c)   Remind children of problem, e.g.,

Remember what our problem was?
Tell me again what the problem is.

(d)   Provide, in some cases, alternatives to be evaluated rather than relying on the ones the children suggest. Select alternatives which have characteristics which will encourage the use of criteria and reasoning you want to foster.

Considerations Involved in This Choice of Strategies
Cognitive Demands

The child must *examine ideas analytically* (rather than globally). The child must engage in *causal thinking* to determine if a given alternative will be effective for solving a problem. The child is required to *represent a mentally desired outcome and the probable one* (from solution being evaluated). He must *compare these and resolve the discrepancy if they are not the same.*

Motivational Considerations:

It is more motivating for the child to evaluate ideas relative to a goal *he* has or perceives vs. having the *teacher* impose standards the child does not understand or accept. The child's evaluation leads to refinements *he* wants to make and sees the need for (because of a discrepancy he himself perceives).

Diagnostic Considerations:

The teacher finds out children's understanding of causal relationships, learns more about how analytic a child can be. These strategies help her to discover which aspects of the problem children focus on and how well they keep the problem in mind.

Becoming a more effective teacher or a different kind of teacher is, as we have said, not an instant transformation. We have suggested that you begin with activities you know children like. As you do more activities with children and begin to build up an intuitive sense of what children like, reflect on why these activities are so appealing to them. In general, if an activity appeals to children, it does so because it is cognitively stimulating. As you acquire experience, knowledge of children, and theory, you'll find yourself choosing activities for their cognitive potentials and their appropriateness for the particular children you're working with. There is a high correlation between the activities children like and those which are good for their development—one reason why teaching *can* be such a pleasure (not *easy*, admittedly, but fun). So as you approach learning encounters with children, remember that when children aren't enjoying something, they won't be learning much.

And finally, we return to the point we made in the beginning of the book when the teachers sat down to talk about a problem. Teaching is a process of making decisions. No teacher can always make the right ones. No teacher ever has. But you *can* commit yourself to avoiding mindless, habit-determined teaching—to always asking the question of *why* you are doing things a certain way, to approaching decisions thoughtfully in relation to your goals. Your job, after all, could hardly be a more crucial one. You are educating the young thinker.

References

Arnheim, R. *Art and Visual Perception* (Berkeley, Calif.: University of California Press, 1967).

Baldwin, C. P., and Baldwin, A. L. "Children's Judgements of Kindness." *Child Development,* 41 (1970): 29-47.

Bandura, A., and Walters, R. H. *Social Learning and Personality Development* (New York: Holt, Rinehart and Winston, 1963).

Berlyne, D. E., *Conflict, Arousal and Curiosity* (New York: McGraw-Hill, 1960).

———, "Children's Reasoning and Thinking." In *Carmichael's Manual of Child Psychology,* Vol. I, edited by P. H. Mussen (New York: Wiley, 1970).

Brown, N. S., Curry, N. E., and Tittnich, E. "How Groups of Children Deal with Common Stress Through Play." In *Play: The Child Strives Toward Self-Realization* (Washington, D.C.: National Association for the Education of Young Children, 1971).

Bruner, J. S. *Beyond the Information Given: Studies in the Psychology of Knowing* (New York: Norton, 1973).

Butterfield, E. "An Extended Version of Modification of Sucking with Auditory Feedback," Working Paper No. 43 (Kansas City, Ks.: Bureau of Child Research Laboratory, Children's Rehabilitation Unit, University of Kansas Medical Center, 1968).

Cataldo, C. Z. A follow-up study of early intervention (Doctoral dissertation State University of New York at Buffalo, 1977). *Dissertation Abstracts International,* 1978, *39,* 657-A. (University Microfilms No. 7813990)

Chandler, M. J. "Egocentrism and Antisocial Behavior: The Assessment and Training of Social Perspective-Taking Skills." *Developmental Psychology,* 9 (1973): 326-332.

———, Greenspan, S., and Barendoim, C. "Judgements of Intentionality in Response to Videotaped and Verbally Presented Moral Dilemmas; The Medium is the Message." *Child Development,* 44 (1973):315-320

Charlesworth, R., and Hartup, W. W. "Positive Social Reinforcement in the Nursery School Peer Group." *Child Development,* 38 (1967):993-1002.

Copple, C. E., Coon, R. C., and Lipscomb, T. J. "Effects of Listener Feedback on the Messages of Kindergarten Children in a Referential Communication Task." Paper presented at the meeting of the Eastern Psychological Association, Boston, 1977.

———, Moore, C., Warman, E. "The Use of 'Distancing' in a Piaget-Based Curriculum:

Exploring the Social-Affective Domain." *Proceedings of the Eighth Annual UAP Conference on Piaget and the Helping Professions* (Los Angeles: University of Southern California, 1979).

Damon, W. *The Social World of the Child* (San Francisco: Jossey-Bass, 1977).

Elardo, P.T. "Project Aware: A School Program to Facilitate Social Development of Children." In *Social Development in Childhood: Day-Care Programs and Research*, edited by R. A. Webb (Baltimore, Md.: Johns Hopkins University Press, 1977).

Elkind, D. "Piaget and Montessori." *Harvard Educational Review*, 38(1967): 15-28.

El'Konin, D. "Symbolics and Its Function in the Play of Children." In *Child's Play*, edited by R. E. Herron and B. Sutton-Smith (New York: Wiley, 1971).

Emmerich, W., Cocking, R. R., and Sigel, I. E. "Relationships between Cognitive and Personal-Social Functioning in Preschool Children." *Developmental Psychology*, in press.

Flapan, D. *Children's Understanding of Social Interaction* (New York: Teachers College Press, 1968).

Flavell, J. H., Botkin, P. T., Fry, C. L., Wright, J. W., and Jarvis, P. E. *The Development of Role Taking and Communication Skills in Children* (New York: Wiley, 1968).

Foreman, G. E., and Kuschner, D. S. *The Child's Construction of Knowledge: Piaget for Teaching Children* (Monterey, Calif.: Brooks/Cole, 1977).

Freyberg, J. T. "Increasing the Imaginative Play of Urban Disadvantaged Kindergarten Children Through Systematic Training." In *The Child's World of Make-Believe: Experimental Studies of Imaginative Play*, edited by J. L. Singer (New York: Academic, 1973).

Funk and Wagnalls Standard Desk Dictionary (New York: Funk and Wagnalls, 1977).

Gardner, H. *The Arts and Human Development* (New York: Wiley, 1973).

Gattegno, C. *What We Owe Children—The Subordination of Teaching to Learning* (New York: Outerbridge and Dienstfrey, 1970).

Gibson, J. J., and Yonas, P. M. "A New Theory of Scribbling and Drawing in Children." In *The Analysis of Reading Skill: A Program of Basic and Applied Research*, Cornell University and United States Office of Education Final Report, Project No. 5-1213 (Ithaca, N.Y.: Cornell University, 1968).

Gilliom, B. C. *Basic Movement Education for Children: Rationale and Teaching Units* (Reading, Mass.: Addison-Wesley, 1970).

Golomb, C. *Children's Sculpture and Drawing: A Study in Representational Development* (Cambridge, Mass.: Harvard University Press, 1974).

Goodnow, J. *Children Drawing*, The Developing Child Series, Edited by J. Bruner, M. Cole, and B. Lloyd (Cambridge, Mass.: Harvard University Press, 1977).

Groos, K. *The Play of Man* (New York: D. Appleton, 1901).

Gross, L. "Modes of Communication and the Acquisition of Symbolic Competence." In *Media and Symbols: The Forms of Expression*, The 73rd Yearbook of the National Society for the Study of Education, Part I edited by D. R. Olson (Chicago: University of Chicago Press, 1974).

Helson, R. "Childhood Interest Clusters Related to Creativity in Women." *Journal of Consulting Psychology*, 29(1965)(353-361.)

Holt, B. *Science with Young Children* (Washington, D.C.: National Association for the Education of Young Children, 1977).

Holt, J. *How Children Fail* (New York: G. P. Putnam's Sons, 1964).

Inhelder, B., and Piaget, J. *The Early Growth of Logic in the Child* (New York: Norton, 1969).

_____, Sinclair, H., and Bovet, M. *Learning and the Development of Cognition* (Cambridge, Mass.: Harvard University Press, 1974).

Isaacs, N. *Children's Ways of Knowing* (New York: Teachers College Press, 1974).

Isaacs, S. *Intellectual Growth in Young Children* (New York: Schocken Books, 1966).

Kagan, J., Kearsley, R. B., and Zelago, P. R. *Infancy: Its Place in Human Development* (Cambridge, Mass.: Harvard University Press, 1978).

Kamii, C. "One Intelligence Indivisible." Paper presented at the meeting of the National Association for the Education of Young Children, Washington, D.C., 1974.

King, M. "The Development of Some Intention Concepts in Young Children." *Child Development*, 42(1971):1145-1152.

Kohl, H. R. *The Open Classroom* (New York: New York Review, 1969).

Kohlberg, L. "Early Education: A Cognitive-Developmental View." *Child Development*, 39(1968):1013-1062.

Krauss, R. M., and Glucksberg, S. "The Development of Communication: Competence as a Function of Age." *Child Development*, 40(1969):255-266.

Laban, R. *Modern Educational Dance*, 2nd ed., revised by L. Ullman (London: MacDonald and Evans, 1963).

Lee, L. C. "Toward a Cognitive Theory of Interpersonal Development: Importance of Peers." In *Friendship and Peer Relations*, edited by M. Lewis, and L. A. Rosenblum (New York: Wiley, 1975).

McDonald, M. "A Study of the Reactions of Nursery School Children to the Death of a Child's Mother." *Psychoanalytic Study of the Child*, XIX (New York: International Universities Press, 1964).

McGillicuddy-DeLisi, A. V., Sigel, I. E., and Johnson, J. E., "The Family as a system of Mutual Influences: Parental Beliefs, Distancing Behaviors and Children's Representational Thinking." In *The Child and Its Family: The Genesis of Behavior*, Vol. II edited by M. Lewis and L. A. Rosenblum (New York: Plenum, 1979).

Minuchin, P. "Affective and Social Learning in the Early School Environment." In B. Spodek and H. J. Walberg *Early Childhood Education*, edited by B. Spodek and H. J. Walberg (Berkeley, Calif.: McCutchan, 1977).

Neill, A. S. *Summerhill* (New York: Hart, 1960).

Neumann, D. "Sciencing for Young Children." In *Ideas that Work with Young Children*, edited by K. R. Baker (Washington, D. C.: National Association for the Education of Young Children, 1972).

Olmsted, P. P., and Sigel, I. E. "The Generality of Color-Form Preference as a Function of Materials and Task Requirements Among Lower-Class Negro Children." *Child Development*, 41(1970):1025-1031.

Olson, D. R. *Cognitive Development: The Child's Acquisition of Diagonality* (New York: Academic Press, 1970).

_____, and Bruner, J. S. "Learning through Experience and Learning through Media." In *Media and Symbols: The Forms of Expression*, The 73rd Yearbook of the National Society for the Study of Education, Part I, edited by D. R. Olson (Chicago: University of Chicago Press, 1974).

Opie, I., and Opie, P. *The Lore and Language of School Children* (Oxford: Oxford University Press, 1959).

_____, and Opie, P., *Children's Games in Street and Playground* (Oxford: University Press, 1969).

Pflederer, M., and Sechrest, L. "Conservation-Type Responses of Children to Musical Stimuli." *Council for Research in Music Education Bulletin*, 13(1968):19-36.

Piaget, J. *The Language and Thought for the Child* (New York: Harcourt, Brace, 1926).

_____, *The Child's Conception of Physical Causality* (New York: Harcourt, Brace, 1930).

_____, *Play, Dreams and Imitation in Childhood* (New York: Norton, 1951).

_____, *The Origins of Intelligence in Children* (New York: International Universities Press, 1952).

_____, *Judgement and Reasoning in the Child* (Patterson, N. J.: Littlefield, Adams, 1959).

_____, *The Moral Judgement of the Child* (New York: The Free Press, 1965).

_____, *Psychology of Intelligence* (Totowa, N. J.: Littlefield, Adames & Co.,. 1966).

_____, "Piaget's Theory." In *Carmichael's Manual of Child Psychology*, Vol. I, edited by P. H. Mussen (New York: Wiley, 1970).

_____, *Science of Education and the Psychology of the Child* (New York: Viking, 1971).

_____, *The Child's Conception of the World* (Totowa, N. J.: Littlefield, Adams 1972).

Pines, M. "Why Some Three-Year-Olds Get A's — And Some C's." *New York Times Magazine*, July 6, 1969.

Pulaski, M. A. "Toys and Imaginative Play." *The Child's World of Make-Believe: Experimental Studies of Imaginative Play*, edited by J. L. Singer (New York: Academic, 1973).

Schaefer, C. E. "Imaginary Comanions and Creative Adolescents." *Developmental Psychology*, 1(1969):747-749.

Selman, R. L., "The Relation of Role-Taking to the Development of Moral Judgements in Children." *Child Development*, 42(1971) :79-91.

_____, "A Structural Analysis of the Ability to Take Another's Social Perspective: Stages in the Development of Role-Taking Ability." Paper presented at the meeting of the Society for Research in Child Development, Philadelphia, 1973.

_____, and Byrne, D. F., "A Structural-Developmental Analysis of Levels of Role-Taking in Middle Childhood." *Child Development*, 45 (1974) :803-806.

Shantz, C. U., "The Development of Social Cognition." In *Review of Child Development Research*, Vol. 5, edited by E. M. Hetherington (Chicago: University of Chicago Press, 1975).

Shapiro, E., and Biber, B. "The Education of Young Children: A Developmental-Interaction Approach." *Teachers College Record*, 74(1972) :55-79.

Shatz, M., and Gelman, R. "The Development of Communication Skills: Modifications in the Speech of Young Children as a Function of Listener." *Monographs of the Society for Research in Child Development*, 38(1973).

Sheehy, E. D. *Children Discover Music and Dance* (New York: Teachers College Press, 1968).

Shure, M. B., and Spivack, G. "Cognitive Problem-Solving Skills, Adjustment and Social Class." Research and Evaluation Report No. 26 (Philadelphia: Department of

Mental Health Sciences, Hahnemann Community Mental Health/Mental Retardation Center, 1970).

_____, and Spivack, G. "Means-End Thinking, Adjustment and Social Class Among lementary School-Aged Children." *Journal of Consulting and Clinical Psychology*, 33(1972):348-353.

_____, and Spivack, G. "A Preventive Mental Health Program for Four-Year-Old Head Start Children." Paper presented at the meeting of the Society for Research in Child Development, Philadelphia, 1973.

_____, and Spivack, G. *Problem-Solving Techniques in Child-Rearing* (San Francisco: Jossey-Bass, 1978).

_____, Spivack, G., and Gordon, R. "Problem-Solving Thinking: A Preventive Mental Health Program for Preschool Children." *Reading World*, 11(1972):259-273.

Sigel, I. E., "The Distancing Hypothesis: A Causal Hypothesis for the Acquisition of Representational Thought." In *The Effects of Early Experience* edited by M. R. Jones (Miami, Fla.: University of Miami Press, 1970).

_____, "The Development of Classificatory Skills in Young Children: A Training Program." In *The Young Child: Reviews of Research,* Vol. II edited by W. W. Hartup (Washington, D.C.: National Association for the Education of Young Children, 1972).

_____, and Cocking, R. R. *Cognitive Development from Childhood to Adolescence: A Constructivist Perspective* (New York: Holt, Rinehart and Winston, 1977).

_____, and McBane, B. "Cognitive Competence and Level of Symbolization Among Five-Year-Old Children." In *The Disadvantaged Child,* Vol. I, edited by J. Hellmuth (New York: Brunner/Mazel, 1967).

_____, and Olmstead, P., "The Development of Classification and Representational Competence." In *Problems in the Teaching of Young Children,* edited by A. J. Biemiller (Ontario, Canada: The Ontario Institute for Studies in Education, 1969).

_____, Roeper, A., & Hooper, F. H. "A Training Procedure for Acquisition of Piaget's Conservation of Quantity: A Pilot Study and its Replication." *The British Journal of Educational Psychology*, 36(1966) :301-311.

_____, and Saunders, R. "An Inquiry into Inquiry: Question-Asking as an Instructional Model." In *Current Topics in Early Childhood Education,* Vol. 2., edited by L. G. Katz (Norwood, N.J.: Ablex, 1979).

_____, Secrist, A., and Forman, G. "Psycho-Educational Intervention Beginning at Age Two: Reflections and Outcomes." In *Compensatory Education for Children, Ages Two to Eight: Recent Studies of Educational Intervention,* edited by J. C. Stanley (Baltimore, Md.: Johns Hopkins University Press, 1973).

Singer, J. L. *The Child's World of Make-Believe: Experimental Studies of Imaginative Play* (New York: Academic Press, 1973).

Smilansky, S. *The Effects of Socio-Dramatic Play on Disadvantaged Preschool Children* (New York: Wiley, 1968).

_____, "Can Adults Facilitate Play in Children?: Theoretical and Practical Considerations." In *Play: The Child Strives Toward Self-Realization* (Washington, D.C.: National Association for the Education of Young Children, 1971).

Spivack, G., and Levine, M. "Self-Regulation in Acting-Out and Normal Adolescents." Report M-4531 (Washington, D.C.: National Institutes of Health, 1963).

_____, and Shure, M. B. *Social Adjustment of Young Children: A Cognitive Approach to Solving Real-Life Problems* (San Francisco: Jossey-Bass, 1974).

Staub, E. "The Use of Role Playing and Interaction in Children's Learning of Helping and Sharing Behavior." *Child Development,* 42(1971):805-816.

Sutton-Smith, B. "The Role of Play in Cognitive Development." In *Child's Play* (New York: Wiley, 1971a).

_____, "The Playful Modes of Knowing." In *Play: The Child Strives Toward Self-Realization* (Washington, D.C.: National Association for the Education of Young Children, 1971b).

Vance, B. *Teaching the Kindergarten Child: Instructional Design and Curriculum* (Monterey, Calif.: Brooks/Cole, 1973).

Webster's New Twentieth Century Dictionary of the English Language, 2nd ed. (Cleveland, Oh.: Collins World, 1977).

Appendix

Sample Lesson Plan: 1

Name of Activity: Reading **Sally's Caterpillar**
Schedule: Large group
Curriculum area/Representational System:

Science	Social/Affective
Art—2 dimensional	Movement
Construction—	Music
3-dimensional	Language Arts

Objective/Goal:

1a. To increase awareness of objects and events and one's reactions to them. *A natural phenomenon which involves striking irreversible transformations (caterpillar →*

  b. To increase awareness of methods for finding out about stimuli. *cocoon →butterfly.*

2a. Elaborate/refine internal representation.

  b. Search store of internal representations (with one or more criteria in mind).

3a. Understand a single representational system as a system (perceive, know about elements, transformations, etc.).

  b. Perceive/understand how that system relates to, refers to, the world.

4a. Understand a variety of representational systems.

  b. Use diverse representational systems to communicate, to encode meanings.

5a. Generate solutions, alternatives.

  b. Seek out, perceive, or identify problems.

  b. Seek out, perceive, or identify problems.

6. Evaluate through reasoning.

Materials and Teacher Preparation

                         The book, **Sally's Caterpillar,** by Anne and Harlow Rockwell

Rationale: (Why those subgoals, this content, this activity, why at this time?)

Exploring a natural phenomenon—the changes of a caterpillar, in this case—to gain a greater awareness of the transformations involved, the details of appearance, etc. The choice of the caterpillar is because of the children's spontaneous interest in them (several brought them to class and because of the marked transformations the awareness of what to watch for in the caterpillar by (a) getting the group to individually and collectively bring to mind what they may already know of caterpillars, and (b) providing new information (about the stages of transformation, etc.) to aid the children in constructing a fuller notion of caterpillars in their several forms.

Activity: Procedure and Teacher Strategies:

Teacher will introduce story by referring to the two caterpillars recently brought into the classroom by children. As the story is read, the teacher will elicit information the children may have about caterpillars from past experience, as well as from observing those in the classroom: "What will the caterpillar that Sally finds look like? How will it feel? How big will it be? What will its legs be like?" (I)

Teacher will point out stages of caterpillars as they are read about and ask children to predict what will happen to the caterpillars brought into class. (II) At the end of the story, she will ask children, "How will we know what's happening to our caterpillar? Will we be able to tell when it's a cocoon? How? How about when it's a butterfly? How will we know? (III)

Reasoning: (Why this procedure, these strategies?)

1.   (Having the children call on what they have seen or heard of caterpillars)

Children have to call on their internal representations (whether mental images, stored verbal information, etc.) and express these in verbal or gestural form. Specific questions are intended to help them *refine the internal representations* and use them as a basis in *anticipating* what Sally's caterpillar (and later the class caterpillars) will be like.

Reading the book is intended to heighten the children's awareness of what to watch for in the caterpillar by (a) getting the group to individually and collectively *bring to mind what they may already know of caterpillars*, and (b) providing new information (about the stages of transformation, etc.) to aid the children in *constructing a fuller notion of caterpillars in their several forms.*

II.   (Talking to the children about changes in the caterpillar and asking them to think about how the class caterpillar will look)

Some transformations and features to *observe* are mentioned to give the children an awareness of aspects to be watching for. When children see things happening, they can relate them to what they've heard.

III.   (Asking the children to predict what will happen to the caterpillar and to think about how one can tell when it's a cocoon, etc.)

Being asked to think about the points in between the caterpillar, the cocoon, and the butterfly, helps the child *decenter from the end states,* which is hard for young children. In so doing, they will be liklier to really understand the process. The how-does-one-know question are good for scientists of any age to specify—what are the identifying earmarks of X? How can you be sure what you are observing is an X? etc.

Sample Lesson Plan: 2

Name of Activity: Using rhythm instruments to help tell Peter Pan
Schedule: Large group
Curriculum area/Representational System:

Science	Social/affective
Art—2 dimensional	Movement
Construction—	Music
3-dimensional	Language Arts

Objective/Goal:

1a. To increase awareness of external stimuli and one's reactions to them.

  b. To increase awareness of methods for finding out about stimuli.

2a. Elaborate/refine internal representation.

  b. Search store of internal representations (with one or more criteria in mind).

3a. Understand a single representational system as a system (perceive, know about elements, transformations, etc.).
The Elements of Speed and Rhythm.

  b. Perceive/understand how that system relates to, refers to, the world.
Speed/rhythm in music in relation to speed/rhythm of movement.

4a. Understand a variety of representational systems.

  b. Use diverse representational systems to communicate, to encode meanings.

5a. Generate solutions, alternatives.

  b. Seek out, perceive, or identify problems.

6. Evaluate through reasoning.

Materials and Teacher Preparation

Children are each given a rhythm instrument, including, if they desire, those which they made themselves. They have already had experience using and caring for these and thinking about the musical element of speed.

Rationale: (Why those subgoals, this content, this activity, why at this time?)

In this activity children are using one specific element of music to represent specific events and transformations in the storyline. Later on they will be introduced to other elements and at some point combine multiple elements.

Activity: Procedure and Teacher Strategies:

I.   After selecting instruments, group will examine ways to vary the speed at which they play their instruments. Then teacher tells them that they will be using the instruments to tell parts of Peter Pan in which the characters do things faster and slower.
II.   During the story, at specific points, teacher tells children to use instruments and tells story in such a way that children can represent speed changes. E g., "They started to fly but Wendy was a little frightened. So first she flew very, very slowly, then she went a little faster, then a little more . . . until she was flying as fast as she could."
III. Rather than just encouraging representation of slow and fast, teacher stresses the gradual change from one to the other. She may have them stop in the middle of one of these transformations and have children go back to starting point then start again. Story is completed using this method of representation.

Reasoning: (Why this procedure, these strategies?)

1.   Introduction to activity and review of speed variations. This helps children to orient their thinking toward this element of music.
II.   Children are required to mentally represent situation verbally described by teacher and transform that into sounds created by musical instruments.
III. Emphasis on transformational aspect of representation requires that children become aware of dynamic changes involved in one state becoming another. This is important for their understanding of how transformations work in the world.

Index